ASCENSION

A Step by Step Guide

Danny Searle

ISBN-13: 978-1545246054

ISBN-10: 154524605X

Most images were sourced from Google Images in the Public Domain unless specified. Credit goes to original uploaders. However, the illustrations in the last meditation, and Chapter 3 were done by Evelyne Park.

Library of Congress Control Number: 2017909028
CreateSpace Independent Publishing Platform, North Charleston, SC

Available from Amazon.com and other online stores

I

DEDICATION

To all those seeking the truth and enlightenment.

Never give up your quest. Never give up hope.

You are never alone.

ACKNOWLEDGMENTS

I would like to thank all the wonderful people who gave me donations over the years, bought my previous books, and watched my videos. Not to mention some of the beautiful comments on my YouTube Channel. This is what keeps me going.

The following people have made donations to bring this book to publication, and without their kind act, you would not be reading this!

- Kerri-Anne Sheehy
- Penn Yap
- Jennifer Neilson
- Craig O'Brien
- Ishik Wittman
- Benjamin Mesvania

CONTENTS

Appendices

1

WORLD ON FIRE: WHICH PATH WILL YOU CHOOSE?

"You can make bad choices and find yourself in a downward spiral or you can find something that gets you out of it."
- RAY LAMONTAGNE

Ascension is the process through which a human, a planet, or even an alien can raise their vibration to a higher state of being. In fact, it is the process of moving from the dense 3rd dimension we are currently in to a much higher vibration in the 5th dimension.

This process is currently taking place by our planet. The Earth is a living, breathing organism with a complex consciousness. Some people refer to this consciousness as Gaia, the Great Mother or simply Mother Earth.

This process has been unfolding for thousands of years, however we are now in the Quickening, or end times. As the Earth Ascends, we too must raise our vibration if we are to follow her.

Many people are quick to mock this philosophy as purely New Age mumbo jumbo. However, I have demonstrated throughout my YouTube videos that the process has begun and that it can be scientifically proven. I presented scientific facts anyone can test for themselves. Yet many still live in denial due to fear, mostly because they are younger souls and, thus, cannot process the information meaningfully.

For older souls, this information is critical if you are interested in joining the Earth in her journey to the higher 5th dimension. As I have shown, this process is not always a peaceful or easy one, however I can explain why certain things are going on in the world and how to prepare yourself for the journey.

2012 and The Shift

2012 was originally meant to be the first time ever that a planet and its inhabitants would Ascend to the 5th Dimension. All that was required was for 25%, yes, just ¼ of humans to embrace the Love vibration. The controllers/globalists know what I know. They did not want this to occur because, firstly, they knew they would not be able to go because of their extremely low vibration. Secondly, if they were the only ones to remain on a 3rd Dimensional planet, they would lose their power and control.

Therefore, they pulled out all the stops, and using their propaganda and control system (the mainstream media) they bombarded the people with a massive "*2012 is the end of the world*" fear campaign. This worked, and did indeed inspire Fear in the minds of the masses, which of course was the complete opposite of the Love vibration we required. Thus, the global Ascension did not take place. I did make a public warning (on YouTube) that as humanity chose Fear over Love and, thus, turned their backs on Ascension, it would now mean that great social and natural upheavals will take place. This was not a threat, or a spiteful "*I told you so.*" This was acknowledging a choice, and the consequences of it. And I was 100% correct.

So, since then, immigrants are raping, stabbing, and looting their way through Europe. Sweden is now the rape capital of the world, closely followed by Germany and France. Wild riots, car burnings, and crimes are everywhere. All the troubles and upheaval in the world right now are a direct result of the 2012 choice. But all was not lost.

The new energy that came through then was also of the Light. Therefore, institutions, organisations and people who have been successfully conducting their wicked business in the shadows, were suddenly thrust into the light of day. Indeed, thousands of paedophile rings and individuals are being exposed. Human traffickers, animal abuse, and corrupt industries like Big Pharma and Big Agra (Monsanto) are all being exposed. The Catholic Church is on the brink of collapse, just like I said it would be at this time 20 years ago on Australian national TV. Islam is now the new force to reckon with, and the globalists still want World War III. Which side will you choose?

2012 was not the end of the world. It was supposed to be an end to the modern, corrupt, society we had all become so used to. A doorway was still opened, and the new wave of high vibrational energy came in. That is why since 2012, we have seen a complete turnaround in world politics and world views. People have woken up to the corrupt political system – the establishment – and have finally begun to reject it. This was started in the UK with Brexit, and later followed by the Donald Trump Presidential victory in the United States.

Now, in 2017, many other countries are seeing the rise of anti-establishment candidates like Geert Wilders in the Netherlands, Marine Le Pen in France and Pauline Hanson in Australia, to name but a few. Whether you support these politicians or not is irrelevant. What is relevant is none of them would have made it this far pre 2012. They are all openly anti-establishment, anti-corruption, and anti-globalism. Thus, like Trump, they are the focal point of people's frustrations over establishment politics. They each have risen on a nationalism platform. But what we have to realise is that these types of politicians have always been around. It is only now that the people are listening to them. I call this the *Trump Effect*, but really, it is the 2012 Effect.

The 2012 Effect

The new vibration that came in 2012 has split the world down the middle. For ease of explanation, I will focus on the US and Trump. On the one hand, since Trump was elected in late 2016, the opposition have been going crazy. At first, people were going on YouTube and saying they were going to kill themselves. Celebrities like Miley Cyrus had very public meltdowns. Then, ongoing riots/protests have ensued, and every dirty political trick in the book has been used against Trump to demonise him and hamstring his administration. Never before in history has such resistance been seen against any political person.

On the other hand, the Trump supporters, who came from both the Left and the Right of the political spectrum, love Trump. They are excited by the fact that he is doing what he said he would do (a first in politics), and if anything, he is over-achieving. The opposition is being run and funded by the globalists, particularly George Soros. These are the same people who blocked the 2012 Ascension. They realise that if they allow Donald Trump to carry out his agenda, it will be the end of their global hegemony.

But there has to be more to it than just evil little men financing and plotting the takeover of the world, right? Well, yes there is. Trump is a catalyst for change. However, the short version is, there really is a battle going on right now between the Light and the Dark. Those that have attuned to the new energies have embraced the change and the new paradigm. Those who do not want to embrace and attune to the new energies of change will go crazy, depressed, or live in complete denial of the new reality. A failure by Trump will plunge the world into darkness once again. If Trump is allowed to succeed, then the world will embrace a new age of Light and prosperity. Trump is just the needle on the compass – we the people and our will is what guides that needle. So, it is really up to the people of planet Earth to guide its own future.

The Human Upgrade

In my YouTube series **The Mechanics of Ascension** I demonstrate scientifically that it is possible to activate your dormant DNA to create the Light Body required to move into the 5th Dimension. In a simple process, you can activate 12 strand DNA, which is required before you can raise your vibration significantly enough to Ascend.

I have also looked at the prophecies of ancient cultures that tell of a time when humanity will progress to a Golden Age. I believe that time is upon us. If humanity chose Love back in 2012, many humans (about 1.3 billion) would have automatically Ascended, without having to do any real preparation or work. They would have Ascended based entirely on their **intent**. Unfortunately, we have missed that opportunity for now. Indeed, I do not believe it will be possible to attempt another mass Ascension for another 120 years, when the Earth is fully attuned to the Age of Aquarius.

But it is not all bad news. In the past, only a very few, select people were able to Ascend. It took a lifetime, a lot of sacrifice and isolation. But since 2012 and the new energies, Ascension got a little bit more simple. Yes, there is still a fair bit of prep, discipline and determination, but what once took over 20 years, can now be achieved in as little as six weeks. And that is what I present in this book. For the first time in human history, we have a step by step Ascension guide book that can fast track an individual's Ascension to the 5th Dimension. Indeed, if you are serious about Ascending, then you cannot afford to miss this significant information. It is your choice.

2

EVERYTHING YOU NEED TO KNOW ABOUT ASCENSION

"Three things cannot be long hidden: the sun, the moon, and the truth." - BUDDHA

The majority of our knowledge about Ascension comes from the Father of Wisdom and Knowledge, **Thoth.** Thoth was the ancient Egyptian pseudonym of Enki's son **Ningishzida** (pron: Nigi-shee-dah). Ningishzida was crucial in the genetic engineering of humans, and it was he who found, then hid (for our own safety) our sacred DNA.

The Ascension process, from our perspective, involves the energizing of our second body. The ancient Egyptians called this the **KA**, and its elevation in vibration allows it to emit more light, eventually becoming the **SAHU**, the Incorruptible Soul, or Immortal Energy Body. There are many ways to raise the vibration of one's KA. Most of the world's Spiritual traditions have their own methods for raising your vibration.

Unfortunately, many of them are riddled with dogma, taboos, and quite honestly, interference patterns created by negative thought-forms (what Christians call demons), so that they can no longer assist in humanity's progress. They were put in place by those who did not and do not desire your freedom, but who profit by your imprisonment.

And, yes, it is sad to say that some of the Spiritual traditions – and especially the religions – are insidious traps, and if you are to rise upward in the Ascension of your own being, you must separate truth from falsehood.

Only you can undertake this task, for it is one of the necessities of mastery. This is a line in the sand of consciousness itself for those who have chosen the Ascension of their own being. They become Masters of truth and do not step aside from ferreting out falsehood from reality. They are not slaves to dogma. They bow to no one but their own divinity.

From an energetic standpoint, the Ascension Process begins when your life force, called **Sekhem** by the ancient Egyptians, begins its ascent up the **Djed**, or sacred pathway of the chakras. This is Ascension in its simplest form. It is the expansion of consciousness and awareness. As your life force enters your higher brain centres and as your KA body becomes energized, you enter another phase of Ascension.

At this phase, you begin to metabolize light itself. By light we refer to Spiritual light, a light that exists in the Spiritual realms. This light feeds the KA body and increases its vibration. When the KA body reaches a certain amplitude, or strength of vibration, without wavering, it ignites with a type of etheric fire, turning it into the SAHU, or Immortal Energy Body, which I refer to as the **Light Body**. This could be viewed as one of the final stages of this particular form of Ascension.

But what I wish to make very clear is that any movement upward in consciousness and movement of life force up the Djed, regardless of the method used, is part of the Ascension process. It is necessary to transform into your LIGHT Body to reside full-time on the 5th Dimension.

What are Dimensions?

First of all, dimensions are not places or locations: they're levels of consciousness that vibrate at a certain rate. There exist numerous dimensions; the fourth and fifth are simply higher than the one we've been living in. Ascension into even higher dimensions will continue even after we've reached the fifth.

Each dimension vibrates at a higher rate than the one below. In each higher dimension, there exists a clearer, wider perspective of reality, a greater level of knowing. We experience more freedom, greater power, and more opportunity to create reality. In order for a higher dimension to be available to us, we need to vibrate in resonance with it. Shifting from one level of consciousness to the next higher one means becoming established on it, so we don't get pulled back.

In order to gain access to higher dimensions, you must cast aside your 3rd Dimensional ideals and understandings. Things like belief in duality, judgment, and fear must be purged. But to do this, you must first understand what the 3rd Dimension is.

The Third Dimension

It's important to understand, first off, that the Third Dimension is not the things you see: the table, the tree, the earth. These are "form."

All things in form are still present in the Fourth Dimension (and to some degree in the 5th); they're simply more light-filled, and not as dense. The Third Dimension is a state of consciousness that is very limited and restricted. Because we've been living in this 3rd dimensional reality for so many lifetimes, we tend to assume that this is the only reality available to live in. We think this is simply how "reality" is, not realizing it is a very limited experience of reality.

The Third Dimensional "operating system" runs on rigid beliefs and a fairly inflexible set of rules and limitations. For example, in the Third Dimension, we learn to believe that bodies are solid; they can't merge with each other or walk through walls. Everything is subject to gravity, physical objects cannot disappear, and we cannot read another person's mind.Furthermore, there is a solid belief in duality, and judgment and fear are all pervasive. These are the things we need to eliminate from our Being if we are to Ascend.

The Fourth Dimension

The 4th Dimension is the "bridge" we're all popping in and out of right now, and will be for a relatively short period of time. In travelling through the Fourth Dimension, we are preparing ourselves for the Fifth. Many of us have had experiences of the Fourth Dimension for a number of years now without realising it.

We know we're experiencing the Fourth Dimension when we have moments of spiritual awakening and experiences of heart opening. Other times, it can happen when we're simply feeling clear and quiet inside. Everything within and around us feels lighter, less rigid. There's a sense of spaciousness and upliftment.

Time is no longer linear in the Fourth Dimension – there's an ongoing sense of being in present time, with no interest or even awareness of past and future. And we can discover that time is speeding up – it can actually stretch and condense, much to our third dimensional surprise. I have even had items disappear off the table, and reappear an hour or so later.

Manifestation is much faster in the Fourth Dimension. Something we simply think about can show up very quickly in our lives. In general, when we're experiencing joy, love, separation, and gratitude, we're experiencing fourth dimensional consciousness.

The Fifth Dimension

The Fifth Dimension is the dimension of Love, and of living totally from the Heart. In order to enter into the Fifth Dimension and stay there, all mental and emotional baggage must be left at the door. No fear, anger, hostility, guilt exists there – no suffering or sense of separation. Mastery over thought is a prerequisite.

The 5th Dimension is humanity's next level of existence. Eventually, all humans will end up there. But because of Soul Ages, this will be a staggered event. So, Older Souls will get there well before the Younger Souls make it. Once everyone is there, the next Shift will begin. That will involve going to the 8th Dimension. The final destination is the 11th Dimension, which will be a couple of million years into the future. If we were to go directly from the 3rd Dimension to the 11th Dimension, we would explode. It is like a diver coming up too fast and getting the bends – not good.

The 5th Dimension is similar to the Spirit Plane, except you have your body. Your body will feel physical like now, but lighter, and can never get sick or hurt. You no longer need sleep, food, drink, or anything. You are sustained by the Divine Rays of Light, emanating from the Great Central Sun.

All will be living in peace and harmony, experiencing oneness with all of life, and love and compassion flowing through all things. People generally communicate through telepathy and have the ability to read each other's thoughts and feelings with ease. The experience of time is radically different: some describe it as "everything happening at once." There is no distinction between past, present or future.

Equality, justice, and respect for all beings: no more hunger, poverty, or crime – abundance available to all. Everyone living without fear – with complete trust in the Divine. Everyone awake to the majestic, divine inter-dimensional beings they truly are.

Using your mind alone, you can create, or manifest, anything. You can travel anywhere in the Universe by thought, and you have full access to the **Akashic Records**. To humans still on the 3rd Dimensional Earth, you would be godlike; but of course, you are not a god – just a very powerful, free Spirit!

The Shift to the Fifth Dimension

This shift will probably be complete within the next couple of decades, however some may decide to stay for the next 120 years until we are in the height of the **Age of Aquarius**. Whatever the date, it will be complete sometime in the future, although individuals will be moving into the Fifth Dimension at their own rate, when their frequency is high enough to match the vibration of the higher dimension. This is known as the **Ascension Process**.

The shift has been "planned" for eons. Not only that, it has already been happening in the last few decades. Indeed, it started at the beginning of the 19th century, and has been progressing to now. We have seen different points in history when consciousness rose: the 1960's Hippy movement, the 1980's New Age Movement, the 2000's with the Body-Mind-Spirit movement.

December 21, 2012 was a date that was given as the mid-point of the shift taking place, and this will continue to unfold in more and more obvious ways, picking up speed, as time goes on.

Imagination, Memory or Intuition?

Much of what has been described about the Fifth Dimension can sound like a fairy tale. And yet, haven't we all had dreams of living in a world like this? Are these dreams just figments of our imagination? Or are they memories of what we, thousands and thousands of years ago, once experienced – and at some point lost – as we descended into the kind of world we know today, filled with struggle and suffering and lack of direct connection with the Divine? Or do these dreams perhaps come from intuitions about the future that is in store for us?

Many of us are having these intuitive feelings; some are having clear visions; others are inwardly hearing about the reality of what humanity's future will be. And our longing to return to this ideal world is simply a yearning to finally return Home to this beautiful world ahead of us. But people often ask, how can this possibly happen?

How Will The Shift Actually Happen?

How can this world turn around from where it is today and become this utopian kind of paradise? There is still so much darkness on the planet – wars, hatred, prejudice, and injustice. Well, that is a twofold answer.

First, thousands of people on the planet are now experiencing an awakening of the heart at an unprecedented rate – and this awakening appears to be speeding up, as time goes by. At some point, the hundredth monkey phenomenon will inevitably take hold.

Secondly, not everyone on the planet at this time is making the choice (consciously or unconsciously) to make the shift into the Fifth Dimension. All souls have the choice to enter the 5D, given they have assimilated sufficient light to hold the energy levels that exist in that higher vibration.

But many will be choosing to leave the Earth within the next couple of years to move on to other third-dimensional experiences in other parts of the galaxy. They will not have finished with what third-dimensional reality has still to teach them.

Those who are choosing to stay and make the shift along with the Earth, will be going through some intense and rapid changes, the radical changes of body and mind needed to shift into the higher consciousness, the requisite for moving into the Fifth Dimension.

Transitional Times

We are currently in what I call the "transitional times" or the "end times." These are the times in which we are experiencing the death of third-dimensional reality, while at the same time beginning to travel through new and unknown landscapes of the 4th Dimension.

In essence, one whole structure of reality is collapsing while a new one is emerging. It's to be expected that some chaos, confusion and disorientation will reign, both within and around us, as we attempt to adapt to a whole new way of experiencing reality. Many of us are beginning to experience radical changes in our lives as we enter into these times. Whatever does not serve us in shifting into a higher dimension has to fall away. This can include:

- Old relationships
- Lifetime careers
- Approaches to life we've traditionally taken
- An out-dated sense of identity
- Any limited or negative thoughts and emotions that hold us in a lower vibration
- Changes in diet

Radical transformation can be hard on the body too, causing:

- Pain
- Aches
- Exhaustion
- Flu-like symptoms
- The inability to physically consume certain foods or drinks

On the up side, releasing old patterns and negative emotions is getting easier and easier, if we have the clear intention of letting them go.

Are You Ready to Make the Shift?

If you feel a resonance with this information, it's likely you've decided – either consciously or unconsciously – to shift with the Earth into the Fifth Dimension in this lifetime.

If so, you have the choice to simply accept and allow, and let life transform you – sometimes in uncomfortable ways if you have any resistance to change. Life will do the job for you. Or you can choose to actively cooperate with the shift taking place inside you.

You can consciously let go of old patterns, release negative emotions, judgments and thoughts, and work on keeping your vibration high at all times. This effort will likely ensure that your journey through the Fourth Dimension will be a lot smoother and even perhaps more rapid.

But there's no right way to make this journey. We each have to do it the way that's best for us. One way or another, we will make it into the new reality that lies before us.

What happens if you do or don't Ascend?

There are three questions I get asked on a very regular basis:

1. What will happen to those that do not Ascend?
2. What will I experience during the Ascension process?
3. What can I expect life to be like on the 5th Dimension?

I will try to address these questions to the best of my knowledge because, in truth, no one knows exactly what will happen or exactly what to expect. My conclusions come from several sources of reliable information and my own experience on the Astral plane.

What will happen to those that do not Ascend?

Firstly, it should be understood that those that do not ascend are not being punished in any way. Every soul on Earth has a choice and some chose not to ascend at this time. In reality, it is mainly because they are younger souls that do not have the experience yet to raise their vibration. Furthermore, their soul may still have experiences it wants to learn that can only be learnt on the 3rd Dimension.

The majority of these Souls also live in a fear based mentality and, as such, will create their own "end-times" scenario. So, I am not trying to sugar coat anything, nor am I trying to fear monger. The fact is, these souls will have chosen to die. Whether that is in an Earth changes scenario, a world war, or just old age, is irrelevant. It will be in a way that each soul has chosen for their experience.

These people will die, but it will not be like the traditional death where they will leave their earthly body and return to the Spirit plane. Instead, they will die on Earth, and simply "wake up" in a bed, in a large hospital-like building. This building (and there will be many like it) exists right now on another 3rd dimensional planet within our galaxy. This planet is similar to Earth, but a little smaller, cooler and has much less native wildlife. The planet mainly consists of rolling hills with sweeping grassy plains. There is one smallish ocean that only harbours very primitive life. On the land there are very simple insect-like creatures and a few small mammals. In fact, it is what the Earth was like about a ½ billion years ago before really advanced life took off.

It revolves around a star very similar in size and make up to our own sun. That is actually why this planet was chosen for these humans.

Not all stars (suns) can sustain human life. Our sun plays a critical role in human wellbeing and health, so something similar needed to be found.

The people who end up here will be in a renewed body. Indeed, they will have the exact body they had before they died, but it will be cured of any injuries, malformations, disfigurements or disease. They will still have the same personality, thoughts and traits (for now).

They will have full memory of what took place. This is so they can grow quicker from their experience. If they know what happened to them, they are more likely to want to change their consciousness.

These souls will be grouped into soul level groups. For example, young souls in one group, child souls in another group etc. For the record, the majority of souls that will Ascend are Mature and Old souls. If you want to know more about Soul Ages, then I have covered this topic in depth in my book *The Truth Chronicles Book 1: Secrets of the Soul.*

Each group will be supervised by very spiritually enlightened entities from the **Pleiades**. These beings are known as **Pleiadians** and they have had a long association with the human soul group. Pleiadians are very tall, about 3-4m/10-12ft. They have high cheek bones, chalk white skin, almond eyes that are indigo to violet, and very straight, long hair. They look suspiciously like Angels and they have a beautiful, visible silver/blue aura around them. Indeed, the younger the soul group, the more Pleiadians will be there to supervise.

The Pleiadians will counsel and guide these souls and help reunite them with other family members and friends. They will teach them how to live and to raise their vibration. This new Earth will have no money, no religion and no government as we currently understand it. All means by which corruption can thrive will be removed. The aim is to get these souls up to the 5th dimension as quickly as possible. With the help of the Pleiadians, some souls will literally ascend in days after they arrive on the new Earth.

In reality, every soul will be exactly where they were meant to be to experience The Shift.

By the way, people who have already died before the Ascension Process has begun have already made their choice. Some will Ascend from the Spirit Plane and others will re-incarnate into their old bodies on the new Earth planet.

That is about all I can tell you about Souls that do not Ascend, so let's look at what happens to the Souls that will Ascend.

What will I Experience during the Ascension Process?

The first thing I can say with certainty is that each person will experience Ascension in a very personalised way. What I mean by this is if you were sitting right next to your best friend and you both Ascended at the same time, you would not be aware of each other, nor would you see each other. After it was all over, you and your friend would be able to swap stories about your experience and they would be completely different.

The first thing you will notice is a raising in your vibration. This will be experienced as a tingling or buzzing sensation. Your body will begin to feel weightless, starting at your feet and rapidly moving up. You will feel an intense (but not painful) buzzing in your Crown Chakra and, by now, you will have lost all sensation in your lower limbs. You will also experience a strong "butterflies" in your tummy kind of feeling.

Manmade objects like plastic, bricks, walls, electrical appliances and even non-natural fibres will begin to slowly vibrate, giving them a washed out, wobbly appearance like they were made of jelly or jello, so it would be like looking at them under water.

These objects will begin to disappear and a cloudy haze will begin to envelope your surroundings. As the haze gets thicker, more things around you will begin to disappear. The haze seems to be lit by an external light but you will not be able to determine the direction of the light source. This is the **Veil** between dimensions. You will have an experience of moving upward, however you will have no sense of direction, nor any sense of time or space.

Suddenly, the haze begins to dissipate and your eyes can refocus. You will notice intense colours of every description (including colours that are not visible on the 3rd dimension).

By now, you notice that your body no longer has any weight. Yes, your body is still there, and will still feel physical to you, but your body has been transformed into a **Light Body**. A light body never gets sick, never ages, and never needs food, water or sleep. In fact, any requirements of the physical body are no longer necessary, including feeling hot or cold. Just like in the movie **The Matrix,** when Neo is inside the computer program, you will project your residual self-image. In other words, you will look like how you view yourself in your mind. Indeed, you will look better than you can ever imagine. Further to this, you can look like anything or anyone you want to look like. For most people, they project themselves as a fit and trim 30-something year old, but of course there are exceptions to this. Some people want to experience being in a child's body again, and others want to appear as a graceful elderly person. The point is, you have free will, and whatever you think, you create – but more on that later.

More than likely, you will appear in a beautiful flower field or forest or standing on a beach facing an endless ocean. There will be birds and animals, but they no longer fear you, nor will you fear them, such as in the case of big cats and bears. You will feel at oneness with all creation. If you quiet your mind and close your eyes you can hear the thoughts of all living creatures. With further practice you can join your mind with the heard or flock and experience group consciousness.

The aromas wafting on the gentle breeze are exquisite and the flowers are like nothing you have ever seen. There are fruit trees heavy with fruit. One particular fruit is similar to a large plum. You may feel an overwhelming urge to eat this fruit. That is because it has incredible healing properties, but more importantly, it can help to ground you to the 5th Dimension. So, in other words, once you eat the fruit, there is no going back to the 3rd dimension, so bon appétit!

Adjusting to the 5th Dimension

Getting back to your body, even though you do not need to eat, you may still want to eat – but this time purely for the sensation and taste. Your mind has not fundamentally changed, so you may still have urges for things you did in the 3rd Dimension. These urges will pass in a short time.

Some people may also feel an overwhelming urge to lie down and sleep. This is because you may have experienced a particularly traumatic event in your 3rd dimensional life, so some extra healing needs to take place to repair your Aura and other subtle bodies. But don't worry, you are not going to miss anything.

Time no longer exists! That's right, linear time only exits on the 3rd Dimension. There is still day and night, but not measured like we do at the moment.

Once you are suitably grounded and healed, your Guides will appear. For some people, they may have been with you right from the start and actually held your hand right through the process. Either way, your Guides will now tell you what the next move is and what to do.

Something they will stress is that in the 5th dimension, whatever you think will manifest. Unlike the 3rd dimension where there is a delay between cause and effect, on the 5th dimension it is instantaneous. Thus, you will be trained in how to control your thoughts. But don't fear this new ability. Once you learn to control it, you will never understand how you got by without it in the past. This is also why no fear based people can enter the 5th dimension. If you were fear based, and began thinking fearful thoughts, you would manifest those things immediately and probably go insane. So, that is why a **LOVE** vibration is so important. Just on another note, if you are thinking, "*oh great, I can manifest a red Ferrari*" – well, yes you could, but those that understand 5th dimensional living realise that this is just folly and dedicate their energies to much higher endeavors.

What can I expect life to be like on the 5th Dimension?

It is now time to be introduced to your new Teachers. That's right, every single person will have two teachers – a male and female. Just like on the 3rd dimensional planet, your teachers will be Pleiadians. So, for the next (equivalent of two years) they will be your full-time companions, teaching you everything you need to know about living in the 5th dimension, along with any other questions you have about the past and some future events. You will probably come to see them as loving parent figures. But don't worry, you will still see your other friends and family members that Ascended.

In fact, at some point there will be a massive **Welcome to the 5th Dimension Party** where everyone who as ever Ascended will be in attendance. Just imagine a party where you can eat, drink and be merry and never get tired, bored or even feel bloated! The finest musicians playing, the greatest talents performing and some of the best conversations this side of the Andromeda galaxy! Speaking of which, don't be surprised if you bump into a few special – nonhuman – entities (what we presently call Aliens) that are there to welcome you to their homeland.

Just like in the movie **Jumpers**, you will be able to move from one side of the planet to the other instantaneously just with a thought! Indeed you can go anywhere in the Galaxy, but that is getting a little ahead of ourselves.

You will be free to study or practice anything you want. You could learn a new instrument, study the healing arts, invent an advanced form of engineering, or try your hand at painting. With access to the vast Universal libraries and teachers, there is nothing you cannot master. After all, you have all the time in the world to perfect your skills.

There are lots and lots of jobs to do, but I prefer not to use that term. Work in the 5th dimension is very different to what you know in the 3rd dimension. For a start, there is no money and no need for money, so any jobs that are based around money, like banking, are suddenly redundant. But there is lots of work in **Service to Others**, roles like creation, invention, growing, healing, caring, recording, teaching, administrating, performing, showing, travelling and many more. The basic guide is anything that will benefit humanity or anything you can share with humanity that is beneficial to the whole. All work is done on a volunteer basis. No one is forced to work in order to survive and no one is forced to do a job they do not like.

Your home will be a creation of your own making, so start practicing now by visualising the type of home and location you would like to live in now! And remember, you can build it anywhere in the world because travel is just a blink of an eye! There will still be cities, but not quite like what they are today, and some will even be underwater cities.

You will still fall in love, get married and have children. But sex is no longer a physical act, but rather, a blending of energies that makes a physical orgasm seem like popping a balloon in comparison to a hydrogen bomb!

We have all been part of an experiment that required us to incarnate for thousands and thousands of years, into thousands of lives, to experience all levels of creation. This helped the **Source of All That Is** learn more about itself. The plan was to see if we, as incarnate souls, could be completely cut off from the Source (via amnesia & the dense 3rd dimension) and still find our way back to it. To cut a long story short, the experiment was deemed a huge success and enough souls were able to achieve a heightened state of Spiritual awareness without ever having any direct knowledge of the Source at birth. Truly remarkable. So, basically, it's all over and it is time to go home! But just like a scuba diver that has been at depth, he must return to the surface gradually or else risk contracting the bends. The same can be said for our souls. We are originally from the 11th Dimension. But if we were to suddenly jump from the 3rd dimension to the 11th dimension we would quite literally be torn apart. So, that is why we are going to the 5th dimension first. We will stay there until **ALL** humans join us. So, remember all those souls still stuck on the 3rd dimension?

Yep, we cannot move to the next level (the 8th Dimension) until the very last soul ascends to the 5^{th}Dimension. But that is a long way away, and I can assure you that once you get to the 5^{th}Dimension, you would feel like you would never want to leave it! Indeed, your soul has been disconnected from the Source, but once you are in the 5th Dimension, you will once again experience the overwhelming **LOVE and UNITY** that is the *Source of ALL That Is*. That's when a lot of you will have the Ah-Hah moment about what I am trying to relate here. It really is a BIG DEAL.

So, the next 12-18 months are going to be really tough (2017-2019). As the Earth's vibration rises, the world will fall further into chaos. Younger souls will literally go crazy. Indeed, there will quite literally be two realities – one for those that will not Ascend, and one for those that have chosen to Ascend. But that is why it is so important to do the work now – meditate, meditate, meditate! 20 minutes a day – every day – that is the bare minimum requirement.

I hope by now you can understand what waits for those that are committed to doing the hard yards. And make no mistakes, it is going to get hard, but stay focused and do your visualisations and do your meditations. In fact, it's those days that you couldn't be bothered are the days you need it most. Push yourself, you won't regret it. This book contains everything you need to know to Ascend. Read it and pay attention. It holds the keys to your salvation.

Indeed, your present life now is just a cheap imitation of what life is supposed to be. In less than 8 weeks, you can trade in your current slavery for paradise! I hope to see you on the other side.

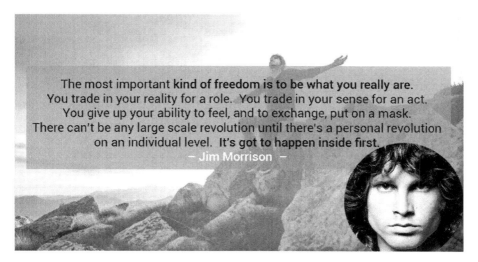

The most important **kind of freedom is to be what you really are.**
You trade in your reality for a role. You trade in your sense for an act.
You give up your ability to feel, and to exchange, put on a mask.
There can't be any large scale revolution until there's a personal revolution on an individual level. **It's got to happen inside first.**
– Jim Morrison –

3

THE HUMAN CHAKRA SYSTEM

"There is one unity, unified wholeness, total natural law, in the transcendental unified consciousness." ~ MAHARISHI MAHESH YOGI

*I*t is said that when you begin to develop your senses, a new and fascinating world opens before you; the hidden world suddenly unveils itself – your perception heightens and your thoughts and feelings are expressed before your very own eyes in colour and form.

There is more to the human body than the physical body. Unfortunately, most people consider the physical body and the material world to be the only reality that exists. They believe this because, for them, these are the only things that can be discerned with their own physical senses, and I might add, understood by their limited, rational mind. But there are numerous energy bodies within and around the human body. These energy bodies are:

- The Ethereal (astral) body
- The Emotional body
- The Mental body
- The Spiritual body

Each energy body possesses its own vibrational frequency, from the lowest (ethereal) to the highest (Spiritual). In addition, there is a complex energy system that is at work, which the body could not exist without. This energy system consists of energy bodies, namely:

- the **Chakras** (or energy centres)
- and the **Nadis** (also known as energy channels)

Nadi is a Sanskrit word meaning "pipe" or "vein." Nadi are akin to a network of channels or arteries that transport **prana** (vital energy) throughout the human being's energy system.

This illustration depicts the chakra system and the large number of secondary chakras including the complex network of nadis. These nadis unite into 14 main channels, which correspond to the main primary and secondary chakras.

Ancient Indian texts say there are 72,000 nadis in the human body, whereas other archaic texts speak of 350,000 nadis. The most important nadis are called the (1) **Sushumna** (2) **Ida**, and (3) **Pigala**. The nadis of one energy body are connected to the nadis of the neighbouring energy body via the chakras.

What Is Prana?

One common description of the "vital force" (field) or "etheric body" is a silvery haze that extends a few millimetres beyond the skin. You can see this field under special conditions using ultra-violet light or with your own eyes.

Prana is the primal source of all forms of energy and manifests itself in various frequencies.Your level of consciousness (awareness) determines the frequencies of prana you are capable of receiving and storing. One form of prana exists in the air, and one way we can retrieve it is through proper breathing (exercises).

Prana is equivalent to the force of "vitality." Vitality is radiated on all levels and manifests itself in the physical, emotional, and mental realms. This force is not electricity, albeit in some ways it represents it. In the 1871 novel by **Edward Bulwer-Lytton**, *The Coming Race*, a strange, subterranean race of humanoids live in a hollow Earth. All of their healing and technology is based on a force they call *Vril*. Vril is a very good analogue of prana.

Is It Possible To See This "Etheric" Energy Field?

Try this little experiment right now. Lie down, or sit, and hold your hands directly out in front of you so a light coloured ceiling is behind your hands. Splay your fingers, and allow them to almost touch. Now, gaze at the point where your two middle fingers are almost touching. Allow your gaze to go slightly out of focus. You should start to see the thin, silvery blue outline around your fingers and hands. This is your life force. When you get good at this, and you have raised your vibration slightly, you will begin to see the colours of your aura. Later, you will be able to see the auras of other people.

How Is Prana Distributed In The Body?

In the dense, physical body, the blood carries chemical material in a liquid solution; the red corpuscles take oxygen to the tissue and bring back carbon dioxide from these and dispose of it. The radiations in the "vital field" or "etheric body" absorb and carry "vitality" or "prana" from the other, multi-dimentional realms and dispose of subtle waste matter in a similar manner.

Vitality action differs from electricity, light, and heat. Vitality causes oscillation of the atoms as a whole, which is enormous compared to that of the atom. The "vitality force" comes to the atom from **within**, **not** from **without**. It enters the atom along with the force that holds the atom together. When this "vitality force" wells up within an atom, it gives it a power of attraction that immediately draws six other atoms around it, thus creating a sub-atomic element called **globules**.

So, globules are charged with the force of "prana." Globules are very good for you. Under certain conditions, they can be seen dancing in the air as tiny points of brilliant light. They are also sunshine dependent for their power of manifestation. You won't see many under cloudy days. Perhaps this is why people are not as jovial or in a depressed or sluggish mood after being exposed to many cloudy and/or rainy days in a row.

What Are Chakras?

Chakras are energy centres. They function like receivers and transformers of the various forms of prana. Through the nadis, the chakras take in the vital energy and transform it into the frequencies needed by the various areas of the physical bodies for sustenance and development.

Each chakra is connected with one of the elements of earth, water, air, ether, and mind – mind being an instrument of consciousness. These elements are states of matter and not elements as we understand them in modern chemistry. They are equivalent to the terms solid, liquid, fiery or gaseous, airy, and etheric – which are somewhat analogous to the physical, astral, and mental and sub-planes.

Chakra is a Sanskrit word, meaning, a "wheel." The human chakras are "wheel-like" vortices, or saucer-shaped depressions that exist on the surface of the *etheric* human body. Traditional writings say there are 88,000 chakras in the human body. Most are extremely small and play a minor role in your energy system. However, there are approximately 40 secondary chakras that are of significance; these are located in your spleen, the back of your neck, the palms of your hands and the soles of your feet. But for brevity purposes, we will only explore the seven primary chakras here.

The **Seven Primary Chakras** are located along a central vertical axis of our spine and open toward the front of the body like a blossom; they also extend mirror fashion out the back. These circular energy centres are in constant motion, rotating, attracting energy – receiving or radiating.

At the centre of each chakra, in its deepest point, is a stem-like channel that extends to the spine and merges with it, thus connecting the individual chakra with the **sushumna** (the most important energy channel), which ascends within the spine to the top of the head.

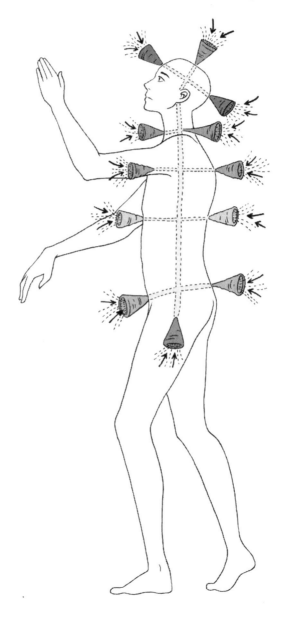

The main seven Chakra positions in the body

Seven Chakra Colours

A journey through the seven chakra colours is essentially a journey through the rainbow. Each of your seven chakras has a corresponding colour that follows the colours of the rainbow: red, orange, yellow, green, blue, indigo, and violet (or white). This is the most widely accepted colour system for your chakras.

In my experience, the colours are not stable and permanent as you would see colours in a picture. The colours are fluid, constantly changing just as your emotions change. The chakra colours can be muddy, faded with very little colour present, or even too saturated – too bright. The colour of a chakra indicates your current physical, emotional, and spiritual state.

We all recognise the connection between colour and emotion. It is reflected in our language, and there is even a branch of psychology, called **colour therapy**, which deals specifically with colour and its emotional impact. There is much you can learn about yourself by learning about colour.

Colour provides you with a mirror of your emotions. What is your favourite colour? Do you wear certain collars of the spectrum more often? Do you avoid certain colours? What do you feel in your body when you see red colour? Or blue colour?

Colour is a universal language – it is simple yet very profound. Before we delve into exploration of colour psychology and the meaning of chakra colours, let's explore the science of colour.

What is colour?

The visible light spectrum is part of the electromagnetic spectrum, and its wavelengths range approximately from 380-740 nm. Colour is a wave travelling through space. Depending on the wavelength, the space between the peaks – measured in nanometres(nm), our eyes register different colours.

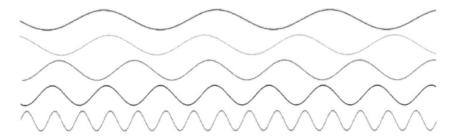

Colour	Wavelength nm	Frequency THz
Red	625 - 740	400 - 484
Orange	590 - 625	484 - 508
Yellow	565 - 590	508 - 526
Green	520 - 565	526 - 606
Blue	500 - 520	606 - 670
Indigo	435 - 500	670 - 700
Violet	380 - 435	700 - 789

How does this relate to your seven chakras?

Each of your chakras is vibrating at a particular frequency and responds to different vibrations (or wavelengths) of light. As you may have already guessed, the root chakra is vibrating at a frequency within the 400-484 THz range, the sacral chakra within the 484-508 THz range, the solar plexus chakra within the 508-526THz range, etc. By knowing these frequencies, you can easily modify your meditations with tones, music, and colour, to work on specific areas.

Within these frequencies and wavelengths, each colour contains information on several different levels: physical, mental, emotional, and spiritual. This information can be used in chakra balancing and chakra healing.

There is no single colour that has more value than the other. The colour is simply what it is – an aspect of the visible light spectrum with its particular frequency.

Like a flower, a "stem" branches out from our spine into the shape similar to that of a lotus flower. Think of our spine like a central stem.

For most people, the chakras extend in a cone shape about 10 centimetres (two inches) from their point of origin.

When undeveloped, they appear as small circles about 5 centimetres (1 inch) in diameter, but when awakened, they are blazing, shimmering whirlpools, akin to miniature suns 20-30 centimetres (8-12 inches) in diameter. As one's development advances, their chakras will extend further from the body, their frequency vibrations will increase and their corresponding colours will become clearer and brighter.

Depending on the sex of the individual, the chakras rotate either clockwise or counter-clockwise. For instance, when a chakra in a man is rotating clockwise, the same chakra in a woman will rotate counter-clockwise, and vice versa. This enables the energies of man and woman to complement each other. Every clockwise rotation is primary male, which is in accordance with the Chinese teaching, Yang, and every counter-clockwise rotation is female, or Ying.

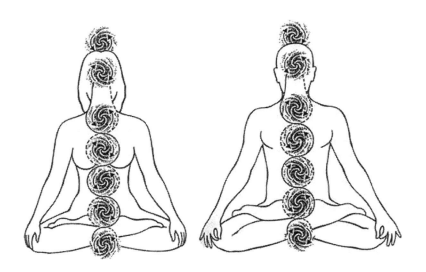

It should be noted, the direction in which a chakra rotates varies from chakra to chakra. Each chakra rotates in a different direction, as these illustrations depict.

The Seven Primary Chakras in the human body are:

(7) Crown Chakra
(6) Third Eye/Brow
(5) Throat Chakra
(4) Heart Chakra
(3) Solar Plexus
(2) Sacral Chakra
(1) Root or Base Chakra

Chakras

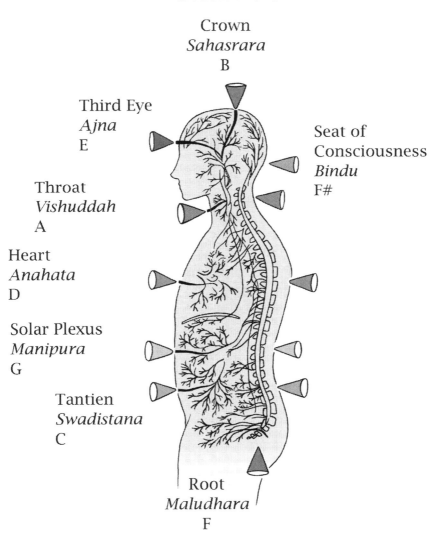

How the Chakras connect within your body and the musical notes associated with them.

7 Primary Chakras
Plus Transpersonal Chakras

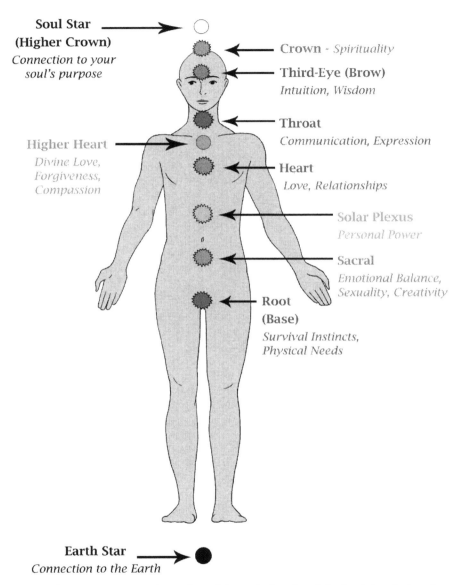

Soul Star (Higher Crown)
Connection to your soul's purpose

Crown - *Spirituality*

Third-Eye (Brow)
Intuition, Wisdom

Throat
Communication, Expression

Higher Heart
Divine Love, Forgiveness, Compassion

Heart
Love, Relationships

Solar Plexus
Personal Power

Sacral
Emotional Balance, Sexuality, Creativity

Root (Base)
Survival Instincts, Physical Needs

Earth Star
Connection to the Earth

In this diagram we can see the Soul Star (above the head) and the Earth Star (below the feet). These Chakras will be used in MERKABA activation.

Root Chakra

The 1st chakra is called the Root Chakra. It is located between the anus and the genitals and is connected with the coccyx. The Root Chakra opens downward. When active with vigour, it is fiery neon red in colour. Parts of the body that are associated with this chakra are the lymph system, teeth and bones, prostate gland, bladder and the legs, feet and ankles. The sense of smell is covered by this root chakra. Security, trust, the home and work are all connected with the root chakra, as the root is where life begins. This chakra also reflects a person's connection with their mother and with Mother Earth.

Sacral Chakra

The 2nd chakra is called the Sacral Chakra. Located below the navel, it is bright, neon orange in colour. It rules the reproductive system and sexual organs and it looks after the sense of taste and appetite. Children are also associated with this chakra. Emotions and the person's willingness to feel their emotions is also guided by this chakra.

Solar Plexus Chakra

The 3rd chakra is called the Solar Plexus Chakra. It is located about three to four fingerbreadths above the navel, and is directly connected to our astral, or etheric, body. Through the solar plexus chakra we absorb the solar energy that nurtures our etheric body, which in turn, energizes and maintains our physical body. This is where our emotional energy radiates, particularly our "gut feelings." Its colour is bright, neon yellow. The parts of the body associated with this chakra include the muscles, skin, solar plexus, large intestine, stomach, liver and the eyes. The sense governed by this chakra is eyesight. Power, control and mental activity are associated with this chakra. The Solar Plexus is an important chakra as it's linked to the personality.

Heart Chakra

The 4th chakra is called the Heart Chakra. It is the centre of our entire chakra system. It is located in the centre of the breast at the level and vicinity of the heart cavity, and connects the three lower physical and emotional centres to the three higher mental and Spiritual centres. It is primarily bright, neon green in colour. The Heart Chakra is associated with the heart, the circulatory system, lungs and chest. This chakra governs the sense of touch and the sensitivity that comes from being touched. When we want to project Love, we do so from the Heart Chakra, and change its colour to pink.

Throat Chakra

The 5th chakra is called the Throat Chakra. It is located between the depression in the neck and the larynx, beginning at the cervical vertebra behind the Adam's apple. It is also connected to a small secondary chakra, which has its seat in the neck and opens to the back, but since the two chakras are so closely related, they have been integrated into one. It is bright neon blue in colour. This chakra controls the throat, neck, the arms and the hands. The throat chakra governs the sense of hearing, and is related to communication and creativity. Often when people have a sore throat, it is because they are holding something back, or not saying something to someone.

Third Eye Chakra

The 6th chakra is called the Third Eye Chakra. It is associated with the pituitary gland, which is a very small, shapeless organ, about 1/8 inch in diameter, located in the forehead about three finger breadths above the bridge of the nose between the eyebrows. Here, conscious perception of being takes place. It is the seat of our higher mental powers. On the physical plane, it is the highest centre of command for the central nervous system. It is indigo in colour – a deep purplish-blue – and is associated with the temples and the carotid plexus. It is related to the act of seeing, both physically and intuitively, and tunes in to our psychic ability. This ability includes clairvoyance (inner sense of vision), clairaudience (inner sense of hearing), and clairsentience (inner sense of touch), and these are all interlinked with this chakra.

The Crown Chakra

The 7th chakra is called the Crown Chakra. It is seated in the pineal gland, which is a small organ of fleshy consistency not much larger than the pituitary. The pineal gland is located near and behind the pituitary gland, almost in the exact centre of your head at the level of your ears. The Crown Chakra opens upward, at the top of your head. Interestingly enough, medical science has yet to conclusively determine the physical influence this gland has on the human body (probably because metaphysics is beyond their rational thinking mind!) Although its colour contains all sorts of prismatic hues, it is predominantly a bright, neon violet.

The Crown Chakra is also known as the cosmic consciousness center. This chakra gives off a sense of empathy and unity, and is calming when centered on.

The Crown Chakra is usually the last to be awakened. It is the same size as the other chakras, but as the person progresses on the Path of Spiritual advancement, it increases steadily until it covers the entire top (crown) of the head.

Like the other chakras, at first the Crown Chakra is a depression in the etheric body and the divine force flows in from without. But when the person realises his position as a being of the divine light through development of this chakra, the Crown Chakra reverses itself and turns itself inside out!

In other words, it no longer is a channel of reception but a channel of radiation; it no longer is a depression but a prominence above the head – it radiates outward like a dome, like a crown of glory!

Chakras in Everyday Life

Each chakra is perpetually rotating. At the mouth of the chakra, a divine force from the higher world flows. Without this inrush of primary energy, the physical body could not exist.

The chakra centres are in constant operation in all of us. In the undeveloped person, they are usually in sluggish motion, just forming the necessary vortex for the force to enter, and not much more than that. Indeed, in the average, undeveloped person, they are said to be living only in their "lower chakras." That is because the lower chakras look after the basics of survival – eating, bodily functions, and procreation.

However, in the more evolved person, they have all of their chakras operating and in balance. Therefore, they may be glowing and pulsating with living light, so that an enormous amount of energy passes through them. The divine energy that pours into each chakra from without sets up at right angles to itself secondary forces in an oscillating circular motion. Think of this like a magnet that produces a current around a coil at right angles to its axis.

After entering the vortex, the primary force radiates from it at right angles as straight lines, as though the centre of the vortex was the hub of a wheel and the radiations of the primary force were the spokes. The force of these spokes seems to bind the astral and etheric bodies together like grappling-hooks. The number of these spokes differs in each chakra, which determines the number of petals each chakra exhibits. This is why the chakras have been described in oriental books as resembling flowers.

Each of the secondary forces, which sweep around the saucer-shaped depressions, has its own wavelength, and moves along large petals of various sizes. The number of petals is determined by the number of spokes in the wheel, and the secondary force weaves itself under and over the radiating currents of the primary force, like a basket might be woven around the spokes of a wheel – the number of wavelengths being infinitesimal.

All the petals have a shimmering effect, like the mother-of-pearl, yet each has its own predominant colour. This silvery aspect is likened in Sanskrit works to the gleam of moonlight on the surface of the water.

> *"Chakras are energy-awareness centres. They are the revolving doors of creativity and communication between spirit and the world."* ~ Michael J. Tamura

If we look down into the bell of a convoluted-type flower, we would get the general appearance of a chakra.

4

THE HUMAN ENERGY FIELD

*"When Your Energy vibrates at a frequency that is
in direct alignment with what the universe has been
attempting to deliver your entire life, you begin to live
in the flow and true miracles start to happen."*

~ PANACHE DESAI

The electromagnetic field around the Earth can be viewed as a stiff jelly. When our bodies move, these movements are transmitted to the environment, and vice versa. Medical science has shown that all living creatures maintain electro-chemical processes in their bodies. These fields not only impinge on our bodies, they also affect the electrical charges inside our bodies. The human body also has its own electrostatic field about itself, usually referred to as the Aura.

Valerie Hunt, a Physical Therapist and Professor of Kinesiology at U.C.L.A. California, has developed a method of measuring the electrical signals within the human energy field.It corresponds to ancient teachings regarding the human aura and the system of vortices known as the Chakras, which you will recall and have now acquired a good understanding of from the previous chapter. Valerie's work involved the study of human muscle movement by means of Electromyography.

This instrument picks up the electro-chemical pulses sent along the nerves to activate the muscles. The strength of the muscle reaction depends solely upon the frequency of such pulses. Valerie was able to filter out muscle signals and their higher frequency components.

After doing this she was left with smaller signals in the range from 100 to 1600 Hz, which did not seem to emanate from the heart, nerves, or brain. By producing a Frequency Spectrum of these signals, she showed that they formed distinct peaks at regular intervals, quite unlike what might have been expected from random noise. This discovery led Valerie to believe that the high-frequency electrical signals were the effect of another, non-physical energy system acting upon the human body. Something intangible, like the human aura and the system of Chakras!

Valerie then expanded her research to include people who claimed to be able to see the colours of the human aura. The aim of her research was to establish whether something immaterial, outside the body, could influence electro-chemical activity in the body. This might be the vital link between body and spirit, which had occupied the minds of all philosophers since the time of Plato.

The human body is composed of 75% water, and so these higher frequencies would be damped out if they originated in the body. In order to affect the body's electro-chemical system, they would have to pass along a separate, non-physical system of special meridians throughout the body. Valerie was able to associate particular peaks of the subtler frequencies, both with a tone scale and with particular colours of the human aura, as seen by sensitives.

By collecting sample fields from many individuals, Valerie was able to relate certain talents or abilities to specific frequency peaks in their energy field spectra.

This chart shows The Relationship of the Human Energy Field Frequencies to the Colours of the Aura and the Chakras:

- Materialistically minded people had no significant peaks above the limit of 250 Hz.
- People with healing ability seemed to have frequency peaks between 400 and 800Hz.
- Persons with extra-sensory perception of some kind or other seemed to operate in a narrow band from 800 to 900 Hz.
- Those with energy peaks above 900Hz are what she called "mystical personalities, "or what we now call Star Seeds.

Chakra	Colour	Approx. Frequency
Root	Red	200 Hz
Sacral	Orange	300 Hz
Solar Plexus	Yellow	400 Hz
Heart	Green	500 Hz
Throat	Blue	600 Hz
Third Eye	Indigo	700 Hz
Crown	Violet	800 Hz
Astral	Cream/White	1000 Hz
Mental	Golden	1400 Hz

For the record, you need to be aiming for a minimum resonance of Violet, 800Hz Crown Chakra (3rd from the bottom), if you have any chance of Ascending. But don't be concerned. You can easily reach that level in 4 to 6 weeks!

The human body is basically an electro-chemical plant. It is influenced by external fields but can also influence external fields. By understanding the frequencies of the human aura, we can begin to back-engineer the system to our advantage. By raising our aura frequencies to resonate in harmony with the Shuman's Resonance, we create a healthy body.

The Human Aura

One of the most well-known healers and teachers in the field of energy healing and aura healing is **Barbara Brennan**. A former NASA physicist, Barbara Brennan studied the energy around the Earth and then applied the theory to the human body.

Through her work, Brennan has identified seven layers of the human energy field. The first three layers are the most dense and easiest to perceive, and they pertain to the physical plane. The higher layers are vibrating at higher frequencies and are more difficult to perceive.

These layers hold different forms of information and correspond to the chakras. The energies from the chakras produce the auras, and the auric layers expand and contract depending on physical, emotional, and spiritual health. Simply put, on the one hand, when you are healthy, well balanced, and meditating regularly, your aura expands, usually out to 2-3 metres (6-9 feet). On the other hand, when your body is physically ill, or you are experiencing an emotional upheaval, or even if you are just never meditating, your aura can shrink inward to as little as 5 cm (1 inch). The seven layers are:

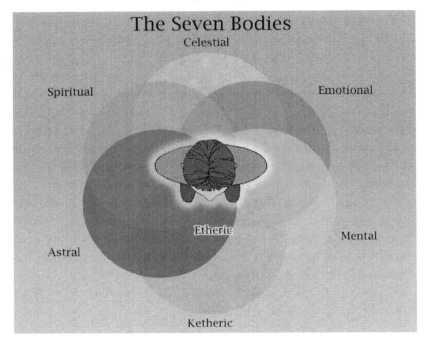

- **Etheric body** - the first layer and most dense of all, is where the physical body is formed.
- **Emotional body** - the second layer is where healing of our emotions occurs and we develop self-love.
- **Mental body** - the third layer comprises the mental aspect: thoughts, ideas and beliefs. Healing of this aura layer is creating positive thought forms.
- **Astral body** - the fourth layer is on the astral plane and contains the records of all our past – childhood experience, conception, pre-conception, our past life experiencesas well as our future plans for this life.
- **Spiritual body** - the fifth layer is the spiritual plane and encompasses our will, our purpose in life in this physical form; becoming our own authority and our sense of truth.
- **Celestial body** - is also on the spiritual plane, and this is the layer of divine love and unconditional love for all of creation.

- **Ketheric body** - the last of the seven layers, vibrating at the highest frequency, also on the spiritual plane. This is the layer of divine wisdom, divine perfection, and oneness with the universe.

The first field, known as the **Etheric Aura,** vibrates closely to the physical body. This field holds information about your physical health. Its colours are shades of blue and extend 2.5 cm – 3 cm/1-1/4 inch to 2 inches outward. A person reading this field may feel physical pain or sensations of pleasure.

The **Emotional layer** of the aura extends about 5 - 7.5 cm/1 to 3 inches from the body. This is the field that holds emotions and feelings. The colours are usually a bright rainbow combination. When negative feelings and emotional blocks are present, this field can appear somewhat muddied. Problems in this aura will have a negative impact at some point in the first and third layers.

The Mental, or third layer, of the aura, can extend anywhere from 7.5 – 20cm/3-8 inches from the body. It contains your ideas, thoughts, and mental processes. Usually, bright shades of yellow are associated with this layer.

The **Astral layer**, the fourth level, spreads out about 30cm/1 foot. It represents a bridge to your spiritual realm and is also the doorway to the astral plane. If your spiritual health is good, the colours are vibrant and reflect that of a rainbow.

The fifth layer, the **Spiritual template**, protrudes about 60cm/2 feet outward. Within this field, there is a blueprint that contains all the forms of the physical world. Because of the negative space it creates, colours can vary.

The **Celestial aura**, or sixth field, can extend up to 80cm/2.5 feet. This level is connected to the spiritual realm. Communication with those in the spiritual realm takes place here, along with unconditional love and feelings of ecstasy. The colours that appear are a brighter shimmering light in a multitude of opalescent pastel colours.

The **Ketheric template**, or seventh layer, can extend to over 1 meter/3 feet. This field surrounds all of the other layers and holds them together. It vibrates at the highest frequencies and is composed of threads of bright, shining, gold colour. It reflects all the experiences and events that your soul has undergone. It is your link to the Divine and to becoming one with the universe.

Experiences of the Human Aura

At one time or another, you have sensed someone's aura. This is often referred to as the "vibes," or vibrations, you get from a person. Aura sensing is demonstrated in children between the ages of four and six.

For example, when drawing family members, some children use a specific colour for each person. They do so because they sense the human aura, although they do not consciously realise it. Parents and teachers often question them about why they have chosen these specific colours. Believing that there might be something wrong about drawing this way because of all the questioning, the children eventually stop. As they continue to mature, the ability fades as logic gets in the way of psychic abilities.

Each one of us encounters many different feelings and situations. These happenstances, negative or positive, are processed and reflected in the auras. They reflect mood, physical and mental health, and even psychic abilities. Auras are not permanent. They change depending on many factors. Being conscious of your own aura is key in developing your own psychic abilities and raising your vibration high enough to Ascend.

The best way to begin learning to interpret people's auras is to become aware of how you are physically affected when you are near them. This is known as *clairsentience*.

When you are in company with someone else, take a deep breath, and as you exhale, take notice of your five senses and your gut reaction. Think about how you are feeling. Are you anxious? Do you want to be near this person? Do you feel relaxed or happy to be with this individual? Does this person make your skin crawl? Try hard not to focus on the verbal conversation that took place. Instead, try to think about what colour you would attach to this person. As your abilities are enhanced, feeling, sensing, and seeing the aura colours become easier.

A good suggestion is to keep a journal of your thoughts and experiences after encountering other people. After meeting someone, write down what appeared in your mind or any colour you associated with that person. You might later find out something about the life or past experiences of the individual you had met.

To understand how your aura is projected from your body, there is a simple exercise that can be done. Take your palms and rub them together rapidly. Pull them apart and then repeat the rubbing. Next, slowly pull them apart again, but hold them approximately 5 cm/one inch apart.

Close your eyes and focus on the sensation happening between your hands. Is there warmth? Does it feel like they are opposing magnets? Is there a slight trembling feeling? Continue moving your palms slightly in and out, and you will begin to feel a ball of energy grow. It should feel warm and spongey.

Your sensations are not solely the result of friction. It is how your energy is emitting from your body. Also, by doing this, you have stimulated the chakras in the palms of your hands, which are important for receiving and projecting healing energies. Focus on this energy field and you will experience several different vibrations and temperatures. These fluctuations represent information about you. All over your body, from head to toe, vibrations are released. An example of how to extend your auric field would be to open up your palms and turn them upward.

Many exercises and techniques, such as meditation, are available to fine-tune your ability to sense and see auras. The process can be slow, so be patient. If you do not see the colours, that is okay. Just focus on the feelings and sensations you are getting when you are around other people. You are on your way to further developing your psychic abilities. Here are some of the signs that you have experienced the Universal Human Energy Field of yourself and others, and our interconnectedness:

- You felt anxious, panicky when you entered a room full of people.
- You turned around, only to find out that someone was staring at you.
- You felt instant calm and peace in someone's presence.
- You felt anxious, angry, and irritable in someone's presence, without any particular trigger or verbal communication from the other person.
- You feel drained around certain people.
- You feel drained or overwhelmed in large crowds, shopping malls, or at events.
- You had a sense of how someone is feeling, despite their behaviour indicating otherwise.

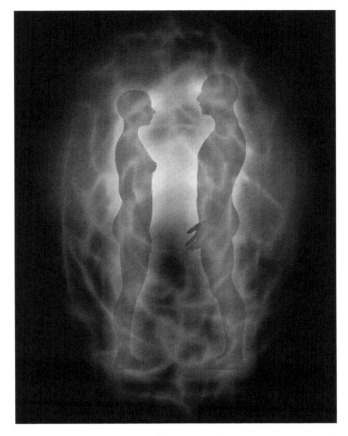

When you are near someone, your auras become interconnected

These are just a few examples. If you have answered yes to any of these, then you have felt and experienced the auric field of another person, which means that you have experienced *interconnectedness*. We can also experience the energy field of animals, plants, rocks, minerals, etc.

Anything that is comprised of atoms (protons and electrons) will have a Universal Energy Field. This is because the protons and electrons are electrical and in constant motion. They are simply vibrating at a certain frequency.

If you have a dog or a cat, you may have noticed that you sense how they are feeling, whether they are calm, relaxed, anxious, or sad. This is your way of sensing their energy field. They do not communicate this to you. In other words, you perceive it through their energy field. You are experiencing *interconnectedness*.

If you are visually perceptive, you can also see auras, or the Universal Energy Field, surrounding trees, plants, flowers and any other material objects.

The Halo

The Human Aura is easiest to see around the head. That is why there are many pictures of saints, mystics, and masters who are depicted in paintings with a halo around their head. In fact, everyone has a halo around their head. The difference is in the degree and intensity of the colour. A golden halo is often seen as a sign of integrated spiritual development.

How to Feel Auras

If you are more of a kinaesthetic (feeling) person, it will be easier for you to feel auras then to see them. In terms of psychic ability, this is called *clairsentience*, the ability to feel and perceive beyond the material realm.The hands are the easiest means for feeling subtle energies. You will need a quiet space and uninterrupted time for this exercise.

1. Begin by sitting in a comfortable position with your back supported by a chair and feet fully grounded on the floor. Close your eyes and connect to your breath. Feel your breath entering your body, moving through the body, and leaving the body. Just follow your breath for a little while.
2. With your eyes closed, rub the palms of your hands briskly together, for about 20-30 seconds.
3. Extend your hands in front of you, elbows slightly bent, palms facing each other, about a 30 cm/1 foot apart.
4. Very slowly, move your hands closer together, without them touching each other.
5. Slowly, move your hands apart again. Do this slowly and pay attention to what you are sensing, feeling, in the space between your hands.
6. Repeat the process: slowly draw your hands closer, and slowly draw them apart. Continue with your eyes closed. If you feel distracted, connect to your breath again. Notice the breath as it enters your body, as it moves through your body, and as it leaves your body. This will ground you again and stabilise your attention.
7. Repeat the process of drawing your hands apart and closer together. Notice any sensations, images, thoughts that come through your mind. What are you noticing in the space between your hands?
8. How does this sensation change when you change the distance of your palms?

There is no right or wrong with this exercise. Whatever you are experiencing is your reality; it is your perception of the subtle field, of your own aura. With practice, you will be able to feel the human energy field with eyes open.

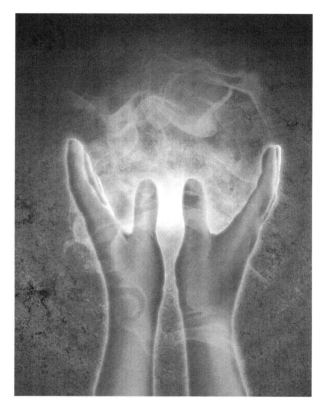

Create a ball of green energy to heal someone

How to See Auras

Seeing auras can be developed with practice. First, you begin to learn how to see your own aura. At the beginning, you will only be able to see the lower layers of the Aura, but with time and practice, you will develop the ability to see the higher layers as well.

For this exercise, you will need a quiet room with a white wall, preferably in low light (use a candle or light dimmer).

1. Begin by sitting down across from the white wall. Your back should be fully supported by a chair, your feet flat on the ground. Connecting to your breath, take a few minutes for relaxation.

2. Extend both arms, palms facing you, fingers slightly apart. Have your index fingers almost touching. Soften your gaze(don't stare) as you look at your hand. It is ok to blink. Hold this soft gaze for 30 seconds and you will begin to see the energy field surrounding your hand.

3. Slowly spread your fingers apart. Continue with the soft gaze, looking at your fingers and the space between your fingers. Move your index fingers back and forth – touch: almost touch. What do you see?

4. With time and practice, you will begin to see an outline around your hand and around your fingers. At first, it may appear as a heat wave, an almost colourless field; later on, you will begin to see the different colours of your aura.

5. Patiently observe. There is nothing to strive for. Just being here, in the moment, focusing softly on the hand, on the fingers, and the space between the fingers.

With practice, you will be able to do this exercise during daylight or in any other light conditions, and eventually without using the white background.

Another exercise I find helpful is to look at your own face/head in a mirror, preferably standing up. Like you did with your hands, gaze at the very top and centre of your head. Eventually, you will see the thin life force field, and then eventually flashes of colour. The flashes of colour will turn to solid blocks after you practise this exercise regularly.

How to See Auras of Others

For this exercise you will need a partner and a white wall.

1. Have your partner stand against the white wall, not touching it, just standing very close.

2. Stand away from your partner so that you can see them from head to toe, including the white space behind them.

3. Feel your feet firmly planted on the ground, and connect with your breath. Close your eyes for a few seconds.

4. Open your eyes, and with a soft focus, look at your partner in a way that encompasses their whole body. Gaze softly, passively noticing whatever arises. There should be no striving to see anything, just allowing whatever arises in the moment.

5. You will begin to see the energy field around the head and upper body. This is the area of the body that is easiest to see. At first, it will appear colourless, like a heat wave. With time, you will begin to see colours and you will no longer need a white background.

Seeing auras takes time and dedicated practice. But anyone can learn to detect the human energy field.

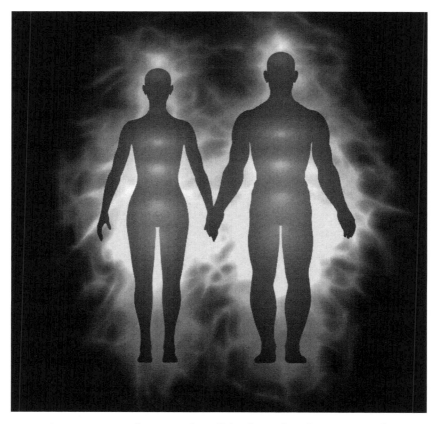

Auras never stay the same colour all the time – they change constantly

Reading Auras

Learning how to see auras is the easier part. Learning how to interpret and understand what they mean is more challenging. One way to learn to read auras is through understanding aura colours and their meaning. But that is not all that is required for reading auras.

We are complex Beings and what we see is usually an interplay of our own perception, our knowledge, experience, biases and ego defence mechanisms, cultural and societal influences,the way we understand the world, the nature of reality, and our own view of spirituality (what I collectively refer to as your "filters").

When I am reading auras, I always take this into consideration: the way I see auras is my own projection based on all of the above mentioned factors. Through many years of personal work, meditation, and the use of a variety of spiritual techniques, I have learned to get "out of myself" when I am working with others.

What does it mean to get "out of myself"?

It simply means entering a state of consciousness that is beyond my identification with the Self. It is a state of Be-ing that is pure consciousness, beyond the boundaries of Ego and the boundaries of the body. In this state, there is no "I" and "You" as separate Beings, there is oneness and openness to see what is presented in the moment.

In this state, the energy field can be seen, felt, and understood for what it is in the moment. I am guided by Universal knowledge that is accessible to all of us.

Ethics in Healing and Reading Auras

When you learn how to see auras, you may be tempted to share everything you see with other people. However, aura colours change throughout the day, with each emotion, a blockage in the body, with thought patterns, energy levels, and the flow of prana through the body. So, what you see in the moment is just that, in that moment. Thus, you need to be careful about interpreting aura colours of other people. Why?

For two reasons. First, when you see the aura of someone else, you are seeing it through your own aura. You are seeing it through your own perceptions, your knowledge, and your beliefs. Jumping to conclusions may not be wise. Use your heart, your mind, and your soul to guide you.

Second, once you develop the skill of seeing auras, you will be able to see auras around people anywhere, on the street, in a shopping mall, at work, at college etc. Seeing somebody's aura is like looking into someone's bedroom and intruding on their privacy. It should not be done without the person's consent.

If you do happen to see auras without consciously focusing on it, then treat what you see with the highest respect for the person. If they have not asked you to read their aura, then do not disclose that you see their aura. Remove yourself and shift your focus away, letting go of what you have seen.

Lastly, you will know immediately when you see the aura of a person who is soon to depart the physical world. They have what I call a "death shadow," mainly over their head, shoulders, and chest area. It is not your place to go and tell them they will die soon! Nor is it right to tell their loved ones.

Indeed, once you develop your psychic abilities, you will have access to all kinds of private information about people. It is not for us to judge, and it is not for us to tell of what we have seen, except when you have been directly asked by that person. Even then, when I see a death shadow, I do not tell them they are going to die. I tell them that there is a concern around their health, and that they should consider seeking medical advice. The last thing you want to do is put fear into people.

Aura Colours

Aura colours, the hues, the sharpness, and the intensity of colours, provide information about your emotional, physical, spiritual, and mental well-being.

Colour is a wave travelling through space. Our eyes register different colours of the electromagnetic spectrum based on the space between the peaks of the waves. The brain interprets these spaces between waves into colours.

Our energy bodies, the chakras and the aura, show colours, because the energy bodies are vibrating at different frequencies. You will see these frequencies, or waves, as colours in the auric field.

Aura Colour Meaning

Red Aura

Red is a strong colour associated with basic, primal urges. It signals connection to the earth, vital energy, and enthusiasm for life on this plane of existence. People with a lot of red in their aura have a zest for life and a desire to succeed and excel in this world. Muddier shades of red can indicate anger held deep within the structure of personality. This anger serves as a protective mechanism for the Being to survive in the world.

Orange Aura

Orange in the aura is associated with ambition, creativity, and sexual energy. It is a passionate colour and people who have a lot of orange in their aura are emotionally expressive. If the colours are muddy, it can indicate emotional imbalance, such as pride, flamboyance, or vanity.

Yellow Aura

One of the easiest aura colours to see is yellow. It is the colour of sunshine, happiness, optimism, and awakening psychic abilities. Yellow around the hairline can indicate spiritual development, growing wisdom, new ideas, intellect, sense of appropriateness, and mental clarity. Muddier shades of yellow can indicate being too critical, overanalysing, and excessive thinking.

Green Aura

Green colour in the aura indicates growing compassion, love, and a desire to be of service, to help others. It is a colour of balance, harmony, and a feeling that I am OK, you are OK, and everything else is OK. This colour reflects personal growth, openness of the heart, and willingness to change and transform. Muddier shades of green can indicate possessiveness and fear of being unlovable.

Blue Aura

Blue colour, one of the easiest to see in the aura, indicates peace, quiet order, and a person who can speak their truth – they know their own authority. It reflects quietness, calm, and seriousness. A person with a lot of blue has a strong sense of purpose, is sensitive, and has a developed inner guide or teacher. It can also indicate loneliness and a journey of coming home, of coming to higher Self, or Essence. Darker blue is an indication of connection to the deep mysteries of spiritual life, intuition, creative imagination, clairaudience, and telepathy.

Purple Aura

Purple in the aura indicates that a person is integrating the physical plane and the spiritual plane. It indicates a blending of heart and mind, as well as a sense of leadership. Purple indicates intuition, high imagination, visualization, and connection to the world of dreams. People with a purple aura have the ability to lucid dream, to astral travel, and they possess other psychic abilities. As we will see later, during the Ascension process, your aura will change to purple around week 5 to 6. That is why it is important to learn how to see your aura now, so you can check on your Ascension progress later.

Gold Aura

Gold in the aura indicates that a person is in the process of higher spiritual development and is coming to their true personal power – her Essence, or Being – without the constraints of the Ego. Gold means that you are connected to a higher power or God, and that you are inspired, devoted, and are coming to a time of revitalization. It is a colour of higher mind, of understanding the patterns of the Universe and of the laws of the Universe. Gold in the aura around the hairline indicates high spiritual development. Your aura will turn to gold about 1 week or so before you Ascend. You cannot ascend until your aura is resonating as gold.

Pink Aura

Pink in the aura indicates softness, of yielding to love for others. It is a colour of growing compassion, tenderness, kindness, and gentle nature. When seen in an aura along with other pastel colours, it can indicate a quiet, modest person, with love for all of humanity. The muddier shades can indicate emotional imbalance. Perhaps the person gives too much and sacrifices their own needs.

Black Aura

Black colour is often thought of as dark, negative energy. In my experience, seeing black in the aura is a sign of drug abuse. Indeed, smoking large quantities of marijuana is known to blow holes in your auric field. These holes always appear black. Demons and low form entities are repelled by bright, luminous colours, so the only time they can approach, and latch on, is when there is an absence of colour – i.e. Black holes.

Depending on the overall colour of the aura, and the vibrancy of the colours, black in the aura tells me that the person is experiencing a level of imbalance, physical blockage or is under psychic attack.

Especially if it is seen close to a body part; for example, a knee can indicate blockage in that area and the person can be experiencing pain in the knee area. Black can also be a sign that death is near.

Grey Aura

Similar to black, grey in the aura can indicate blockages in certain body parts, especially if darker and muddier shades of grey are found close to a body part.

Colours Are Not Always What They Seem

You need to use wisdom when interpreting aura colours of other people. You will never see one colour and one solid colour only. It is always patches of colours, and sometimes they cross over.

Green is a secondary colour, a combination of the two primary colours of blue and yellow. Secondary colours always match the colours that comprise them. Each subsequent combination echoes a similar one in the natural world. Hunter green and eggshell blue, for example,evoke a forest and sky, respectively, or emeralds and blue topaz. Green and yellow might be like foliage on a tree beginning to turn during fall.

Red and green are complimentary colours. When matching green with red, or green with yellow, orange, blue, or brown, it is best to pair different shades in terms of their intensity. Light green and pink, for example, or olive green and mustard yellow. A dark green with a light accent colour is also a handsome match, such as pesto green and ruby red.

Beyond complimentary colours are analogous colours, of which chartreuse (green), aquamarine, indigo, magenta, vermilion and amber are a single set. These are essentially other shades of blue, purplish-blue, red, orange, and brown.

Once you get good at seeing colours, you will literally see all the colours I just mentioned at one time or another. This is why it is critical to have a well-tuned psychic ability to interpret the meanings correctly. How do you fine tune your psychic ability? Meditation.

Aura Cleansing

An important part of maintaining overall well-being, and also in developing your psychic abilities, is to be aware of your auric field and how aura cleansing will protect it. Everyone has an aura, an oval energy field that, as we have seen, is made up of several layers, extending approximately 1 metre/3 feet around you. Aura awareness and cleansing are achieved through techniques, including the balancing of your chakra system.

Unbalanced chakras are reflected in your aura but, at times, you might be unaware that an imbalance exists. Sometimes you just feel out of sorts and do not know where those feelings are coming from. Another sure sign is if you are feeling scattered, confused, or overwhelmed. Whether or not there is an imbalance, it is a good idea to cleanse it periodically, just in case any negative energies are lingering.

Furthermore, your aura is very susceptible to taking in another person's energies, without you even knowing it. For example, you may be in a great mood before a party, in anticipation of connecting with old friends and their acquaintances. While having a great time at the party, you may suddenly find that your mood changes and becomes one of sadness or anger, for no apparent reason. When you arrive back home and reflect on your unexplained mood swing, you may deduce that there had been some type of intrusion or invasion of your aura. This type of incident is an indication that your aura needs cleansing.

To cleanse your aura is an act of personal healing because it holds information about your physical, emotional, and spiritual well-being. It continually processes positive and negative information about your personal experiences, your five senses and even your sixth sense – your intuition.

How can you cleanse your aura and keep it safe from another negative invasion? Try the following technique. This is where chakra awareness comes into play.

1. To begin, focus on your root or base chakra, which is the first of the seven major chakras, located at the base of your spine and associated with the colour red.
2. Envision it having a red light extending beneath it, anchoring it to the earth.
3. Next, imagine yourself engulfed in a shower of brilliant, golden light extending down from the sun. This light penetrates throughout your body and your aura.
4. Imagine this light engulfing you for some time.
5. Then envision a violet light extending from the soles of your feet to the top of your head and that acts as a warming, protective blanket.

6. Believe that this violet light has the capacity to heal and protect any gaps within your aura. These gaps need to be closed, as they inadvertently allow negative energies to flow through. This imagery will begin the aura healing and cleansing process.

7. At this point, you should begin to feel that you are becoming stronger, starting to release the negative energy and feeling more at peace with your mind, body, and soul. Also, you will now be more open to attracting heightened divine energies. Meditate on this sensation for some time.

8. When you feel comfortable, imagine a white light surrounding your cleansed aura for additional protection. This should help remove all of the negative energies you may have attracted.

You can now reap the benefits of a cleansed and healthier aura. However, this meditation takes practice and you may have to repeat it several times before you will be comfortable using these healing lights. If you find this cleansing process difficult and not giving you the results you were looking for, there are individuals who specialise solely in aura cleansing.

That is why we want to cleanse our aura regularly. There are many ways to do this; drinking plenty of fresh, clean water every day is one way to keep your energy field humming. Taking time for yourself, meditating, engaging in arts, and anything that nourishes your soul, helps your energy field as well.

How to cleanse your aura using the Earth's energy

One of my favourite ways to cleanse my aura is to use the energy of Mother Earth. I spend a lot of time in nature and at least twice per week I go for long walks in the woods.

The Earth is a living, breathing, pulsing organism that emits her own energy. You can use this energy to cleanse your energetic field, to balance the vibrational frequencies of your chakras and to bring equilibrium to your subtle body.

Just being in nature, away from electromagnetic pollution, will aid in cleansing your aura. You don't have to do anything else. Slowing down, being present, sensing the Earth, the trees, the vastness of the sky, and taking deep belly breaths will help to cleanse your aura.

Sometimes I also incorporate the following ways of using the Earth's energy for aura cleansing:

- **Hugging a tree** - closing my eyes and sensing the aura of the tree, allowing it to merge with my own aura.

- **Walking barefoot** on grass - being present, sensing my feet on the ground, sensing the temperature, the softness, settling into the quietness and the humming of Earth's energy. Letting the energetic frequency of Earth merge with my own frequency, very quickly cleanses unsettling energy.
- **Meditating** under a tree, sensing my auric field, sensing the energy of nature, and sensing the body's boundaries merging with Earth's energy, into oneness.

Aura cleansing with sea salt

You can also cleanse your aura by taking a sea salt bath. Sea salt has wonderful electrical and cleansing effects on the body and the energetic field. If you don't have access to the ocean, then try this at home: Draw a warm bath and add a cup or two of sea salt. You can buy sea salt in a health food store. Avoid adding commercial bath products into the water as they can contain many chemicals. If you wish to use something fragrant, use pure essential oils in your bath.

Aura cleansing with a smudge stick – "smudging"

Another way of cleansing your aura is with smudging. Smudging is used in many native traditions and shamanic practices as a process of cleansing. Oftentimes it is used as part of a ritual to begin or conclude ceremonies. The shaman or the healer will use a smudge for this process.

A smudge is a bundle of dried herbs, also called a "smudge stick." You can make a smudge stick on your own or you can buy one at a metaphysical store.

Most commonly used herbs for smudging are sage, cedar, and sweet grass. Any herb can be used instead of these. My friend sometimes uses rosemary as it grows abundantly in her garden. First, she lets it dry and then ties the branches together into a tight stick.

The smudge stick is burned in a way that it produces smoke rather than a flame or fire. For your own aura cleansing, it is best to have someone to help you. If you would like to do it alone, I recommend placing the smudge stick into a safe porcelain container in order for you to have both hands free.

Light up the smudge stick; once there is smoke, scoop it up with your hands (or have a friend to do this) and with smooth rolling hand motions bring it over to the body.

Start at the top of the head and continue down towards the legs. Scoop up more smoke as you move along the body. You do not touch the body; rather, you bring the smoke over to your auric field. Let your intuition guide you how far or how close to bring the smoke to the physical body.

Smudging can also be used for cleansing a room, an entire house, your car, your sacred meditation space, or basically anything, since all objects have aura. The smudging ritual purifies energy, the auric field of all objects and spaces.

Aura healing with Colour

A very simple way for aura healing is with colour. Colour is a wave traveling through space. Depending on the wavelength, the space between the peaks – measured in nanometres (nm)– our eyes register different colours.

Sine wave is the measurement of energy, used to depict frequency, vibration, and waves. It is a waveform, a single frequency repeated indefinitely in time. Your subtle body, the aura, and the chakras, vibrate at different frequencies.

The colour of your aura is determined not only by your internal state –your thoughts and feelings – but also by your external environment, your clothing, and your surroundings. Since everything is energy, everything interacts with everything else. There are a number of ways you can use colour to support your aura healing:

- **Wearing colourful clothes** - you can use different colours on different days to have a full spectrum of colour healing.
- **Eating a rainbow food diet** - this is not only healthy for the physical body, it is also beneficial for the other layers of the aura, including the spiritual layers.
- **Charging water with colour** - coloured glass (you can often find coloured bottles in thrift shops), or covering the top of the bottle with a transparent filter. Fill the bottle with pure spring water (not tap water) and put it in a sunny location. Leave the water in the sun for about two hours. My two favourite colours for charged water are blue and orange. Blue water (water charged with blue colour) is healing for the physical body, the first layer of the aura, and orange water is healing for the emotional body, the second layer.

Using Crystals

Crystals like clear quartz and amethyst are very good to clear and strengthen your aura and Chakras. Simply sit with a crystal in your hands. Listen to gentle music, or be in nature. Sit for about one hour for the crystal to do its work. The longer the better. To recharge the crystal, either leave it outside on a full moon, or place it in fresh ocean water, or salted water, for about one hour.

White Light Yourself

The best way to protect your aura, yourself, your loved ones, your house, your car or whatever, is to white-Light it. The principle is the same for everything. Visualise a brilliant, white light surrounding, or filling a person or object. Try this simple exercise on yourself:

1. Sit in a comfortable position and close your eyes.
2. Imagine a bright white light entering through your Crown Chakra.
3. This light fills your head, inside and out.
4. Now imagine this light travelling down from your head, through your body.
5. Imagine the light filling your neck, your shoulders, your arms, your chest, your solar plexus, abdomen, pelvis, and all the way down through the legs to the tips of your toes.
6. Imagine this white light now hardens into the hardest element in the universe. Nothing can penetrate it.
7. You are now cocooned in Light, and totally protected.

Practise this White Lighting technique daily, as every future meditation will begin with it.

Aura healing affirmations:

Another tool for aura healing is affirmations. Affirmations work on the third layer of the aura, the Mental Body, where you can heal your thought forms. You can use these affirmations anytime during the day or as you are falling asleep. Just like during meditation, when you are falling asleep, you are accessing deeper layers of consciousness, and you begin to re-pattern the thought forms embedded in the aura.

Repeating healing affirmations as you are falling asleep also helps to quiet down the nervous system and calm an overactive mind. Here is a short mantra I use regularly:

I open my heart to Divine healing.
Healing light surrounds me.
Healing light is within me.
I am filled with light.
I AM Healed.
I AM Whole.
I AM Light.
I AM.

5

SHIFTS IN THE PHYSICAL BODY

"Love is the energy from which all people and things are made. You are connected to everything in your world through love." ~ BRIAN L. WEISS, M.D.

A shift in consciousness creates a shift in your physical biology as well. For example, when you are stressed, your adrenaline and cortisol levels heighten, along with a lot of neuropeptides, causing physiological chaos. By default, the body then switches off the immune system every time the stress hormone cortisol is released. Therefore, during unnatural, lengthened episodes of stress, the body will eventually get sick because the immune system is constantly switched off!

Think how many times you have been stressed, on the one hand, and working back late for several weeks. Almost always, you will end up with a viral infection and spend two days in bed recovering.

On the other hand, if you are calm and meditate regularly you can experience an internal state of bliss and euphoria, with the simultaneous release of serotonin, dopamine and opioids as well as oxytocin, which just happens to be an immune modulator.

Thus, I have known many people who have meditated for years, who have never had a day off sick. They can have the same pressures and stresses of any job, but they are able to cope better with those times. When you meditate regularly, the little things that used to bug you just don't seem so important any more.

The Pineal Gland

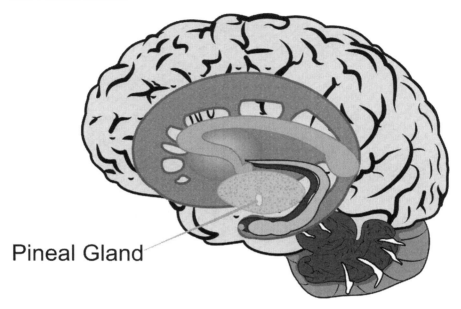

Pineal Gland

Dr. Dean Hamer, a molecular geneticist, claims he has identified the "God" gene in human DNA. It is called **VMAT2,** and its job is to release the feel good chemicals into our body, called dopamine and serotonin, which give us the feeling of bliss and euphoria. VMAT2 is the gene of our *pineal gland*. What's the pineal gland?

It is a gland about the size of a pea, located directly in the middle of your head. It is called the pineal gland because it resembles a tiny pinecone. This powerful gland is the seat of our Soul and the gateway to the Universe and higher realms. Because its structure is remarkably similar to our eyeballs, it is often referred to as the 3rd eye or the "mind's eye." It actually has a lens, cornea, and retina.

The Elites revere it, calling it the "all-seeing eye," and have featured it on the US $1 bill. Strangely, the pineal gland is tucked away in the dark recesses of our brain and is bio luminescent and sensitive to light.

Like a mobile phone, it has a built in wireless transmitter and is the connecting link between the material and Spiritual worlds and higher frequencies (via the Crown Chakra).

By awakening our pineal gland we can speed up our memory and learning abilities; enhance our intuition, wisdom, creativity; and trigger our psychic healing abilities and experience bliss.

Court of the Pinecone, Vatican, Rome

The symbol of this pinecone shaped gland is the pinecone! It is so revered by the Vatican that a special court was built, called the *"Court of the Pinecone"*, where the symbol for the world's largest pineal gland is on display. The symbol is also found on the staff of the Pope and the Egyptian god Osiris. Considering the power and function of the pineal gland, why has it been ignored and given so little mainstream attention? Why? Because it is our power source, and the ruling class know this.

Medical science refers to the pineal gland as the atrophied 3rd eye. By the age of 12, it is already calcified and hardened, and by adulthood it is dormant and atrophied through lack of use. Recent research reveals that **fluoride**, which is a toxic additive to our water supply and toothpaste, accumulates in the pineal gland where it wreaks havoc. Outdoor activities, eating less sugar, and eliminating processed foods and fluoride from our diet can help to revitalise it.

DMT

During periods of stimulation like heightened awareness and stress, the pineal gland secretes a hormone called **dimethyltryptamine**, or DMT. DMT is also produced in certain plants from the *tryptamine* family which are used by the Maya to make a brew called **ayahuasca**. Shamans drink the DMT laced drink to see into the future, or to go on "dream journeys," to learn about higher universal knowledge.

In recent years, unscrupulous drug barons have been producing a synthetic drug they market as DMT. Unsuspecting young people then smoke it, with sometimes devastating results. The lab-made concoction they falsely call DMT can lead to brain damage, blindness, and insanity. So, it is best to stick to the natural form of DMT, and meditate!

Pineal Gland Activation

There is an ancient technique that has been preserved and passed down through the centuries for reactivating the pineal gland. The technique produces the same result that Tibetan monks achieve through trance meditation. This exercise technique should not be attempted by anyone who does not feel ready to explore higher realms of consciousness beyond the five senses.

To begin the exercise you need to find the right vibrational tone of voice. Hum the word "love." Not a low or high pitched voice but somewhere in between. When you find the right tone it will feel like your mouth and/or head is vibrating.

1. Sit comfortably with your back straight and your eyes closed and scan your body for any sign of tension.
2. Take three long, deep breaths through your nose and exhale all the tension through your mouth. Now think about opening your third eye and entering a loving Universe where all that exists is bliss.
3. Take another deep breath through your nose and hold it for a few seconds. Just before you exhale, begin your tone, making everything in your mouth and lips vibrate.

4. As you slowing exhale through your pursed lips loudly hum the word Love and vibrate the "v" sound until all of the air is expelled from your lungs.

Repeat this exercise four more times, taking a few moments rest between each repetition. To awaken your pineal gland you need to repeat this exercise again for two more days in a row at 24 hours apart. The entire exercise only has to be done once to be effective, but depending on how calcified your gland is, it may take longer. After activation, it can take six weeks or more to experience your newly awakened abilities.

The Link between Emotions and DNA

The intangible parts of our existence, such as emotions, are part of the true reality of our higher consciousness. If emotions are part of a realm that we cannot experience with our five senses then how is it that we are all aware of our emotions?

What people believe to be emotions is not truly the emotion but a physical manifestation of these emotions. Anger causes disturbance in the psyche, which manifests itself in the Ego. These manifestations cause the heart rate to increase, body temperature to rise, and they spawn many other physical traits that signify anger.

Just as music on the radio is a physical manifestation of an intangible signal, our experience of emotion is the physical manifestation of an intangible signal, as well.

Emotions have a Vibratory Frequency

It has been demonstrated that our emotions have a vibratory frequency to them. **Hans Jenny** first published *Cymatics: The Study of Wave Phenomena* in 1967.

Jenny created an experiment where he passed vibrations of sound through a form of media like sand or water. Each time he did this at a set frequency there was a set pattern that would follow.

When the frequency increases, the media develops into a more complex pattern. This is exactly how emotions work!

 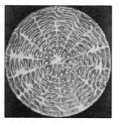

Slow vibration   **High vibration**

Hans Jenny's experiment with Cymatics

Emotions create waves of energy through your entire body. Fear based emotions manifest as (but not restricted to): anger; hate; jealousy; greed; vanity; self-loathing; addictions; manipulation; over control; OCD; narcissism; judgment; hypocrisy; racism; bigotry; living in scarcity; an unwillingness to change; and many more.

Love based emotions manifest as (but not restricted to): compassion; happiness; self-love; kindness; support; unconditional love; balance; calmness; politeness; nonjudgment; and many more.

There is a hard digital link between emotions and genetics. This is the first time we have ever seen the patterns of emotion directly and physically linked to the human genome.

Emotions have a Direct Effect on your DNA Structure

As stated, it has been shown that our emotions have a vibratory frequency to them. Furthermore, there are only TWO emotions that humankind experiences: FEAR and LOVE. All other emotions branch directly or indirectly from these two emotions. Fear has a long, slow vibratory frequency, and Love has a rapid and high frequency.

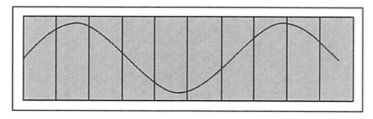

Fear has a long and slow vibration frequency to it

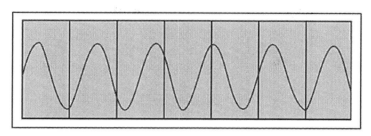

Love has a very rapid and high frequency

DNA Phantom Effect

Researcher **Peter Gariaev** (Russian Academy of Sciences, Moscow 1985 – findings published in 1991) measured tiny particles of light, called photons, inside a vacuum tube. The photons were scattered, as expected. A sample of DNA was then placed inside the vacuum tube and the photons were measured again. They found that the particles of light aligned themselves along the axis of the DNA. Then, as they removed the DNA sample, the photons remaining aligned with the same form as the DNA, even though no DNA was present. This is what is known as the **DNA Phantom Effect**.

Emotions are Directly Connected to our DNA

Science has now bridged a very important gap between the physical and the ethereal, or Spiritual. Emotions directly affect the structure of our DNA, which directly shapes the physical world we experience every day.

After 2012, the Earth started vibrating at 21 GHz (more on this in the next chapter). It had been steadily rising from the original Earth frequency of 7.8 GHz. The frequency increase has followed the Fibonacci sequence. Just as Cymantics shows us, the higher the vibration, the more complex the patterns become. The Schuman's Resonance remained constant at 7.8 GHz until 1986, then it rose to 9 GHz in 1996, while in 2006 it was about 13.8 GHz. When the major Shift occurred in 2012, the vibration moved up to 21 GHz. It has been steadily rising so now, in 2017, it is around 34 GHz.

Fibonacci sequence: 0, 1, 1, 2, 3, 5, 8, 13, 21, 34, 55, 89, 144…

0	1982	1982	2002	2012	2017
0	10	10	20	30	50
0	7Hz	7Hz	14Hz	21Hz	34Hz

The Earth's vibration has a direct effect on us. If we are unable to attune ourselves with the Earth, then we will literally go crazy, and society will become chaotic - just as we are seeing now in 2017! Indeed, as we have seen, our emotions directly influence our DNA. If you are not in sync with the Earth, then your mental state will become unstable and your DNA will be impacted in a very negative way. Furthermore, it will also impact on your physical wellbeing.

Indeed, you may develop any number of chromosomal diseases and, in particular, endocrine diseases and autoimmune disorders. We are already seeing the signs of this with the highest level in history of youth suicide, drug and alcohol addiction, violence, greed, and general unhappiness in society. On a more positive note, we have also seen a global move away from the corrupt globalisation structure and a move toward nationalism and solidarity.

To attune yourself with the Earth, you need to spend more time in nature, on a beach or in the woods. Drink more clean water, eat less processed food, and above all – meditate!

6

THE BIO-PSYCHOLOGICAL EFFECTS OF ASCENSION

"Your personal vibration or energy state is a blend of the contracted or expanded frequencies of your body, emotions, and thoughts at any given moment. The more you allow your soul to shine through you, the higher your personal vibration will be."

~ PENNEY PEIRCE FROM FREQUENCY

The Schumann's Resonance

Do you feel inner peace and generally happier when you're out in nature, or in the country, or on a secluded beach? When you're out in nature, it's not just the fact that you've left the city behind, but also that, out in nature, your body tunes into the Earth's frequency and can repair, rejuvenate and heal itself more efficiently. So, what is the Earth's frequency?

Our planet is surrounded by a layer of electrically charged particles called the ionosphere. The lower layer of the ionosphere is roughly 50-95 km (30-60 miles) from the crust. This charged layer is known to reflect radio waves.

In 1953, Professor W.O. Schumann discovered that the Earth's cavity, which is the area between the crust and the Ionosphere, produces a very specific pulse.

This is the vibrational pulse, or heartbeat of planet Earth.

Schumann fixed the most predominant standing wave at 7.83Hz. Therefore, the term Schumann's Resonance refers to the frequency or vibration of the Earth set at 7.83Hz. The Schumann's resonance (7.83 Hz) was so constant that the US Navy based all of their communication technology on it. In the early 1980's, their communication equipment began to fail. After some intense fault finding, the technicians made a startling discovery: the Schumann's resonance was no longer fixed at 7.83 Hz – it had gone up! As the Earth's background base frequency, the Schumann's Resonance is rising dramatically. The rise in the Schumann frequency has followed the Fibonacci sequence.

By 2012, the Earth was vibrating between 21Hz and 24Hz. It is now at around 34Hz, and climbing. 21Hz is the critical point that the Earth and humans must reach to begin the final Ascension process. So, we are well and truly past the point.

The Earth's vibration has a direct effect on humans, like when you feel relaxed out in nature. However there can also be a downside.

Therefore, we will next look at the Schuman's Resonance effect on human health and brain activity.

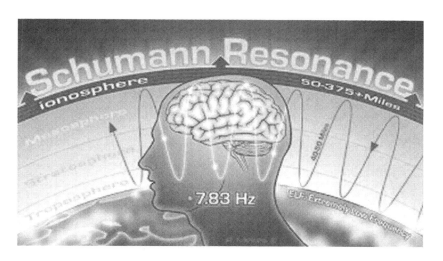

Human Brain Waves

The brain has its own set of electrical frequencies it uses to communicate with itself and the rest of the body. The electroencephalograph (EEG) measures brain waves of different frequencies within the brain. Waves can overlap somewhat, merging seamlessly into one another.

Brain waves are measured in cycles per second (Hz). Raw EEG frequency bands include: Gamma, Beta, Alpha, Theta, and Delta.

These frequencies are linked to behaviours, subjective feeling states, physiological correlates, etc. The frequency bands and wave characteristics are described as follows:

- **Gamma waves** relate to simultaneous processing of information from different brain areas. They are involved in memory, learning abilities, integrated thoughts, or information-rich task processing. Gamma rhythms modulate perception and consciousness, which disappear with anaesthesia.

- **Beta waves** dominate our normal waking state of consciousness when attention is directed towards cognitive tasks and the outside world. Beta is a "fast" activity, present when we are alert or even anxious, or when engaged in problem solving, judgment, decision making, information processing, mental activity and focus.

- **Alpha waves** are triggered during dreaming and light meditation when the eyes are closed. As more and more neurons are recruited to this frequency, alpha waves cycle globally across the whole cortex. This induces deep relaxation. In alpha, we begin to access the wealth of creativity that lies just below our conscious awareness. It is the gateway, the entry point that leads into deeper states of consciousness. Alpha waves aid overall mental coordination, calmness, alertness, inner awareness, mind/body integration and learning. Alpha is also the home of Schumann's Resonance 7.83Hz! When we intentionally generate alpha waves we go into resonance with the Earth frequency. We naturally feel better, refreshed, in tune, in sync. It is, in fact, environmental synchronization. That is why you feel relaxed and at peace when you are in the country, or on a secluded beach – your brain is resonating with the Earth!

- **Theta waves** occur most often in sleep but are also dominant in the deepest states of meditation (body asleep/mind awake) and thought (gateway to learning, memory). In theta, our senses are withdrawn from the external world and focused on the mindscape – internally originating signals. Theta waves are associated with mystery. It is that twilight state which we normally only experience fleetingly as we rise from the depths of delta upon waking or drifting off to sleep. Theta meditation increases creativity, enhances learning, reduces stress, and awakens intuition and other extrasensory perception skills.

- **Delta waves** are the slowest but highest in amplitude. They are generated in deepest meditation and dreamless sleep. Delta waves confer a suspension of external existence and provide the most profound feelings of peace. In addition, certain frequencies within the delta range trigger the release of a growth hormone which is beneficial for healing and regeneration. This is why deep restorative sleep is so essential to the healing process.

Brain waves affect the way we feel, our health, and our ability to learn. Alpha waves induce feelings of peace and harmony and just happen to be the same frequency as Schumann's Resonance. This is no coincidence; after all, our brains did evolve on this planet within the Schumann's cavity. However, as we have learnt, the Schumann's Resonance is rising, so our brain waves are no longer in sync with the Earth!

Schumann's Resonance Effect on Human Health

Electrical engineer **Lewis B. Hainsworth** of Western Australia, first discovered the relationship between Schumann's resonances and human health and well-being. In 1975, **Dr Robert O. Becker**, noted electromagnetics pollution expert, along with several Harvard neurologists, took up Hainsworth's study. What follows is the outcome of their combined research. Hainsworth posed a series of questions, all of which are answered with a resounding "yes."

a) Does the human biological system contain, use, or generate any forms of electrical signal?

b) Does it respond to any of these signals?

c) Does it respond to audible signals at these frequencies?

d) Does it respond to optical signals at these frequencies?

e) Do human signals change with psychological or mental states, such as stress or problem solving?

f) Does the human system respond to any very, very low-power electromagnetic signals?

The scientists discovered that all biological processes are a function of electromagnetic (EM) field interactions. EM fields are the connecting link between the world of form and resonant patterns. They store gestalts or patterns of information. Earth's resonances and our brain frequencies co-evolved.

Thus, human health is linked by way of the naturally occurring Schumann's Resonance. Having answered the questions posed by Hainsworth's study, the researchers identified how Schumann's Resonance determines the frequency spectrum of human brain-wave rhythms:

> *"The frequencies of naturally occurring electromagnetic signals, circulating in the electrically resonant cavity bounded by the Earth and the ionosphere, have governed or determined the 'evolution' or development of the frequencies of operation of the principal human brain-wave signals. In particular, the alpha rhythm is so placed that it can in no circumstances suffer an extensive interference from naturally occurring signals."*

Hainsworth concluded that the frequencies of human brain-waves evolved in response to these signals. This is self-evident given that Alpha Waves and Schumann's Resonance are at the same frequency! As the Schumann Resonance rises, it can be expected to lead to the appearance of "new" diseases, probably accompanied by a decline in resistance to many minor infections. There will be an increase in conditions related to abnormal cell development, including conditions such as cancer, birth defects, and infertility. There will be an increase in psychological disturbance problems; for example, drug addiction, depression, and suicide.

In recent decades, there has been a massive rise in diabetes, thyroid, and gall bladder problems. The majority of health issues show up as stress-related conditions. There have been increases in mental disturbance, antisocial behaviour, psychosomatic conditions, and neurological disturbances. Some electrical field phenomena have already been linked with abnormal cell growth and a decrease in immuno-competency.

The rise in Schumann's Resonance explains the riots and protest going on all over Europe and the United states since 2016. These people are no longer in sync with the new Earth energies, so they have quite literally gone crazy.

The brain is a massive source of Extra Low Frequency signals that get transmitted throughout the body through the nervous system, which is also sensitive to magnetic fields. So, when the brain is out of sync with the Earth's resonance, eventually the whole body is affected. By understanding how our bodies are connected to the Earth, we can begin to re-synchronize ourselves with the Earth.

Harmonic Synchronization

Entrainment is the process of synchronization, where vibrations of one object will cause the vibrations of another object to oscillate or vibrate at the same rate. As we have already learnt, the brain is a massive source of Extra Low Frequency signals that get transmitted throughout the body through the nervous system. So, just as the brain can influence the entire body's vibrational frequency, so too can the Schumann's resonances influence the brain!

Brain waves and natural biorhythms can be entrained by strong external ELF signals, such as Schumann's resonances. During meditation you may experience fleeting moments where the brain resonates in Alpha, Delta or Theta, but it is difficult to maintain this frequency since the Schumann's resonances begun to rise.

However, entrainment, synchronization, and amplification via an external source can promote coherent large-scale activity. There is a harmonic relationship between the Earth and our mind/body. Schumann's resonance forms this natural feedback loop with the human mind/body via our brain and our DNA. The human brain and body developed in the biosphere, so our body's Electro Magnetic field was environmentally conditioned by this cyclic pulse or Schumann's resonances.

Indeed, this pulse acts as a "driver" of our brains and can also carry information, much like the cable that connects your computer to the Internet. Therefore, functional processes may be altered and new patterns of behaviour facilitated through the brain's web of feedback networks.

Harmonic synchronization occurs when your body/mind transfers information back and forth with the Earth. This can only be achieved if both bodies are vibrating at the exact same frequency. However, since the Earth has begun her Ascension, as is evident by the rise in Schumann's resonances, most people are out of sync. There are 3 obvious behaviours that determine if you are out of sync:

- **Under arousal** leads towards unipolar or reactive depression, attention deficit disorder, chronic nerve pain and insomnia.
- **Over arousal** is linked with anxiety disorders, sleep onset problems, nightmares, hypervigilance, impulsive behaviour, anger/aggression, and agitated depression.
- **A combination** of under arousal and over arousal causes anxiety and depression as well as ADHD, and autism.

So, think for a minute. Does over arousal,in the list above,describe the rioters and protestors against Trump and the burning down of Europe? Does a combination of under and over arousal describe the epidemic of ADHD and autism diagnoses in the last decade? As for under arousal, I personally know many, many good people suffering from nerve pain and insomnia like never before...as I sit here at 03:10AM typing this! Hahaha (but no depression or ADD thank goodness!)

The brain responds to inputs at certain frequencies. Computers can create certain frequencies that compare with the mind's neural signals in terms of mind patterns. If people can control their mind patterns, they can enter different states of being – for example, mental relaxation. So, what happens when the mind is entrained with a sound or vibration that reflects those thought patterns?

Remember what we learnt earlier, entrainment is the process of Harmonic synchronisation, where vibrations of one object will cause the vibrations of another object to oscillate at the same rate. It becomes obvious that in deep meditation, when waves of alpha and theta rhythms cascade across the entire brain, a resonance is possible between the human being and the planet. Energy and information which are embedded in a field are transferred. Perhaps the planet communicates with us in this primal language of frequencies? Next, we are going to learn how we can train our brain to accept the new Schumann's Resonances no matter how high it rises!

Training Your Brain

Sound waves are examples of rhythm. Sound is measured in cycles per second (hertz or Hz). Each cycle of a wave is, in reality, a single pulse of sound. The average range of hearing for the human ear is somewhere between 16Hz and 20,000Hz.

We cannot hear extremely low frequencies, but we can perceive them as rhythmic vibrations. I am sure you have stood in front of a large bass speaker or drum and "felt" it as well as heard it. External rhythms can have a direct effect on the psychology and physiology of the listener. Slower tempos from 48 to 70 BPMs have been proven to decrease heart and respiratory rates, thereby altering the predominant brain-wave patterns.

Binaural beats are continuous tones of subtly different frequencies, delivered to each ear independently in stereo via headphones. If the left channel's pitch is 124 cycles per second and the right channel's pitch is 114 cycles per second, the difference between the two equals 10 cycles per second, or 10Hz. When these sounds are combined, they produce a pulsing tone that waxes and wanes in a "wah wah" rhythm. Binaural beats are not an external sound; rather, they are subsonic frequencies heard within the brain itself.

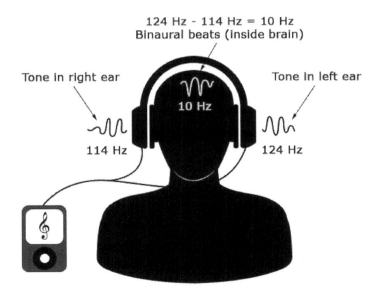

The brain waves respond to these oscillating tones by following them (entrainment), and both hemispheres begin to work together. Communication between the two sides of the brain is associated with flashes of creativity, insight, and wisdom. Alpha-wave biofeedback is considered a consciousness self-regulation technique. Through the self-regulation of specific rhythms, we begin to control those aspects of consciousness associated with that rhythm.

When the goal is alpha, either in meditation or in biofeedback, it means entraining with the primary Schumann's Resonance. In other words, by listening to binaural beats in the frequency of Alpha, we can begin to train our brain to resonate predominately in that frequency.

In my experience, I have listened to Alpha binaural beats for a minimum 1 hour a day for 12 days, every few months. I sometimes put earphones in and listen while I drop off to sleep. Even asleep, the brain is still entrained.

This literally re-sets my brain to start resonating with the latest new Schumann's Resonance frequency.

I also regularly use other binaural beat frequencies, such as Delta – for sleep, intuition, wellbeing – after I have reset my Alpha frequency.

Binaural beats can also be embedded into music. So, you will hear the music instead of the tone. Some people prefer this method. There are thousands of free binaural beats soundtracks and tones on YouTube that cover every frequency for every occasion.

We are complex electro-dynamic beings sensitive to natural and artificial Electro Magnetic fields. Schumann's Resonance frequencies coincide with human brain waves regulating homoeostasis, healing and Psi (psychic ability). There is a strong correlation between human behavioural disturbance and Schumann's Resonance frequencies. By adjusting our brain's alpha frequencies using binaural beats, we can once again harmonize with the Earth. This is essential if we are to make the shift to the 5th Dimension, which will occur during the Ascension process.

Seven Rules of Life

1. Make peace with your past so **it won't screw up** the present.

2. What others think of you **is none of your business.**

3. Time heals almost everything, so give it time.

4. Don't compare your life to others and don't judge them. You have no idea what their journey is all about.

5. Stop thinking too much, it's alright not to know the answers. They will come to you when you least expect it.

6. No one is in charge of your happiness except **you.**

7. Smile. You don't own all the problems in the world.

7

DECODING 11:11

"Sometimes it takes a wake-up call, doesn't it, to alert us to the fact that we're hurrying through our lives instead of actually living them; that we're living the fast life instead of the good life." ~ CARL HONORE

D o you find that every time you glance at a digital clock that the time says 10:10 or 11:11? Maybe you see 12:12, or any double number for that matter. Many people are witnessing this phenomenon, but do not understand the significance of it.

Physical reality is a consciousness program created by digital codes. Numbers, or numeric codes, define our existence. Human DNA, our genetic memory, was encoded by Ningishzida (Thoth) to be triggered by digits at specific times. Those codes awaken the mind to the change and evolution of consciousness. When you see certain number patterns, your DNA is being activated to move you to a higher frequency vibration. Many believe awakening comes through healing and the creation of balance through: one, one – 11.

- 11 is double digit and is, therefore, considered a Master or Power Number in Numerology
- 11 represents idealism; vision; refinement of ideals; intuition; revelation, artistic and inventive genius; the avant-garde; refinement fulfilled when working with a practical partner.
- 11 is a higher octave of the number two.

- 11 carries psychic vibrations and has an equal balance of masculine and feminine properties.
- 11 contains many gifts such as psychic awareness and a keen sense of sensitivity

Ultimately, 11:11 is a wake-up code/alarm to unlock the subconscious mind, our genetic encoded memories, and it is our final "upgrade" to Ascend. It is also a sure sign that the Alpha waves in your brain are changing frequency!

- **10:10** = Moving into a new beginning
- **12:12** = a higher octave of 6 or 3+3=6= Spiralling of Consciousness
- **15:15** or 33 represents Christ Consciousness; universal nurturing; social consciousness raised to a world class; global responsibility; master teacher and healer

People all over the world are seeing 11:11, 10:10, 12:12 on digital clocks. These are wake-up calls to initiate changes to your DNA. If you are one of these people then you have already started your transition to a higher vibration.

You will experience a sudden awakening after which reality is never the same. You are going to create clarity, healing, and balance for yourself. Do not expect others in your life to be on this journey with you. It is yours alone, as it is for most souls. You will have to seek new friends of like mind who are also being triggered by the digits – once you open the Digital Door there is no going back! Your soul will automatically and quickly move you from level to level of experience until you 'get it'.

Your consciousness is expanding, and therefore, you will manifest faster and with greater comprehension, becoming more aware of the meaning of the synchronicities that will become more and more frequent. These are created by your Higher Self, as they help you to remember that you are a soul spark in a physical program that is about to end and evolve back to higher consciousness.

Once you see your numeric codes, you have activated something in your DNA codes, and they will continue to appear until you 'get the message' that it is 'time' to move on. Upon seeing your digit encoded numbers, you may feel a sense of urgency or related emotions. Don't panic! For now, there is time. The numbers can also signal changes in the patterns of your life.

10 Second Tune-Up

Next time you glance and see 11:11, 10:10 etc. – PAUSE: look into your mind and tune in to a message. It can be about anything. STOP – THINK – don't close your eyes: see an image in your mind. Try to remember the first thing that pops into your head. It only takes 10 seconds of your time. With practice, you will move forward. This simple exercise will help you unfold very quickly. It might be fun to do in a boring office situation, or at a boring meeting or class.

8

THE SPIRITUAL PLANES OF EXISTENCE

"To care about your outward appearance is important, but what's more important is to have a beautiful soul."

~ ROY T. BENNETT

If you have read my first book, **The Truth Chronicles - Book I - Secrets of the Soul,** then you will remember that the Spirit World consists of seven concentric spheres around our planet, and that each of these spheres is separated into seven sub-levels. Since you will have access to some of these planes during the Ascension process, we will take a brief look at each of them now.

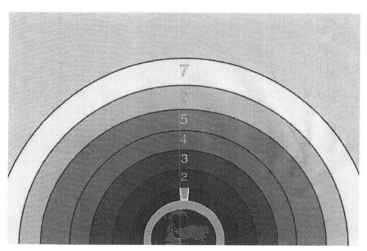

The spirit planes around the Earth

1. The Physical Plane/Etheric Plane

Prior to the first sphere, there is a "buffer zone" (the grey band nearest the Earth), which is not a numbered sphere. It is a neutral space between the Earth plane and the first sphere. The Physical plane (Earth) and the etheric plane are connected to make up the First Plane.

This is where lost souls (ghosts) reside, as well as Diva (nature spirits), Faerie, and other creatures, such as Sasquatch, chupacabra, and it is even where Grey aliens and Reptilians can hide out. They can change their vibration by only a fraction to appear on the Earth plane then to disappear again. It is as easy as breathing for these beings. Indeed, think of it like moving the dial on a radio set from one station, then going up or down to the next available station. Dolphins and Whales also have the ability to do this. They can reside on the Earth or Etheric Plane at will. In fact, many whales escape Japanese whalers by slipping into the Etheric world and hiding there.

The Etheric Plane is more or less an analogue of the Earth Plane, with a few distinctions. Colours are much more vibrant, and you can see in ultraviolet. In fact, the whole place has a light blue tinge to it. As stated, many other creatures exist there. Faeries, devas, unicorns, dragons, etc. Others are too weird to describe. The Reptilians and Greys do more than hide out there; they use it as a home base. For that matter, they also have subterranean bases on the Earth Plane.

It is not unusual to see many itinerant travellers there. They come from all over the galaxy, either to observe planet Earth, or to use it as a stopover on route to somewhere else.

Light and Dark beings exist there, and battles are fought constantly in some regions.

> *"The sky is filled with good and bad, that mortals never know…"*
> ~ Battle of Evermore by Led Zeppelin

The US Military have been engaged on the Etheric Plane, and involved in battles there since the late 1960s. These operations come under **Project Star Gate.** This program went officially public in 1995 just after it had been turned over to the CIA. The CIA, then through its FOIA system, released 12,000 files totalling 89,000 pages of material from the entire twenty year history of the program.

This is not where your soul comes from, and it is not where it stays after you die. Younger Souls do hang around on the Etheric Plane after death so they can witness their funeral and/or try to comfort those loved ones left behind.

The Etheric Plane is the place where most people go to when they "Astral Project." Indeed, most have not raised their vibration high enough to go to the Astral Plane, for it is still much more Light filled then the Earth Plane is. So, to the uninitiated, it would seem like a very high plane of existence. But the fact is, it is not – it is "just" above this third dimensional plane you are in right now.

The next sphere (black band) is still part of the Earth/Etheric Sphere. Think of it as another region. It is actually an exclusion zone or quarantine area to keep the really bad (low vibrational) beings out of the Etheric Plane proper.

It contains the least light and is the habitat of spirits who are of a very low vibration. This is the realm of the creatures called demons, dark entities, and poltergeists etc. It is also the realm where negative thought forms manifest, and where they can then filter back down to Earth. It is not hell – hell is NOT a real place, and does not exist. Nor can human souls be sent to this sphere. It is, however, the place where negative human thoughts manifest.

Yes, when you think very negative thoughts, they do go somewhere, and that somewhere is this sphere. You see, every thought you have becomes manifest on the etheric Plane. Fleeting thoughts manifest then quickly dissolve away. But obsessive thoughts will form and take root – good or bad. This is where the (incorrect) New Age movement idea of "manifesting abundance" on Earth comes from.

And it is also where all these Fear based thoughts go to and take root. Some filter back as cancer or other "mishaps" (Karma), while mass fear can create thought forms so powerful that they can take on a life of their own. They usually return as a world war or as a conflict throughout a particular country that had created the thought form.

I have often wondered if it was the human negative thought forms that, over time, morphed into demons, dark beings etc., or if those creatures were part of the natural balance of the Universe.

Anyway, so we don't get a runaway negative thought form debacle happening, these very low vibrations are quarantined as best that can be. Some still do filter back to Earth from time to time, but as more people "wake up," the less will filter down. This, by default, will raise the vibration on the Earth Plane, which is awesome for everyone!

Later, you will learn how to activate your MERKABA. The Earth/ Etheric plane is the initial plane where the MERKABA is activated. That is why I am covering this information now, so you know what to expect. For the record, as stated earlier in the Chapter 4 (Auras), if you are vibrating at a high frequency, you radiate Light. The dark entities cannot stand to even look at this Spiritual Light. So, in other words, if you explore the Etheric Plane in a Light filled MERKABA, the low vibrational creatures will scurry away in every direction when they see you coming. You have nothing to fear.

2. The Astral Plane

The Astral Plane, also known as the **Emotional Plane**, is where consciousness goes after physical death. Indeed, you leave the Etheric Plane via the Tunnel of Light, and you exit on the Astral Plane. Here you are greeted by loved ones, debriefed by your Guides, and eventually "graded" as to which level of the Spirit Plane you will end up on (see, **The Truth Chronicles - Book I - Secrets of the Soul** for the full story).

The Astral Plane can be visited consciously through astral projection, meditation, and mantra, near death experience, and lucid dreaming, or through other means such as the MERKABA. Individuals that are trained in the use of the MERKABAcan separate their consciousness from the physical body, at will.

From here, it is much easier to tap into the **Akashic Records.**

3. The Spiritual Plane

The Spiritual Plane is split into many sub-planes. This is the place where your soul ends up living in between lives on Earth. Depending on your vibration at death, such as high, medium, low etc. this determines which sub-plane you end up on. Some are better than others, obviously, as each sub-plane is a slightly higher vibration than the one below it.

It is your choices, actions and thoughts, as well as every emotion you caused someone else that decides on which level of the Spirit Plane you end up on. You are not judged – your final frequency determines your fate. Indeed, part of your final "grading" is to experience every emotion you made other people in your life feel. So, if you gave a lot of love, you will feel mostly love. But if you caused a lot of pain and suffering, then that is what you will feel. It is this vibration that determines which sub-plane you end up on.

During your life between Earth lives, this is where you gain spiritual knowledge and experience. I give a full description of this in **The Truth Chronicles - Book I - Secrets of the Soul.**

4. The Mental plane

The Mental Plane, also known as the **Causal Plane**, is the third lowest plane. In the mental world, one formulates a thought, and it is instantly transmitted to the mind of another without any expression in the form of words. Therefore, on that plane, language does not matter in the least.

The Mental Plane, as its name implies, is that which belongs to consciousness working as thought; it is not of the mind as it works through the brain, but as it works through its own world, unencumbered with physical spirit-matter.

On the Astral Plane, you still have a light, Astral body, but on the Mental Plane, there is no body, only thought.

5. The Buddhic Plane

The Buddhic Plane, also known as the **Unity Plane**, is described as a realm of pure consciousness. It is described as such because it means to become unselfish, especially in the sense of letting go of solving any or all problems with the ego. Indeed, it is on the Buddhic Plane that one casts off the delusion of the self and enters a realisation of unity consciousness. Annie Besant defined the Buddhic Plane as "*Persistent, conscious, spiritual awareness.*" This is the fourth, or middle, state of consciousness. Some people incorrectly refer to it as the *Super Mind*.

6. The Logoic Plane

The Logoic plane, also known as the **Monadic Plane**, is the second highest plane. It has been described as a plane of total oneness, the "I AM" Presence.

The Monadic Plane (hyperplane) or continuum/universe, enclosing and interpenetrating grosser hyperplanes, respectively, is the plane in which the monad or Holy Spirit, or Oversoul, is said to exist.

In other words, Soul Groups (Oversouls) that have finished all of their Earth incarnations return here. These Oversouls can contain as many as 1000 individual souls. Here, they are united back into one consciousness, or **Super Mind**.

As a Super Mind, they can become the consciousness that incarnates into planets and stars i.e. **Logos** or **Agathon**. After you have served, learnt, and grown as a planet, star and galaxy, you can finally return to the Source on the Divine Plane.

7. The Divine Plane

The Divine Plane is where new souls come from, and this is also where all souls eventually merge – back with the Source of All that Is (God). This is where your journey began and, now that you have come full circle, where it ends. You now become part of the mind of God.

It is the plane in which Brahman and Om, or Aum, stem from, the Spirit of Deity (as God, Brahman, etc.,); the creative Word (as the Pranava Om or Aum, Tikkun, etc.); and the ideal, exists. Who knows, maybe the Source will project you into another existence. But I know one thing for certain – it will be a very long time before any of us get a ticket into this place!

9

15 LIFE CHANGING LESSONS

"We are not our bodies, our possessions, or our career. Who we are is Divine Love and that is Infinite."

~DR. WAYNE W. DYER (1940-2015)

There are people in this world who can touch our hearts in very profound and meaningful ways, and that's exactly the impact Wayne Dyer had on me when I first discovered his work many years ago.

Wayne W. Dyer was one of the most humble and authentic people who ever walked on this Earth in modern times. He taught me how to be humble, how to live in love and truth, and how to always honour who I truly am. He taught me how to be better than I used to be and I will always be thankful for this.

Thank you for sharing your love, your knowledge, and your wisdom with all of us. The world was, is, and will be a better place just because you have lived. You will be greatly missed.

What follows are my favourite Wayne Dyer quotes that I have incorporated into my own life. I have given each a small explanation of how I understand his message. I believe these messages are essential for purging your being of negative vibration. If you can incorporate these small lessons into your life, you will have a much higher success rate of Ascending.

1. Cooperation is healthier than competition.

> *"If you're always in a hurry, always trying to get ahead of the other guy, or someone else's performance is what motivates you, then that person is in control of you." ~ Wayne Dyer*

Work on improving your own person, and be so busy doing so, that you don't have time to compare and compete with others. We are all in this together, and this sense of separation will only weaken us, creating more pain and suffering.

2. If you love people you don't try to change them.

> *"Love is the ability and willingness to allow those that you care for to be what they choose for themselves without any insistence that they satisfy you." ~ Wayne Dyer*

When you love somebody you love them for what they are, not for what you want them to be, without imposing your will and without constantly trying to change them.

3. Ignorance is not bliss.

> *"The highest form of ignorance is when you reject something you don't know anything about." ~ Wayne Dyer*

Allow yourself to expand your mind a little more day by day: give up labels and you will be happier. If you constantly say NO to "strange" ideas, things, events, and people, how can you expect to progress through life? Try new things, and if it makes your life better, stick to it,and if it doesn't, let it go. It's that simple.

4. You are not a victim of the world.

> *"How people treat you is their karma; how you react is yours."*
> *~ Wayne Dyer*

When you react to people and situations in a certain way and affirm those reactions with words or thoughts, such as, *'you make me mad'*, *'this situation is upsetting me'*, *'I can't believe you are treating me this way'*, etc., you start playing the victim game. Take responsibility for your own thoughts, your own feelings and actions, and by doing so, you will no longer give your power away to forces outside yourself. When something negative comes your way you will pause, and, instead of reacting, you will **RESPOND,** to everything and everyone. You will no longer be a victim, but rather, a person who is aware of his or her inner strength and power.

5. You find yourself in solitude.

> *"You cannot be lonely if you like the person you're alone with."*
> *~ Wayne Dyer*

If you are comfortable in your own skin and really love your own person, you will not be afraid to spend time alone. You will enjoy the time you spend alone as much as you do when you are surrounded by people you dearly love.

6. Rejection makes you stronger.

> *"Be grateful to all those people who told you no. It's because of them that you managed to do it all yourself." ~ Wayne Dyer*

If you trust and listen to your own heart and intuition, you will always know where to go and what to do with your life. No matter how many doors close in your face, you will not give up: you will allow rejection to make you stronger and better, not bitter.

7. Self-worth cannot be verified by others.

> *"Self-worth cannot be verified by others. You are worthy because you say it is so. If you depend on others for your value it is other-worth."*
> *~ Wayne Dyer*

If you constantly seek outside yourself for approval and validation, you will never be happy. We have some control over the way that we are all different and we all perceive things in different ways. But your reputation is not something you can really control. Your reputation is not really in your hands, so stop trying to please everyone around you and start pleasing your SELF. You are the person who matters the most, and if you yourself are not happy with who you are, chances are others will not be happy with you either!

8. You don't attract what you want in your life, you attract what you are.

> *"If you're obsessed with defeating the other guy and winning at all costs, then you're guaranteed to attract the vibrational equivalent of this thinking into your life-- even if you do yoga and stand on your head chanting mantras every day." ~ Wayne Dyer*

People often think that if they focus long enough on something they want, with the Law of Attraction and such, they will get whatever they want in life, but that's not how things work. On the one hand, if you purify your mind and heart, you will attract many beautiful things into your life, and abundance will not be something you will have to chase because it will chase you. On the other hand, if your mind and heart is full of negativity, negativity in all forms will show up in your life.

9. There are no limits to what you can achieve – you are a no-limit person.

> *"When you argue for your limitations, all you get are your limitations." ~ Wayne Dyer*

There are no limits to what you can achieve; only those you choose to impose on yourself.

10. "Heaven on Earth" is a choice you must make, not a place you must find.

> *"Loving people live in a loving world, hostile people live in a hostile world. Same world." ~ Wayne Dyer*

Focus on the **BAD** and that's all you will see and attract into your life; focus on the **GOOD** and that's all you will see and attract into your life.

11. No need to stress over everything

> *"Good morning, this is God. I will be handling all of your problems today. I will not need your help. So have a miraculous day." ~ Wayne Dyer*

Believe it or not, there is an invisible force who created the whole world and the whole Universe. This force becomes available to us the moment we stop trying to do it all by ourselves, the moment we decide to allow events to take their natural course and just go with the **FLOW.**

12. All that you need is already within you

> *"You have everything you need for complete peace and total happiness right now." ~ Wayne Dyer*

In this moment you have it all, right NOW and right here – there is nothing lacking. Take time to be quiet at least five minutes per day, and, in time, you will discover that you do have access to **HAPPINESS, PEACE, ABUNDANCE** and all that is good, at all times.

13. There is no end to personal growth.

> *"Individuals who use self-labels are stating, 'I'm a finished product in this area, and I'm never going to be any different.' If you're a finished product all tied up and put away, you've stopped growing."*
> *~ Wayne Dyer*

Personal growth doesn't end when you finish school. The moment you've stopped growing you can say that you've stopped living. Indeed, once you have a "belief", you stop learning about that subject.

14. Be realistic, expect miracles.

> *"Once you believe in yourself and see your soul as divine and precious, you'll automatically be converted to a being who can create miracles."*
> *~ Wayne Dyer*

There is a great power in the Universe, the Source of All That Is, and this power makes itself available to you the moment you align with who you really are deep down inside, creating miracles for you and those you love.

15. Follow your heart and you will be successful

> *"Doing what you love is the cornerstone of having abundance in your life." ~ Wayne Dyer*

If in doubt, follow your heart. If in Fear, you will follow your Ego. One will bring you to your true destiny, and the other will create obstacles, hurdles, hurt, frustration, and ultimately failure. The choice is yours.

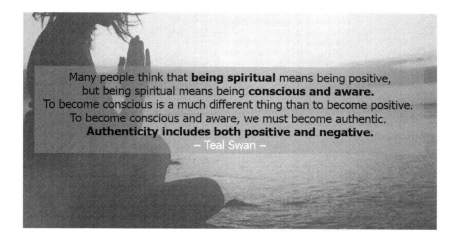

Many people think that **being spiritual** means being positive, but being spiritual means being **conscious and aware.** To become conscious is a much different thing than to become positive. To become conscious and aware, we must become authentic. **Authenticity includes both positive and negative.**
— Teal Swan —

10

SHIFTING YOUR CONSCIOUSNESS

"World is a multi-dimensional reality. At lower level it is full with unconsciousness and competitiveness. At higher level it is full with beauty, BLISS, and divinity. Focus on higher dimensions." ~ AMIT RAY

God is Love. We do not have a contract with God. A Covenant is what some religions claim they have with God. However, a Covenant is a contract. Contracts force the parties to compromise and do things against their Will.

God gave humanity Free Will. So, God would never impose a contract. What we have with God is a relationship. In a relationship, you may allow your partner to do whatever they want. Sometimes they do things that you do not like, but you continue loving them in the relationship.

If God is Love, and Trust holds hands with Love, then Trust is our relationship with God. Trust is very different to Faith. Faith, on the one hand, allows people to carry out heinous crimes and acts of hatred, all in the name of God. Trust, on the other hand, is either there or it is not. You trust your doctor to care for you. You trust your mechanic to fix your car. You do not have "faith" that your doctor may heal you. Faith is subjective – Trust is not.

Imagine you are at a very busy market, or state fair. People are everywhere. You are a small child again, and you are holding your mother's hand. Because your mother is taller than you, she can see much further ahead. You hold hands with your mother because you Trust she will lead you in the right direction.

But sometimes we get distracted. Sometimes we see shiny things, so we let go of her hand, just for a minute. When the distraction has passed, and consciousness returns, we look around and our mother is gone. Panic sets in. You run around trying to find your mother, not realising you are moving further away. You ask for guidance along the way, but the people do not know your mother, so how can they help? Then you remember something she told you. If you ever get lost, go back to the last place you remember holding my hand and I will meet you there. Even if it took you 10 years to find her, your relationship would still be strong. She would still hug you and love you. Love holds hands with Trust.

Some children never find their way back to their Mother/Father. They blame their Mother/Father for all the ills in their life. But what they do not see is that the further they move away, the worse their life becomes. Even so, the parent never stops loving them. Even if that soul never finds the parent in life, they will certainly find them in death, and once again, they will hold hands with God.

Soul Lessons and Choice

Free Will means Choice. Your whole life is a series of choices. What will I have for breakfast, what clothes will I wear today, how will I react when I find out that my girlfriend cheated on me?

It is our choices that determine our life lessons – our Soul Lessons. It is how we choose to respond to a challenge that determines the outcome of the lesson.

All Soul lessons usually revolve around relationships. Not just romantic relationships. You also have relationships with many people in your life, such as Mother, Father, Brother, Sister, friend, co-worker, shop assistant etc. Obviously, some of these relationships are more emotionally charged than others. Nevertheless, they are all relationships, thus they require a degree of Trust. If you or the other person violates that Trust, then it usually ends the relationship – but not always. And that is a choice. Do I end this relationship? Do I try to understand it? Do I examine why it collapsed? Do I go crazy and shoot up a shopping mall?

When you feel a person has betrayed your trust, they have really just exercised their Free Will and let go of your hand. They are now in free fall, falling away from you. Now you have a choice, do you let go of God's hand and free fall as well? When you sit there thinking about how you did so much for them and how could they do this to you, what you are really doing is going through a check list of a contract. Yes, you were in a contract with this person. You fooled yourself by calling the contract a relationship. But if you remember back, a Contract imposes restrictions on our Free Will. Trust does not.

By not accepting that person's Free Will to leave you, cheat on you, or dishonour you, you are really saying, "*I am more powerful than God.*" You see, God never tries to restrict our Free Will, because God loves you. God continues to Love you, no matter what you choose. That is because Love holds hands with Trust. Rather than cherry pick what is acceptable behaviour in a relationship, which is really a contract, we may choose to Accept and Allow.

When we Accept and Allow, we chose Love. It means the relationship has come to a natural conclusion, and we should move on. When we Accept and Allow, we have just completed a Soul Lesson.

Accept and Allow

There is a huge difference between Accept and Allow, on the one hand, and just accepting something, being bitter, or just putting up with something, on the other. To Accept and Allow means we choose Love.

So, what does that mean? Like I said before, you have Free Will to choose whatever response you employ to any given challenge. Most people, purely through lack of experience have a knee-jerk reaction. They will either emotionally collapse, or use blind rage. They may capitulate, which is very different to accepting. These choices are made from a Fear based mentality. Whenever we make a choice from a fear based mentality, we let go of God's hand. So, the outcome will never go well, even if you believe you have gained the upper hand or enacted some form of revenge. Revenge is a fear based emotion.

When a relationship breaks down, you must accept – and allow – their Free Will choice, even if their choice was made from a fear based mentality, which is often the case. Does this mean it will not hurt as much? No chance. You bet it is going to hurt, but believe it or not, that is how we learn. The difference is how we process the hurt. Grieving is a natural and necessary process. You must allow your body and mind to grieve. Cry your eyes out, eat a tub of ice-cream, and watch sad movies all day long in your pyjamas. Allow the pain to pass through you, and wash over you – then LET IT GO.

As Wayne Dyer often said, for the first nine months of your life, everything was taken care of for you. So, why would God stop caring for you once you were born? Once you begin to "take over" control of your life, you gradually edge the Source of All that Is out of your life. If you just stop interfering with your life, and just Be, everything will fall into place.

A Spiritual person is someone that holds hands with God in Love and Trust. They will give these painful emotions over to God in perfect Love and perfect Trust. The difference between a Spiritual person and a non-Spiritual person is the length of time it takes to heal. True Spiritual people bounce back much quicker. The sooner you heal, the sooner you get your life back again. Healing is when you Accept and Allow, let go, and let God.

Balance

The final ingredient to a happier life is Balance. If you apply balance in every aspect of your life, then things will run a lot smoother. So, in a relationship, your partner may choose to get drunk and bash you every night. Should you accept and allow this behaviour? No, because it is not in balance.

When people gain too much weight, or lose too much weight, they are out of balance, so they get depressed. When you work long hours without rest, your body gets sick and forces you to slow down because it is out of balance. When you talk too much and listen too little, you are out of balance, so people avoid you. When you already know everything, and refuse to open your mind, you stop growing.

For every action, there is an opposite and equal reaction. Some people call this Karma. I like to think of Karma as a balance sheet. All of my good Karma and my bad Karma is recorded in a book. Eventually, the book will balance and then I will stop incarnating on Earth. Because that is what Karma really is – Balance. It is not punishment or reward. The Universe is always trying to maintain balance. It does not favour Light over Dark, or Dark over Light – it just wants balance, to maintain equilibrium.

In your relationships, you should always be aware of balance. Do you take too much of someone else's time, do they take too much of yours? Does your partner take you for granted? Do you keep secrets from them?

Remember, the people you conduct relationships with can only do what you allow them to do. So, if they are doing something that you don't like, it is because you allow them to do it.

Choose Love

The next time you find yourself in a frustrating situation, or a hurtful confrontation, or maybe you just got some bad news, say the words in your head, "*I Choose Love*." This stops the natural fear based emotion rising to the top. Cut off the fight or flight response with a reminder that Love holds hands with Trust.

By keeping things simple, and applying these three basic tools on a daily basis, you will notice an immediate change. Take each day as it comes. Practice these three tools every day.

Live in Love and Trust, Accept and allow, and be mindful of maintaining balance in all areas of your life.This is part of the Ascension Process.

Love and Trust
Accept and Allow
Maintain Balance

11

THE 12 PRIMARY LIFE LESSONS

"Though nobody can go back and make a new beginning...
Anyone can start over and make a new ending."

~ CHICO XAVIER

During our incarnations on Earth, and in every Soul Age, we work to master twelve primary life attributes in our experience as humans. With each lifetime, we choose one primary life lesson to work with and may have some side projects that we have already started in previous incarnations, or ones we want to do some preliminary work on in this life. While we do not concentrate on these other life lessons fully, they are still there and can have an effect on our lives.

As for the main life lesson, however, we continue to work on it in consecutive lives until we achieve mastery of that single attribute. Then we move on to choose another primary life lesson to work with in the following incarnation.

In the past, we generally only worked with one primary life lesson at a time. There are certain instances where we may work with two or more, but most of the time we have confined ourselves to only one.

For instance, if people come very close to mastering a life lesson at the end of a lifetime but don't quite achieve full mastery, they may choose to continue working on it as a secondary life lesson in their next incarnation.

When trying to identify your primary life lesson, it is important to know that there are no hard and fast rules. For example, a woman who grew up with sexual abuse as a child will not always be working with a life lesson of Trust, even though this form of abuse provides a perfect foundation for learning Trust. She may, in fact, be working with a life lesson of Acceptance, or Definition, or even Love.

Similarly, an individual's persona and behaviour will change dramatically with each step they take towards achieving mastery of their life lesson. For example, people working with a life lesson of Charity are generally very sensitive, but in order to protect themselves, they often unconsciously disconnect from others. This will make them appear as if they are extremely selfish and interested only in themselves. Yet, once they begin to reach a higher level of mastery, they will become more comfortable with displaying their sensitivity towards others.

People will think they have changed, but all that has really happened is that they have evolved as a result of the work they have done. An interesting side note here is that, in such cases, they themselves will not recognize that they have changed.

Human Evolution

There is no doubt that humanity is evolving at an astounding rate. Spirit suggests that most of us have advanced as souls more in the last 10 years than we have in the last 10 lifetimes!

To differentiate between these different levels of evolution, I use the terms higher and lower vibration. It's important to note that this is not actually a vibration that can be physically measured in the body, but rather, is best described as a state of mind.

When people become interested in seeking a deeper meaning to life, they are actually raising their overall state of awareness. This is what I mean when I refer to raising their vibrational level. Like Soul Ages, it is important to bear in mind that one vibrational level is not better than another, they are merely different. In the same way that the sixth grade is not better than the third grade, so too is a 'higher vibration' not better than a 'lower vibration'.

So, if we are advancing so rapidly, what effect does this have on the Twelve Primary Life Lessons? Actually, the Twelve Primary Life Lessons have been around as long as we have. Whereas we used to take anything between 60 and 100 lifetimes to master a single life lesson, our rapid evolution has now made it possible for us to accomplish this in a single lifetime.

I often get asked, is it possible to master several Soul Ages in one life? The answer is always no. What people are mistaking as Soul Age advancement is actually completion of Primary Lessons, which are relative to each Soul Age. So, the Primary Lesson of Trust is less challenging for a Young Soul compared to an Old Soul. Think of it like when you were at school. You did math in every year, or grade, but each year the math problems got more difficult; still, you were able to pass the test.

With this in mind, let us never forget that even those life lessons that may look particularly disgusting might have a purpose that ultimately benefits us all. The person panhandling on a street corner, the homeless person rifling through a trash can for food, even the thief or murderer that repels us, may, in fact, already have achieved mastery of many more life lessons than we will ever know. This helps us to remember that, with our limited vision, none of us have the overall perspective to judge another soul on their path. The person we may be looking at with such abhorrence may be a master who has returned to start working on their final life lesson. The reality is, if you see something or someone that is particularly repellent to you, this generally means that they are working on a primary life lesson that you have already mastered. Thus, there is a natural intolerance and even a sensitivity to these attributes.

Young Adults and Children

Children born in the last thirty years are more advanced and, therefore, process in entirely different ways and at an entirely different rate than previous generations. These children, who have been labelled **Indigo** and **Crystal** children, are much quicker and more direct than most adults are. In order to catch their attention, information must be honed down to its very essence. In recent years we have been seeing a vast increase in the number of children with learning challenges, such as ADD and ADHD.

In my experience, many of these conditions are simply the result of children being born with advanced attributes in a society that is not ready for them. Even though many of these children may appear to have difficulty at school, they are actually very bright. In fact, the biggest challenge for these advanced humans is boredom.

When it comes to the Twelve Primary Life Lessons, I have found that most young people intuitively understand what I am saying. Even though they may not yet have had the chance to see the underlying patterns of their actions, they are generally aware of their weak points or blind spots. They simply need someone who can help them understand why they don't fit in.

About Responsibility

One human attribute that is not listed here is responsibility. That's because responsibility is actually the result of an action, rather than an attribute in itself. It is the resulting action of mastering, or not mastering, as the case may be, life lessons. In other words, one either takes responsibility for working on one's life lesson, or one doesn't. The action of responsibility generally shows up in the life lessons of Be-ing, Creation, Trust, and most common of all, Truth.

Collective Life Lessons

Life lessons are always personal in that they are always focused on the individual. However, many life lessons have also been facilitated by groups of people who have contracted to master the lesson collectively.

For instance, socioeconomic groups, religious groups, and so forth, have created specific conditions purely in order to facilitate a particular life lesson. Let's say that you wanted to work with a life lesson of Acceptance. This could be facilitated much more easily if you were to place yourself in a black community in Alabama in the 1960s when racial discrimination was at its height in the United States.

Likewise, being born into any poor family would provide the perfect conditions for mastering the life lessons of Trust, Creation, or Adaptation.

In all instances, we not only choose the best circumstances to facilitate each life lesson, we also place ourselves in precisely the most appropriate era. Let me explain. When we are in Spirit planning our next life, we organise the first stage, which is planning our life contracts and set-ups. We have the ability to see the direction in which things are heading, and thus, can place ourselves in exactly the right point in the time-line that will provide us with the best conditions to work on a specific life lesson.

As an example, in the early 1920s, the most common life lesson was that of Charity, which concerns learning about our connection to other people. We chose to work on this lesson at that time because we saw that the Great Depression that lay ahead offered us the best opportunity to strengthen our connections to each other by helping one another through those difficult times.

In the 1960s, we collectively worked on the life lessons of Communication and Love. Today, there are many diverse groups working as collectives on different life lessons. Because the way we typically advance is to act like a pendulum, swinging from one extreme to another, we have swung from working collectively on the life lesson of Charity, to working collectively on the life lesson of Definition(see description of Definition on following pages). The reason for this is because working on Charity not only taught us to recognise and honour our connection to each other, but also to think of others before we thought of ourselves.

Now the pendulum is swinging in the other direction and we are finding that we have become so wrapped up in taking care of others that we have forgotten to think of ourselves. Thus, the collective life lesson of Definition is necessary right now to help us learn to place ourselves first (*there is that need to maintain Balance thing again!*).

It is also common for a family bloodline to have a general attraction to specific life lessons. You will find that some families seem to pass down life lessons through generations almost as if it were genetic. This is known as **lineage intent**.

Many times in the first stage of life, we place ourselves in a specific bloodline because the lineage intent will help us facilitate a lesson we are working on. Definition is often a product of lineage intent and is most common among healers.

In many ways it's like being born into a family of healers. It is the tremendous sensitivity that is an attribute of this life lesson which makes it possible for healers to facilitate healing for others. It is only when people begin to master this life lesson by learning to place themselves first, and defining where their energy ends and another's begins, that they can fully step into their healing work.

In the old paradigm, when we were taking between 60 and 100 lifetimes to master one life lesson, we had no use for knowledge of the Twelve Primary Life Lessons. Now that we have started to advance very rapidly, however, this knowledge is becoming extremely helpful to the evolution of our species.

Indeed, the reason I have included this topic at all is because you must master at least your two main Primary Lessons if you are to Ascend, but more on that later.

Relationships and the Twelve Primary Life Lessons

Relationships can be the most challenging of all human experiences. To hold someone so close that you can see every detail of your own reflection is both extremely rewarding as well as extremely difficult. In this section, I will not attempt to deal with relationships in general, as that is a topic that could take up a whole book on its own. Instead, we will look at the ways in which the Twelve Primary Life Lessons affect the establishment and growth of our relationships.

The general appearance of a person has a lot to do with where they are at in the mastery process of their primary life lesson. For instance, people working with a life lesson of Trust will appear shy and reserved in the early stages. Once they start to attain mastery, however, these people's demeanour will appear to be quite confident. The same rule applies to relationships. If two people are both working on their individual life lessons simultaneously, they will have a tendency to grow together. But if they are working on their primary life lessons at different rates they will more than likely grow apart. That said, the gaps that often occur during these difficult times could be bridged if the couple can communicate openly with one another.

Certain life lessons usually tend to attract counterparts inside relationships. For instance, I have seen the life lessons of Definition and Communication being worked on by many couples. The real challenge in relationships occurs when one partner starts advancing rapidly in their life lesson and the other person makes no forward movement at all; or, worse, resents their partner's growth.

Even though all other areas of such a relationship may be healthy, the differences in advancement will place these two people at vastly different vibrational levels. This will almost certainly cause great strain on the relationship and quite often will lead to its breakdown altogether.

Even where both partners' commitment is strong enough to hold the relationship together, outside forces will often conspire to push them apart if they continue to remain at different vibrational levels for a prolonged period. The reality is that not all relationships are meant to be for the long term. This is just as true of some successful relationships as it is of many difficult ones. I have seen many relationships that have just run their course and were complete, but neither party was willing to walk away from what was familiar to them and face the unknown.

Imprints and Inherent Attributes

There are two major factors that govern every person's behaviours which can be mistaken as life lessons. **Imprinting** and **Inherent**. The first is *imprinting*. This is when your behaviours are modelled on what your family follows or believes, or what your friends, community or country believes etc. For example, everyone in your street may paint their front door red, so you paint your front door red. But perhaps this red door makes you feel ill every time you look at it. You can easily fix this situation by changing your front door to a different colour. You may have to deal with your neighbours not liking it, but it is not a deal changer. The same can be said when your parents follow a political party, but you follow the opposition.

The second life lesson is *inherent*. An Inherent attribute is one you cannot change. For example, let's say you are born with brown eyes. Nothing you do can change the colour of your eyes. Yes, you can use coloured contacts, but that is just a temporary fix.

As you will see, these two factors are very important when trying to master your Life Lessons. Imprints can be changed, but with an Inherent attribute, you must learn to master it. What do I mean by to master it? Simply own it, to love it and to accept and allow it. The following descriptions are largely based on the great work done by Steve Rother and his team.

The 12 Primary Life Lessons are:

1. **Acceptance:** Self-Esteem, Self-Acceptance and the Art of Graceful Acceptance
2. **Adaptation:** Change
3. **Be-ing:** Wholeness
4. **Charity:** Harmony
5. **Communication**: From the Heart
6. **Creation:** Expressing Self-Power
7. **Definition:** Expressing Individuality through Boundaries
8. **Integrity:** Walking in Harmony with Self
9. **Love:** Love of Self
10. **Trust:** Trusting Self
11. **Truth:** Responsibility to Self
12. **Grace:** Walking in Harmony with All Things

Primary Life Lesson #1 Acceptance: Self-Esteem, Self-Acceptance, and the Art of Graceful Acceptance

---

Although not restricted to it, this life lesson is most often experienced in female form. If there is a negative catalyst in this life lesson, it is that people can become habituated to seeing themselves as victims and then get caught up in that drama.

Energy blockages in this area may manifest as self-sabotage, whereby a person will appear to 'do everything right, but still nothing seems to work.'

The person can learn to create quite well, but as the energy they transmit starts returning to them, they have difficulty accepting the rewards. Outwardly, these people may appear to be suffering from a general lack of self-esteem, but the underlying reason for this is due to a belief system that they are unworthy.

If this belief system stems from Imprinting, it can be rewritten and changed by uncovering the origin and then working consciously to change the script. If it is part of their Inherent Attributes, it can only be mastered through learning the Art of Graceful Acceptance and understanding that energy is a flow and not a destination.

Acceptance is the art of allowing energy to flow through you. By definition, energy does not exist if it does not move. Until energy starts moving, it is purely a potential. In the experiences of life, the ability of your Spirit to feel comfortable in your 'bubble of biology' will be directly related to the amount of energy that flows through you. This is the Art of Graceful Acceptance.

If you look carefully at the areas where energy is blocked in your life, you may recognise that Acceptance may be the missing piece. The souls who choose Acceptance as a primary life lesson may have difficulty taking responsibility for their own reality. They see things as they believe them to be in two dimensions.

Since this Inherent Attribute is often best facilitated with feminine energy, it is not uncommon for these gentle people to set up contracts to become victims. They often have difficulty making sense of events and experiences and may subconsciously harbour very deep resentments towards others.

Acceptance can be a difficult attribute to master, for, once a life pattern is set,it is difficult to change it. Even when people claim full responsibility for creating their own reality, they can still be stuck in specific patterns that conspire to provide a steady supply of people willing to victimise them in one way or another. This is not just about those who are victims, however.

The lesson of Acceptance can manifest in many different ways and areas. For example, a recurring pattern of money problems can indicate that people have still not learned how to accept. They may be adept at sending out all the energy required to start the flow moving in their direction, yet when that energy returns full circle, they find it difficult to accept the abundance it brings.

If you are working with Acceptance as a primary Inherent Attribute yourself, it's important to start allowing energy to flow through you in every possible way. Look for areas where the energy may be stuck and work to release it. Practice the Art of Graceful Acceptance. Get good at accepting.

Another important aspect of this life lesson is the acceptance of responsibility. Responsibility is the balance to personal power. The equation is simple: *If you wish to create more success in your personal life, then you must accept more personal responsibility for your own happiness.*

Likewise, if you wish to create more success in your relationships, you must take more responsibility for building the relationship. For example, those always looking for their soul mate and their perfect match will have less success in relationships than those who consciously work to nurture and transform what may seem like a less than perfect match into a relationship that works for them.

Primary Life Lesson #2 Adaptation: Change

Our natural physiology is capable of great change in a very short time period. It is our psychology that often resists change. Therefore, we don't cope well with change.

The life lesson of Adaptation is about learning to adjust and to become comfortable with change. Few of us are comfortable with change, because it represents the unknown. If we do not know what is going to happen, we feel out of control. We equate giving up control with being powerless.

When faced with change, and the fears it naturally engenders within us, it may be helpful to re-member that it is impossible to achieve a higher vibrational status without change.

Souls that have chosen this area of mastery generally do everything possible to keep everything in their life on an even keel. They believe that in order to succeed they need to keep everything just the way it is, under their control, unchanging.

They often tend to attract teachers who think just the same way they do. These are also people who have a difficult time balancing their hearts and their heads. They tend to think instead of feel, rationalising every bit of information before making any decisions.

In fact, they often have a very hard time making any decisions at all. This particular attribute can be very deceptive because it does not always appear to be a hindrance. Quite often, it is not until these people are faced with drastic change that they realise they are totally unprepared and unequipped for it. The paradox is that the comfort they seek is often best served by becoming comfortable with the process of change itself.

Primary Life Lesson #3 Be-ing: Wholeness

When we first began the game, it was necessary for us to leave the first dimension of unity and travel through the second dimension, to land in the third.

As we passed through the second dimension we acquired a field of polarity. This is where we separated ourselves into the sexes and started seeing things as separate from one another, when, in fact, every single thing that exists is an integral part of everything else.

The illusions of the field of polarity in which we still reside conspire to make us believe that we are not whole. People who choose a life lesson of Be-ing have an especially difficult time with this.

Like all life lessons, this too can be facilitated either by an Inherent Attribute or by Imprinting. Those who choose an Inherent Attribute to facilitate this life lesson spend a lot of time looking for external things to add to themselves or their lives in order to make themselves feel whole.

In some instances, these are people who feel they must find something, or take something, or add something, to themselves in some way in order to enhance their mood. Some people in this situation use food to make themselves feel safe. Others may become obsessed with self-enhancement, i.e., making themselves look prettier or 'better' in some way. Still others become 'study junkies' in the belief that acquiring credentials will make them all they wish to be.

Whatever they choose, it can easily – and in fact, often does – turn into an obsession or an addiction. Obsessions, addictions, and compulsive behaviours generally present the perfect opportunities for mastery of this Life Attribute.

Addictions

The Primary Life Lesson of Be-ing many times leads to addictions. In the case of any addictive behaviour, it can be very helpful to first identify whether the life lesson is being facilitated by an Inherent Attribute or Imprinting. So, often a person attempts to heal an Inherent Attribute rather than finding ways to master it.

The life lesson of Be-ing lends itself well to addictions. Since the main pattern of this life lesson is that people look outside of themselves for things to make them whole, it is easy to see how this attribute can easily turn into a reliance, and even addiction, upon the things they think will make them whole. This does not mean that every addictive person has a Primary Life Lesson of Be-ing, however addictive behaviour is often precipitated by this life lesson.

Leaning Relationships

In the case of those who are constantly seeking to find wholeness through their relationships, this often results in a '*leaning relationship*'.

Leaning relationships are those in which two people lean on one another, both believing that neither of them is whole on their own, and thus, can only become whole by having the other to complete them. The problem is that it's virtually impossible for two people to grow at exactly the same rate, so it's only a matter of time before one person grows and the other, inevitably, falls.

Master Manipulators

There are situations in which people have become so badly injured that they spend much of their life in self-defence mode. People who have chosen to combine several lessons in one experience may find themselves being severely emotionally wounded at a very early age.

Sometimes these souls build walls around their hearts and then expend a great deal of their energy manipulating other people from behind those walls. As they grow into adulthood, they can become what I term 'master manipulators.' Of course, this is rarely done intentionally or even consciously. The problem is, they get so good at it, they are not even aware they are doing it. Frequently, the people they tend to attract into their life to subconsciously 'manipulate' are those who have poorly defined boundaries.

Weight Problems

Are you fat? This may sound like a strange question, but I have found that it's often those with the biggest and most loving hearts who are battling with weight problems. In many cases, these people find it almost impossible to see their own beauty. If you are one such person, here's a perfect opportunity to view your situation in a different light. First ask yourself, is your extra weight the result of Imprinting or an Inherent Attribute? If it is from Imprinting, i.e., something you learned or acquired due to your life experiences, remember those experiences can be healed, and when they are, your weight will automatically change. If your weight issues are the result of an Inherent Attribute, however, you could stop eating all together and still find that you may keep putting on weight. This is because an Inherent Attribute cannot be changed, it can only be mastered.

The lesson here is to first learn to see yourself in a completely different light, i.e., as being whole and complete just the way you are at this very moment and to learn to bless and to love your body.

If you search for the key to mastery and find all the gifts that this Inherent Attribute is affording you, and then learn to use these gifts to their fullest, I guarantee you will see a difference. The very first difference you'll see is that your weight will become less important to you. When that happens, your body will finally be free to adjust itself.

I often help people with this life lesson by encouraging them to find the sacred space within, where they can simply be, instead of always trying to be something, or someone, they are not. Find the place where you can learn to appreciate what you already are and just be with that. The art of simply Be-ing is foreign to most of us, but with practice they will see real change, first in their energy field and then in their life.

From Be-ing into Truth

The life lesson of Be-ing often precedes the life lesson of **Truth**. The experience gathered in a life that requires one to master the Lesson of Be-ing can easily set the stage for a life lesson of Truth to follow. People working with a life lesson of Truth will always be looking for someone else's truth, or the latest and greatest truth, or the newest concept, etc. That's a bit different from this life lesson, however, because that life lesson relates specifically to Truth, whereas this life lesson relates to the entire being. Thus, it's about always looking for what you think is missing within you.

Primary Life Lesson #4 Charity: Harmony

As we evolve as individuals, we go through phases, taking on lessons that relate to each other in some way. Since we also go through different phases as a collective, it's not uncommon for certain life lessons to become popular at different periods in time. Right now, the life attribute of Charity is not popular in our society. That does not mean it is not important, however. On the contrary, the life lesson of Charity holds the key to our next level of advancement as we progress toward becoming Human Angels.

The lesson of 'Definition' or 'centering one's own energy' would appear to be somewhat in contrast to the lesson of Charity. But once our energy is centred to the degree that we can function well, it then becomes essential for us to reach out to others. Thus, both these attributes, Charity and Definition, can coexist and be employed simultaneously in one lifetime. As we become more evolved, we are becoming more unity conscious.

Our fascination with the search for extra-terrestrial life shows that our hearts recognise a fundamental truth, which is that we are not alone. We all are an integral part of each other and what each of us does has an effect on everyone else on Earth, as well as beyond.

The word Charity has become synonymous in our society with 'giving'. However, although this can be one expression of Charity, true Charity is not just the art of giving alone. Our governments are learning very quickly that giving, by itself, only results in creating dependencies that feed on themselves, thereby breeding further dependencies. True Charity, in terms of a life attribute, means honouring the connection we have to all people and practicing this in all our actions. When our actions honour all people we are the ones who rise.

In order to apply Charity, however, we must first learn to centre our own energy. Depending on where a person focuses these attributes, this lesson can appear very differently. With these attributes focused inward we see people working with a life lesson of Charity appearing to be selfish and self-serving. With the lack of connection, they focus inward, as if no matter what they try, they simply can't get their own needs met.

In the lower levels of mastery, their own needs and feelings are foremost because their disconnection to those around them means they simply can't feel much else. This makes them appear to others as inconsiderate. The paradox is that it is only possible to feel whole when we make connections to others, yet it is extremely difficult and awkward for them to do so.

While many in this situation have already mastered the attribute of Definition (see the Primary Life Lesson of Definition), they have not yet learned to apply it to others, because with this disconnection they haven't learned to relate to those outside of themselves. Although it will seem to them that they became this way as a means of survival, their task is to learn to understand their true connection to those around them.

On the other hand, if these attributes are focused outwardly, in the lower levels of mastery this will appear as a person who over-compensates in relationships. They may appear to be in your face, demanding to be the centre of your attention. They often appear as the person who tries too hard to be liked. They don't have the feedback from people around them, so they don't know when to quit. Their inner belief is that they will have what they need if everyone likes them. It is here that they over-compensate and quite often unintentionally alienate themselves.

These people have the ability to drain others around them. As they master this life lesson, they will find that it is through honouring this connection, not by trying to make everyone love them, but by learning to feel the connection, that they achieve mastery.

Please keep in mind that the way I have described the above examples in the lowest levels of mastery, I have done so purposely for the simple reason that it is much easier to see these attributes in their most difficult state. As a person works with this life lesson, they learn to master it in stages, and therefore, you will see varying stages of these attributes. Mastering the attribute of Charity lies in strengthening the connection that already exists between all things around us.

Primary Life Lesson #5 Communication: from the Heart

The Lesson of Communication from the Heart is defined within the sphere of relationships. Although this can apply to relationships of all kinds, relationships of love are the primary area in which we choose to work on this life lesson.

However, it must be said that mastery of this particular life lesson has eluded many people because the objective is not, as so many believe, to complete one's self with another, but rather, to learn to walk alongside another, and share your life together without either of you leaning too much on the other.

Sharing truth is the essence of what creates a good relationship. But in truth, there is only one relationship in the new energy – that is the relationship of You with You. This life lesson is more commonly undertaken in male form.

Quite often, people working with a life lesson of Communication will have difficulty talking as a small child. They may have a speech impediment, or they may be slow to learn to speak. After overcoming such early challenges, many will choose to place themselves in situations where they have to communicate for a living.

If they should make good progress in mastering this lesson, they usually do quite well with communications. Even so, speaking what is in their hearts may always prove difficult or challenging, because voicing their feelings honestly and letting their needs be known is not easy for them. If this life lesson is being facilitated via an Inherent Attribute, they may be prone to retreating behind a wall of silence whenever they become tired or stressed. These are people who will stick their heads in the sand at every opportunity.

Even in cases where two lovers who have shared several previous lifetimes together are reunited, the key to mastering this attribute still lies in not assuming that words are not necessary to express their feelings. The reason that most souls working on this attribute often elect to incarnate in the male gender is because it is men who generally experience the most difficulty expressing their feelings.

For several thousand years, men in our society have had their emotions anesthetized. Thankfully, this is changing fairly swiftly now as the new energy filters in. Emotions are the bridge between the Inherent Attribute and mastery.

Indeed, all of the Primary Life Attributes that we are working on will trigger strong emotions within us. Whether it is the Inherent Attributes or the Imprints that is the chosen vehicle of facilitation, both will be played out through our emotions. Because of this, mastering the attribute of Communicating from the Heart is one of the Primary Life Attributes that helps to facilitate all the others. As we learn to master the art of always saying what we feel, the attribute of communicating from the heart will become the foundation of every relationship.

Primary Life Lesson #6 Creation: Expressing Self-Power

Living within a field of polarity, we cannot see that we are creators, and therefore, we alone hold the power of creation within our own thoughts. We all have this blind spot to a greater or lesser degree.

But it is even more true of people working to master the life lesson of Creation, as not only are they often oblivious to their own creations, but they also are blind to their own ability to create. Even though these people have tremendous abilities of creation, they have great difficulty channelling this into practical creations in their own life.

Depending on how they set it up, people working with this life lesson can find themselves in several situations. For example, they may be artists who work for months or years on a brilliant piece of work, and then when they have their first showing, are so shocked that someone actually wants to buy their work that they accept the very first offer they get.

Or maybe they are a really bright secretary or assistant who does all the important work on a project and lets the boss take all the credit. They may be people who everyone knows has great creative abilities, and everything they touch is an effortless masterpiece, yet they have never been able to make a living at anything steady.

Their blind spot always keeps them from seeing their own creations or their creative ability. Even so, they can often find themselves successfully teaching the creative arts.

In our society, it is the male who has traditionally been supported to create, thus many souls working on this life lesson choose to incarnate as females. Add to this the lack of self-confidence that many women seem to have, and what we often end up with is wives who hide their own creations from their mates. Or, we find wives who create through their spouses, thereby giving the illusion that it is the spouse who is doing all the creating. In this situation, the husband will often appear to be extremely successful, while the wife will appear to be unable to support or create for herself.

Remove this relationship, however, and it often transpires that the husband's 'successful' business or project starts to fail without any apparent cause. This is one of many popular scenarios for mastering the difficult life lesson of Creation.

A belief in lack, and also sometimes perfectionism, often provide the perfect excuse for these people to not even try to create for themselves. The key to mastering this life lesson is to find the balance to personal power, which lies in **RESPONSIBILITY**.

Finding a way to take more personal responsibility will increase an individual's sense of personal power, thereby helping him or her to master the life lesson of Creation. Learning to hold our own power of Creation while in physical form is second only to Grace as the most difficult life lesson to master. The illusions of living within a field of polarity make it very difficult for us to see that we are actually creating our own reality in every single moment. Add to this the lack of self-worth that many of us suffer from and it's easy to see why we are blind to the greatest secret of the Universe: which is, we are God.

Once we learn to understand the simple meaning of these three magic words, we will begin to balance our own power with responsibility. When this happens, we will learn to master the Art of Creation very quickly.

Somewhere along the way, we assumed the belief that to hold our own power as creators means that we cannot make mistakes. The truth is, we are incapable of making a mistake, for the simple reason that if we are unhappy with the reality we have created, all we have to do is claim responsibility for our creation, and then undo it and start again.

All too often, however, we become so caught up in and obsessed by our need to make the 'perfect' choice that many opportunities completely pass us by. Those who have Inherent Attributes that facilitate this Lesson may find it difficult to even begin engaging their own creativity. Often, they become so overwhelmed with getting everything right that they fail to do anything at all.

The problem begins when creative energy is stifled in this manner and soon builds to a critical pressure. This creates a reversed flow of energy, which in turn can put the body under such stress that it ultimately becomes vulnerable to any number of ailments to which the individual may have a genetic predisposition.

A belief in scarcity is also something that those experiencing this life lesson often 'set up' for themselves as an aid to mastering this life attribute. In truth, the natural state of Heaven is abundance. There is no greater abundance than that which we experience when we are Home.

Abundance is an excess of energy in any given situation. It is the opposite of scarcity. It is only the veil of forgetfulness we live behind that causes us to believe that we are finite in form and energy, when the truth is we are actually infinite in energy. When we accept that we are infinite in energy, abundance is no longer an issue.

When we are so fully in the flow that we can tap into our creative energy at any given moment, we have no need of anything. Besides perfectionism, scarcity, and the life traits described above, there are many other contracts that we set up to help us fulfil a life lesson of Creation.

With the veil in place, it is hard to remember who we are. Thus, rarely do we have a sense of just Be-ing while in biology. This is why self-confidence issues are so pervasive among those working with this life lesson. Add to this situation any negative Imprints from a misdirected parent or teacher who failed to support us during childhood, and we have the perfect conditions in which to learn to master the Lesson of Creation.

Those working with the life lesson of Creation will have very pronounced creative abilities, but they cannot always see it. A lot of these people have the ability to be successful, famous writers and authors, but they never let their creative expression out. When we are repeatedly told that we cannot do something and, in spite of that, do it successfully anyway, the feeling (emotion) of power becomes stamped on our soul, to be carried with us always.

Every time we have an opportunity to take and hold our own power, this Imprint will get called into action and, thus, become reinforced. The real challenge lies in learning to alter this Imprint in a positive direction. For one thing, most of us are unaware that we can intentionally create positive Imprints for ourselves.

For another thing, many of us are so afraid of making a wrong move that we make no moves at all. In other words, we become so afraid of falling that we never learn to stand.

The balance to personal power is **RESPONSIBILITY**. Thus, the key to mastering the life lesson of Creation lies in increasing our personal power by finding ways to take more personal responsibility.

Primary Life Lesson #7 Definition: Expressing Individuality through Boundaries

This primary life lesson is particularly common with women at this time. Most people engaged in mastering this lesson tend to be healers with great emotional empathy. They tap into others' emotions, thought patterns, and energy so easily and unconsciously, they often do not even realize that it is not their own energy that they are feeling.

Because of this, they invariably have some difficulty setting proper boundaries for themselves. Having weak boundaries, they often attract a series of master manipulators into their life. What usually happens is that when these souls leave or are removed from one overbearing relationship, without mastering the attribute of Definition, they will unconsciously pull another into their field to help them facilitate their incomplete lesson.

Most often the catalyst for this life lesson appears in these people's lives during childhood. If, on the one hand, the catalyst is a negative influence, it will threaten their boundaries so thoroughly and consistently they cannot help but discover that their primary challenge lies in creating strong boundaries for themselves.

Because their boundaries are weak or non-existent, the definition of self for these souls will also be weak or non-existent. If, on the other hand, the catalyst is a positive influence, the people working on this life lesson will be encouraged from an early age to set very clear boundaries for themselves.

The key to mastering this very popular but difficult life lesson lies in learning to place one's self first. This is not an easy thing to accomplish, particularly since society teaches us from an early age that it is wrong to be selfish. The fact is, despite society's efforts to persuade us otherwise, placing ourselves first in all areas is the most important of all.

To treat ourselves in any other manner is a misdirection of our energy. Placing ourselves first means placing ourselves before our children, partner, parents, siblings, friends, and co-workers. If you find this a shocking concept, remember, there is a huge difference between those who are selfish and those who put self-first.

Granted, both are placing themselves first in the flow of energy, but the similarities cease there. In the case of the former, the intent is to fill one's self at the expense of everyone else. In the case of the latter, the intent is to fill one's self first in order that one has even more to give to others. The key to Mastering the life lesson of Definition lies in learning to define one's own boundaries and becoming accustomed to placing one's self first in all situations.

There is another aspect to this attribute. The reason many people engaged in this life lesson experience such difficulty defining their own boundaries is because they have no concept of where their own energy field ends and another's begins. The paradox is that this extreme sensitivity is precisely what makes these people such powerful healers.

If they can learn to define their own energetic boundaries, they will also find that they can use this same sensitivity intentionally to tap into another's emotional energy field to facilitate healing. Those who master the life lesson of Definition are very powerful healers. And 'no' is the most powerful word they can learn to use.

Primary Life Lesson #8 Integrity: Walking in Harmony with Self

Have you ever watched someone making a speech on television and felt that, while everything they said made perfect sense, for some reason you couldn't buy what they were saying? Have you ever been talking to someone and got the distinct impression that they were speaking one way yet feeling another? If so, you were probably dealing with a person who was working with a life lesson of Integrity.

As we are aware, we all have many different facets. Aligning each of these facets to send out a single congruent vibration is the challenge. The attribute of Integrity is defined as being able to align all these different facets and aspects to form one single, harmonious, vibrational line of Integrity.

There are four lines of vibration within every person's energy field. These are the subtle vibrations that we transmit without conscious knowledge or thought. This is the 'energetic vibration' that precedes us before we walk into a room, or that allows friends at the other end of a telephone to 'pick up' on the fact that it is probably us who is calling. Mastering this life lesson depends on our ability to integrate these four lines. These Four Vibrational Lines of Integrity are:

1. What we speak
2. How we act
3. What we think
4. What we believe

If one or more of these energetic lines do not match the others, the vibration we transmit will become blurred and unclear. At times, one line of vibration will cross over the others, cancelling them out and blurring the overall signal that is transmitted into the universe. When that happens, a blurred result is returned in all our creations, which in turn results in people having difficulty trusting or understanding us. In addition to being confusing, this also causes us to doubt ourselves, which of course blurs our energy field even further.

A good example is the actor who is not totally convincing in a role. He may be perfectly competent, but for some reason that we can't quite put our finger on, we just can't quite believe in the character enough to become fully engaged, either with him or the movie. In most cases, it's the fact that we know that something must be out of alignment for us to feel this way, but can't work out what it is, that prevents us from believing the performance. The actor is not being congruent. And try as they might to conceal it, the misalignment will be broadcast in their energy field.

It is precisely this incongruence that often causes those uneasy feelings of mistrust when someone else is lying to us or being insincere.

Aligning our own personal lines of vibration is all that is required to place ourselves in a state of vibrational Integrity. When we are in vibrational Integrity, we interact well with others. Not only will this assist us in our dealings with others, it also makes it easier for us to fully connect and integrate with our higher self.

Learning to walk consciously in total harmony is the most important step in the mastery of Integrity. Interestingly enough, many people working with a life lesson of Integrity will actually choose a profession that puts them in the public eye. Some choose the stage, others choose politics, and some become sporting heroes. Surprisingly enough, many even become Spiritual leaders.

They don't know they are not in integrity, of course. And because they don't see it, it's all too easy for us not to be overtly aware of it either. This is why it's so easy for people to be taken in by charlatans, false gurus, and other prominent leaders who have ulterior motives.

But by and large, most of us do pick it up on some level. It's as if our 'antenna' picks up on the fact that their energy field is being 'muddied' by a form of static.

Ironically, it is this very incoherence that is often responsible for making such people so attractive to us. We are not consciously aware of what it is about them that we find so fascinating. When we see something that's absolutely perfect, we barely give it a second thought as we pass by.

Then we see something that is equally attractive, but has just one teeny tiny imperfection that causes it to be a fraction out of alignment, and we're mesmerized. We simply cannot take our eyes off of it, because we are transfixed by the incongruence in it.

So it is with those people who, despite not being in integrity, still become movie stars or get elected to high office. In truth, people who are in integrity get nowhere near as much attention, because it is the flaws in a person's makeup that make them interesting.

Primary Life Lesson #9 Love: Love of Self

The key to mastering the life lesson of Love lies in learning to Love ourselves unconditionally, and first. Love is the base energy of all that we call Universal Energy. All energy emanates from a foundation of Love, and we all experience this base energy as the emotion of Love.

Emotions are the connecting link between the physical world and the spiritual world, on which all life experiences are carried. Living in a field of polarity, we humans need to experience one polarity in order to understand the opposite polarity.

The strongest of all emotions is Love, and the opposite (or polarity) of Love is Fear. This is why those working with a primary life lesson of Love will often get stuck in a cycle of fear. Some draw the fear in through some form of drama. An example of this would be a person who gets wrapped up in fire and brimstone religions and in dramas in general.

Depending on where they are on their path to mastery, these people often appear to give love to everyone and everything. The problem is, in many instances, their motivation for doing so stems from their fear of being alone. There are many aspects to this life lesson, the foremost of which involves developing the ability to love oneself.

In order for people to see and experience love, they must be able to experience the direct opposite of love. The opposite of love is the vacuum that is left when no love is present. This vacuum is experienced as the emotion of fear. In the same way that love is the base of all energy, so too is fear the base of all lack.

Fear is the origin of all negative emotions. But in the same way that darkness disappears when light shines upon it, so also can fear be overcome by the presence of love. Darkness is only a lack of light.

Fear is only a lack of love. The very first expression of Love, which is the most difficult for those learning to master this life lesson, is the love of self.

To take this one step further, it is only possible to love another to the degree that you love yourself. Throughout history, innumerable books have been written, songs have been sung, and wars have been fought in the name of, and supposedly for the love of, God. Ironically, if we could only learn to direct our search for love inward, instead of outward, we would find that the oxymoron phrase, 'holy war', would quickly disappear from our vocabulary.

God is within and not without. This is why we must learn to love self-first. The expressions of love we will find in the new energy will be a direct reflection of this simple truth. How many times have you heard people complaining of feeling unloved and lonely? They desperately want to find another person to share their life with, but love seems to keep eluding them. What they fail to understand is that the love they seek cannot be found when they are in a negative state.

By telling themselves that they cannot be whole until another completes them, they are placing themselves in a vacuum. And what loving person would be attracted to a vacuum? So many people say they are looking for love, when what they really mean is they are looking for someone to love them.

They would have a lot more success if, instead of looking for a partner to love them, they concentrated on looking for ways to give love. For it is only through the act of giving love that we can set up the energy to be love and, therefore, to receive love.

In the higher vibrations of the new planet Earth, we will start experiencing more unconditional love. In the past, most of our relationships have been based on conditional love. Even our marriage vows are a statement of conditional love. This isn't to suggest that there is anything wrong with this. It is neither good nor bad. It is simply that the more unconditional love we incorporate into all our relationships, the easier it will be for these relationships to evolve into higher dimensions.

Primary Life Lesson #10 Trust: Trusting Self

The life lesson of Trust is a simple lesson to understand, but a very difficult one to master. If those experiencing this life lesson choose a positive catalyst to help facilitate this lesson, it will generally be in the form of a mother or father who encourages them to believe that they can do anything they want to, if they only put their mind to it. If people set up a contract for a negative catalyst, however, it will often appear in the form of a parent who abuses them, thereby ensuring that they quickly learn to not trust anyone, least of all themselves. In this instance, the life lesson would be facilitated as Imprinting.

Ultimately, the life lesson of Trust is about learning to trust one's own self above all others. When we lived in the lower (First Wave) vibrational energy, we believed in the concept of 'follow the leader.' But all that is changing. Now that we are moving toward a higher vibrational level, there's a new 'Second Wave' concept that dictates, 'follow yourself.' People working with a primary life lesson of Trust will often have a very difficult time both learning to trust themselves and learning to accept and hold their own power. Once this life lesson is mastered, however, they often appear to walk through life with an inner sense of direction, always looking and acting as if they know exactly where they are going. In actuality, they will finally have learned to trust themselves enough to no longer need to know.

The interesting thing about Trust is that few of us have a problem placing our trust in God. But virtually all of us have a big problem accepting that we are of God. Trust is an extremely important life lesson to master, for Trust allows us to become part of the whole by placing us in the flow of Universal Energy.

When we lack trust, we lack faith. Once we learn to Trust, we can allow ourselves to be vulnerable. When we allow ourselves to be vulnerable, we turn our weaknesses into strengths. In fact, as we are going to learn from the Crystal Children who are now being born, our vulnerability is the source of our greatest strength.

Primary Life Lesson #11 Truth: Responsibility

As we proceed from one life lesson to another, it is important to remember that each life lesson can look quite different depending on the level of mastery an individual has attained. Truth provides us with a vivid example of these differences. The life lessons of Truth and Trust are very close to each other and, thus, are often confused. When people choose to master Truth, their energetic wiring is such that they will have difficulty discerning and standing in their own Truth.

Since this can appear, at first glance, as if they do not trust themselves, I ask more questions than usual in order to determine the larger picture of overall patterns before deciding which of these two similar life lessons they are working with. Sometimes, I even use the simple direct technique of asking: *"If I asked you to describe the main focus of your life as being one of Trust or Truth, which would it be?"*

When they have difficulty standing in their own truth, they will always have a tendency to adopt the truth of others in place of their own. They will always be looking for the newest book, or the latest concept, idea, or system to follow.

Truth - A Blind Spot

When we are at an early stage of mastery, we usually are incapable of being truly honest with ourselves. This is a very difficult place for anyone to be at since we never really know where we are, and therefore, we will always feel compelled to measure ourselves against others. Not only is truth elusive to us, but we will often create illusions to rationalize our choices. At this stage of mastery, those of us who choose to facilitate this life lesson as an Inherent Attribute will seek any way possible to avoid taking responsibility for our actions. We often get caught in a loop, looking outside ourselves for guidelines, rather than discerning our own.

Sometimes this will create a problem with honesty towards others. We may tell lies and create excuses, rather than be honest about what is really going on in our life. In many cases, we may live in a fantasy world. The big challenge comes when we really start believing our own lies, as this creates a full disconnection from ourselves.

When we are working with Truth at a higher level of mastery, it is quite common to become a teacher or a leader who is capable of encompassing many varied flavours of truth, without attachment to any one flavour in particular. Mastery of this life lesson also leads to the understanding that truth is based entirely on our own perception, and that it is through the art of shifting perception that we can see many truths beyond our own.

Brutal Honesty

Mastery of this attribute can only be accomplished through brutal honesty with yourself. This means taking full responsibility for your own thoughts and actions. It does not mean that those thoughts or actions need to be perfect; they need only to be your own. Once you start taking responsibility for your own reality, your mastery of Truth will begin. These people will be permanent seekers, always looking for answers to their questions. They will deny their own impressions, feelings, and thoughts and take on others' instead.

Through the Eyes of Others

Those new to this life lesson usually see themselves entirely through the eyes of other people. They can clearly see from the perspective of others, but they have a blind spot when it comes to their own truth. These are the people who always judge themselves by what they think others are thinking of them. Truth is a very difficult attribute to master. So, rather than judging those who are working on this life lesson, we should love them unconditionally and applaud their courage, because the challenges are very great. Even if it takes several lifetimes, mastering this life lesson has a massive effect on our overall learning.

Primary Life Lesson #12 Grace: Walking in Harmony with All Things

Grace is the final step to Mastery. In addition to being the very last life lesson we work to master, Grace is also the most beautiful. In this life lesson, a person learns that it really is not the destination that is important. What really matters is the journey itself, as well as the grace with which we experience the journey. To understand the importance of this life lesson, it may help to ask yourself this question: How often do I awaken in the morning and say, "*I love my life, I can't wait to see what today holds?*"

This may sound like a simple exercise in positive thinking, but in reality it is much more. When you truly see yourself as a player of the game, and allow yourself to play the game with Grace, then the mastery of all the remaining energy matrices becomes not only much easier but also much more enjoyable.

Do you find that you long for Home? Do you feel like you woke up one day in that uncomfortable body you inhabit and spend the majority of your energy trying to find your way back Home? If the answer to these questions is yes, then you have not yet mastered the life lesson of Grace. Few people have, as not many people get to work on this life lesson. Grace is the one life lesson that very few people choose or get to work with. In fact, it is only Old Souls that take on the life lesson of Grace.

What's really important to understand about this life lesson is that most people believe that once we have mastered this final lesson, we become so 'perfect,' we can almost walk on water. We don't. We still have our challenges, as do people working with a life lesson of Grace.

Grace is the connection to what Spirit calls the Universal Energy, the energy that connects all things. A life lesson of Grace strengthens your connection to the energy that runs between and connects all things. In human form, we naturally have the illusion that we are separate from one another. Although this is not yet proven scientific fact, it is widely understood that there is a connection between everything that exists. The connection to the Universal Energy is often experienced as your connection to your higher self, or your Spiritual connection.

At first glance it's easy to confuse Grace with the life lesson of Charity (which is walking in harmony with other people). When we walk in mastery of this life lesson, we intuitively know and work in harmony with all things, on all levels. Many of the stories of master teachers throughout our history accurately describe a person who is stepping into mastery of this exact life lesson.

This connection will allow an understanding of time, space, and energy that very few have ever experienced up to this point in the history of humankind. Due to the nature of the Grace attributes, it is always the final life lesson to be mastered. In fact, since most souls are complete with the Earth experience after they master eight to ten life lessons, very few people ever work with the life lesson of Grace. This draws a picture of a very sacred contract only taken by the elite of souls.

Believe me when I say that the brave souls who do work with a life lesson of Grace rarely feel as if they are special. Instead, they feel like they have a handicap that no one else has. Those working with Grace as a primary life lesson always look for the largest picture possible since they are looking for how everything is connected. They aren't the slightest bit interested in the secrets of life; they want to know the secrets of the Universe.

They will deal with people perfectly well but will also see the inter-dimensional parts of each one of us, and internally know truth when they hear, see or experience it in any form.

In lecturing on Spiritual Psychology in the past, when I speak about Grace, it is everyone's first choice in identifying their own life lesson. Please keep in mind here what I said earlier, that you will see yourself in every life lesson, and because you have a built-in blind spot in order to facilitate your life lesson, it is most difficult to identify your own. In Grace, everyone can see a little of themselves, yet it is extremely rare that a person is ever working with a life lesson of Grace.

The Big Picture

In understanding the larger picture of our experience as Spirits in human form, it is helpful to keep in mind that we are not here to learn lessons per se. In fact, it may even be said that the Twelve Primary Life Lessons themselves are only a distraction to keep us busy, while we are learning the larger attribute that encompasses our Spiritual beings. To put it simply, what we are really here to learn is the Art of Mastery itself. The definition of Mastery is finding positive uses for all energy in all situations. When we attain this, we will finally remember our true power as Creators.

We are experiencing an evolution on a scale never before seen. I truly believe that when we look back on this time two hundred years hence, we will clearly see that humanity went through an exceptionally rapid evolutionary jump. This is what we are in the middle of right now. These are exciting times, indeed, and they will only become even more exciting as we move forward.

What's Next?

With our evolutionary process now on such a fast track, it is quite natural for us to immediately want to take this information to the next evolutionary step. The next questions then become: ***Where are we going?*** And ***what is ahead*** with the **Twelve Primary Life Lessons?**

I believe that the Twelve Primary Life Lessons can now be mastered in one lifetime. Therefore, the following questionnaire is designed to help you discover what your Primary Life Lessons are for this life.

Indeed, the questionnaire will grade your Life Lessons from highest score, those top two being your Primary Life Lessons for this life, to the lower scores which are lessons you have either mastered previously, or that you are close to finishing.

I strongly believe that in order to Ascend, you must master at least the top two Primary Life Lessons you set out to achieve in this lifetime. You are probably already on track to mastering them already, so this is really just a confirmation. The trick is you must be brutally honest in answering the questionnaire; otherwise, the results will be meaningless.

LIFE LESSONS QUESTIONNAIRE

_____

Subject's Name: _____

Date: _____

Gender: M/F

Age: _____

If you are answering these questions regarding someone else, please enter your name: _____

Instructions: Take this Life Lesson test yourself and give it to someone who knows you well or for a long time. Ask them to fill it in about you, being objective and honest in their answers. When you receive the questionnaire back from them, DO NOT question them on their answers, but simply take the totals from their questionnaire and add them to yours. This should give you a good idea of the two highest ranking primary life lessons you may be working on in this lifetime. For even better results, give the test to two or more people, and add the scores to your own.

To the person answering these questions for someone else: As humans, we cannot generally see ourselves, except through the eyes of those who act as our mirrors. Therefore, we usually have a blind spot when it comes to our own life lessons. Most of us will see ourselves in every life lesson as we read the descriptions, yet when we get an outside view, our life patterns may become clear. Armed with that knowledge, we can then begin effective change and intentionally create a life of our own design. This is why you have been asked to complete this survey.

It will be most helpful to answer these questions as an honest mirror, without regard to feelings or beliefs. Honest, rather than kind, answers will be most helpful. Keep in mind that there are no right or wrong answers, and no life lessons are better than others.

General Instructions: Read the questionnaire over completely before starting. In life, it is easier to identify negative situations than positive ones; therefore, most of the following questions ask you about negative attributes. Please know that all negative attributes also have positive counterparts. Spiritual Psychology is looking for major patterns in the subject's life, even if these patterns have changed. The level of mastery of each life lesson will indicate whether these attributes are past or present in the subject's life. Therefore, past and present tenses are always interchangeable. EXAMPLE: "Do they" vs. "Did they," "Have/Had/Has," "Is/Was," etc. Once you have read them, respond to each question by placing a score from 0 - 9 in the corresponding space. The highest two totals of the combined surveys will generally indicate the primary and secondary life lessons of the subject. You can download a full size, printable version of this questionnaire from my website: http://www.dannysearle.com/Books/Downloads

Strongly Disagree 0-1 | Somewhat Disagree 2-3 | Neutral 4-5 | Somewhat Agree 6-7 | Strongly Agree 8-9

Question A	Score
There is a history of being unlucky in love	
Loses self in relationships, trying too hard, at times ignoring the obvious	
Has a huge heart and an abundance of love to give	
Often remains friends with the other person when a love relationship breaks up	
Thinks that most of his/her challenges in life are related to love relationships	
TOTAL for A:	

Strongly Disagree 0-1 | Somewhat Disagree 2-3 | Neutral 4-5 | Somewhat Agree 6-7 | Strongly Agree 8-9

Question B	Score
Is a collector of information, seeking outside validation of what they know inside	
Has an inner guidance system that often tells him/her when something does not match the truth they carry inside, rather than one that tells him/her when it does match	
Has or did have major beliefs that he/she is unworthy or less than others	
Though he/she often denies it, is a natural teacher and others want their knowledge	
Has or did have life events that give them special opportunities to stand in their own truth, even though that stance may be against popular belief	
TOTAL for B:	

Strongly Disagree 0-1 | Somewhat Disagree 2-3 | Neutral 4-5 | Somewhat Agree 6-7 | Strongly Agree 8-9

Question C	Score
Has/had a magic touch of creation, yet has difficulty paying the rent	
Has/had created through others, e.g., wife behind the successful man, friends, etc.	
Is/was perfectionist (especially if as children in the 4 - 12 year range)	
Is a very bright personality and very well-liked by almost everyone	
Has enhanced gifts of creation, being able to create art, music, words, sports or just the ability to create life situations out of nothing, yet cannot see his/her own creations	
TOTAL for C:	

Strongly Disagree 0-1 | Somewhat Disagree 2-3 | Neutral 4-5 | Somewhat Agree 6-7 | Strongly Agree 8-9

Question D	Score
Has or did have addictions or compulsions	
Feels or once felt incomplete, looking for something to add to him/herself	
Is an overachiever	
His/her actions indicate a need to add something outside of themselves to be whole	
Is/was a searcher, looking for the one thing that will make his/her life perfect	
TOTAL for D:	

Strongly Disagree 0-1 | Somewhat Disagree 2-3 | Neutral 4-5 | Somewhat Agree 6-7 | Strongly Agree 8-9

Question E	Score
Has/had difficulty gaining a sense of self worth	
Has had major event(s) that had a devastating influence on the circumstances of his/her life	
Has (had) major difficulty accepting money, love, compliments from others	
Has had more than normal opportunities to be a victim, and may even be accustomed to it	
Outwardly expresses doubt about own abilities	
TOTAL for E:	

Strongly Disagree 0-1 | Somewhat Disagree 2-3 | Neutral 4-5 | Somewhat Agree 6-7 | Strongly Agree 8-9

Question F	Score
Seeks knowledge from the highest perspective, wanting to know more about the universal applications of something rather than its global, national, local or personal applications	
Walks in full harmony with nature. The grass grows better after they walk on it	
Is (or seeks to be) one with all things everywhere and acts accordingly, even to the point of alienating others	
Gets bored with other people dealing with normal life lessons and situations	
Tries to teach but is too far ahead of his/her students and is often misunderstood	
TOTAL for F:	

Strongly Disagree 0-1 | Somewhat Disagree 2-3 | Neutral 4-5 | Somewhat Agree 6-7 | Strongly Agree 8-9

Question G	Score
Has had more than normal opportunities to learning to adapt or go with the flow	
Has (had) difficulties adjusting to changes	
Has (had) unusual events or circumstances that push him/her into major change	
Feels (felt) comfortable keeping things the way they are at all costs avoiding change	
Runs (ran) his/her life by rules or systems, including beliefs fitting everything into boxes	
TOTAL for G:	

Strongly Disagree 0-1 | Somewhat Disagree 2-3 | Neutral 4-5 | Somewhat Agree 6-7 | Strongly Agree 8-9

Question H	Score
Has a history of abandonment, even due to a death, or to emotional withdrawal	
Attracts people into his/her life who blindside him/her	
Thinks everyone else can do things he/she cannot	
Blames negative life events on some outside uncontrollable circumstance	
Rarely takes risks concerning own abilities to create	
TOTAL for H:	

Strongly Disagree 0-1 | Somewhat Disagree 2-3 | Neutral 4-5 | Somewhat Agree 6-7 | Strongly Agree 8-9

Question I	Score
Thinks of everyone else before thinking of him/herself	
Has (had) a pattern of attracting master manipulators into his/her life	
The most difficult word for him/her to say is "NO"	
Picks up others' feelings, emotions, thoughts etc., and takes them as his/her own	
Often has difficulty in busy crowded places where there is a lot of mixed energy	
TOTAL for I:	

Strongly Disagree 0-1 | Somewhat Disagree 2-3 | Neutral 4-5 | Somewhat Agree 6-7 | Strongly Agree 8-9

Question J	Score
Has difficulty relating to others or being understood	
Either: (a) is a recluse because no one ever understands him/her, or: (b) overcompensates by coming on too strong	
Complains that others often misunderstand him/her or take him/her wrong	
Has/had more difficulty in all types of relationships than most people	
Other people perceive him/her as self-centred	
TOTAL for J:	

Strongly Disagree 0-1 | Somewhat Disagree 2-3 | Neutral 4-5 | Somewhat Agree 6-7 | Strongly Agree 8-9

Question K	Score
Tells other people what he/she thinks rather than what he/she feels	
Has/had a tendency to hide his/her head in the sand until emotional events blow over, pretending they he/she is not involved	
RARELY tells other people he/she loves them, even when he/she does	
Is especially good at communications in other areas, e.g., at work	
In emotional confrontations, usually makes it the other person's fault	
TOTAL for K:	

Strongly Disagree 0-1 | Somewhat Disagree 2-3 | Neutral 4-5 | Somewhat Agree 6-7 | Strongly Agree 8-9

Question L	Score
Believes his/her own lies or rationales	
Often says what others want to hear rather than what he/she truly believes	
Easily rationalizes all of his/her actions, no matter the consequences	
Tries to think out what he/she feels	
Has the potential for being successful in public view	
TOTAL for L:	

Score Card

Scoring: Use the two highest scores or three for Ascension Activation.

Question	Life Lesson	Score
A	#09 LOVE: Love of Self	
B	#11 TRUTH: Responsibility	
C	#06 CREATION: Expressing Self-Power	
D	#03 BE-ING: Wholeness	
E	#01 ACCEPTANCE: Self-Esteem, Self-Acceptance…	
F	#12 GRACE:Walking in Harmony with All Things	
G	#02 ADAPTATION: Change	
H	#10 TRUST: Trusting Self	
I	#07 DEFINITION: Expressing Individuality through Boundaries	
J	#04 CHARITY: Harmony	
K	#05 COMMUNICATION: From the Heart	
L	#08 INTEGRITY: Walking in Harmony with Self	

(Notes: *1. Trust and Truth are often cross diagnosed. 2. It is extremely rare that someone would have Grace as a life lesson.*)

I hope this process has led you to another view of yourself and your experience as that of a Spirit living a human life.

DO SOMETHING TODAY THAT YOUR FUTURE SELF WILL THANK YOU FOR.

12

MINDFULNESS: LIVING IN THE NOW

"Feelings come and go like clouds in a windy sky. Conscious breathing is my anchor." ~ THICH NHAT HANH

(*NB For any practise exercises, try to conduct them sitting up straight, feet flat on the ground or cross legged.)

Mindfulness is the first step in the meditative practice, the most valuable instrument in your Ascension toolbox and the key to personal development. In other words, it's the shortest path to actualising your fullest potential – your real You. With so much talk and literature about the subject, it is easy to get confused on what mindfulness really is or is not. Some think of mindfulness as an esoteric eastern practice reserved only to Zen Buddhists, who have spent years secluded in a monastery away from any cares of the world.

Yes, although mindfulness is very intimately related to Zen meditation, it is certainly not exclusive to such a practice. The simplest way it can be explained is not through a formal definition but by real world experiences. Think of a time or situation where you felt really in 'sync' with your inner feelings and thoughts, and felt collected, centred and 'in one place'. Your emotions were balanced and your mind was not scattered everywhere. You were simply there. Things were still happening around you but you were totally still, even if only for a short while. Your awareness wasn't quivering but set on whatever you put your attention on. That was being mindful in its broadest sense.

There are many valuable and comprehensive resources about the subject – from metaphysics to practical guides – and a lot of masters in the practice of meditation. But what I am hoping to achieve here, is a quick and simple way to get people started.

The 3 Breaths Experiment

It is as easy as it sounds – your breath is a vehicle to mindfulness. Breathing comes naturally and automatically, whether we want it to or not. But putting your awareness on your breathing will ground you to the inner stillness situated beneath the frenetic stream of thoughts or feelings constantly arising in your waking consciousness. In short, breathing can be used to 'anchor' your awareness to a place, to keep your awareness still. This is of course a very common method for meditation practice. However, the purpose of this experiment is to experience the stillness and centre of power that comes from mindfulness. You don't need to spend an hour in deep meditation to experience this.

As **Eckhart Tolle** suggests in 'A New Earth', it only takes the awareness of one single breath to connect to your state of mindfulness and inner peace. Well, let's make it three! Do it right now:

1. Take three deep breaths – in through the nose, out through the mouth (purse your lips) and put your awareness on to it…just your breathing, nothing more.
2. Focus on the air going in. Feel it fill your lungs.
3. Hold it for two heartbeats.
4. Let it out under slow control.
5. Feel your lungs empty.

Can you feel a sense of stillness and peace, even if perhaps subtle for now? Do you sense a shift in awareness and focus, albeit briefly? This is mindfulness. The good news is that it can be practised anytime, anywhere, and extended to how long you feel fits your situation.

'The 'I' inside my Body

Another 'anchoring' method for meditation, in general, is being aware of your body – whether of your body as a whole, as a certain part of your body, or else as proprioception (the feeling of space and position your body is occupying). Personally, for me, my chest area always works as a good anchor. The feeling is that my awareness suddenly 'locks' in that area.

My sense of 'I' (or rather the awareness behind the 'I') feels centred and strongest in that place in the body. It can then be extended to other areas, even outside the body, but that is beyond the purpose of this mindfulness experiment for now.

Like the three breaths, the purpose of this exercise is to access mindfulness briefly from anywhere, anytime. As I mentioned, you can focus on any part of your body but there are areas which are particularly useful to access mindfulness – the gut, stomach, the chest, and the throat. These are places where emotions, tension, or unresolved issues tend to manifest certain sensations. Not coincidentally, these are some of the seven energy centres, or chakras, in the body. For instance, a sense of powerlessness from a difficult relationship will manifest in a feeling of constriction around the chest area (Heart Chakra), or in a feeling of anxiety,such as 'butterflies' around your stomach area (Solar Plexus). Placing our awareness briefly in these major energy centres can help you connect much easier to your inner being, which, in turn, will centre you in a state of inner calm and mindfulness.

For example, you are in a coffee shop somewhere watching the world around you go by in a frenzy. Take a few minutes to place your attention to one of the areas of the body to access mindfulness. How does it feel? Is it tense, or constricted, or 'cramped'? Keep putting your mindful awareness to it – do you feel the energy centre, or chakra, opening up and relaxing? Let's go one step further. Focus on your Heart Chakra. Feel it start to rotate, slowly at first, then feel it pick up the tempo. What do you feel? Practise this little exercise every day. Eventually you will feel it, and when you do, move to the other Chakras and repeat. Finally, start to visualise the colours of each Chakra.

The above suggestions are meant to ground your awareness and to become mindful in short time windows, wherever you are. Yet mindfulness is, or ought to be, a continuous practice and an extremely beneficial one. Next, we will continue with breathing exercises that you can use in your daily life.

Ancient Sanskrit names for the Chakras

13

LEARNING TO BREATHE AGAIN

"If you want to conquer the anxiety of life, live in the moment, live in the breath." ~ AMIT RAY

Falling asleep is as simple as 4-7-8. Or something like that. But, tell that to someone who is exhausted and stressed and cannot sleep. Being stressed and sleepless is becoming more and more common. A quarter of Australians report feeling moderately to severely stressed. One survey found 51 per cent of those who suffer insomnia blame stress for their lack of sleep. A lack of sleep exacerbates stress, and so the merry dance continues.

Stress affects sleep because it switches on our body's fight or flight response. Our heart starts racing, our blood pressure rises, our muscles tense and our breath quickens in anticipation.

The mechanism is healthy when we need a hit of energy to get us through real or perceived danger, such as a deadline, exam, or crappy day. It is less helpful when we are trying to wind down for the day. However, a simple breathing technique can switch off the stress response and settle us into sleep. Harvard-educated doctor and best-selling author **Dr Andrew Weil** explains.

> "Breathing strongly influences physiology and thought processes, including moods," Weil says. "By simply focusing your attention on your breathing, and without doing anything to change it, you can move in the direction of relaxation."

By souping-up the experience, further benefits can be achieved. The 4-7-8 breath technique is utilised by yoga and meditation teachers (there are various other pranayama or breath works used in yoga to charge the oxygen in our bodies and extend our breath beyond the 10 per cent of capacity we typically breathe to). The technique is also championed by Dr Weil.

> "This exercise is a natural tranquiliser for the nervous system," Dr Weil says. "Unlike tranquilising drugs, which are often effective when you first take them but then lose their power over time, this exercise is subtle when you first try it but gains in power with repetition and practice. Do it at least twice a day. You cannot do it too frequently."

The 4-7-8 Count

Simply breathe in for four seconds, hold the breath for seven seconds, and exhale completely to a count of eight. It only takes a few seconds, and Weil suggests repeating the technique up to four times. Some users have said the technique helps them fall asleep within one minute. It can help users relax and fall asleep, but breathing deeply, and the knock-on effect this has on our nervous system, offers plenty of other benefits too.

> "The ability to breathe so deeply and powerfully is not limited to a select few. This skill is inborn but often lies dormant," Harvard medical school points out. "Reawakening it allows you to tap one of your body's strongest self-healing mechanisms."

It improves our immune system, blood pressure, overall physical health and even helps us burn fat more effectively. And of equal importance, it is a completely free technique that we can all use to change our response to stress.

> "Once you develop this technique by practicing it every day, it will be a very useful tool that you will always have with you," Dr Weil says. "Use it whenever anything upsetting happens--before you react.Use it whenever you are aware of internal tension. Use it to help you fall asleep. This exercise cannot be recommended too highly. Everyone can benefit from it."

Breathing to Reduce Stress

Breathing exercises are a wonderful way to reduce anxiety, agitation, and stress, while promoting relaxation, calm and inner peace. It may take some practice – and requires some commitment on your part to achieve results. However, the long-term benefits are well worth the effort – a calm and relaxed body and mind are less prone to health issues.

Breathing strongly influences physiology and thought processes, including moods. By simply focusing your attention on your breathing, and without doing anything to change it, you can move in the direction of relaxation. Too much attention on upsetting thoughts may cause anxiety, guilt, and unhappiness. Get in the habit of shifting your awareness to your breath whenever you find yourself dwelling on stressful situations.

The 4-7-8 breath is utterly simple, takes almost no time, requires no equipment, and can be done anywhere. Although you can do the exercise in any position, sit with your back straight while learning the exercise. Place the tip of your tongue against the ridge of tissue just behind your upper front teeth, and keep it there through the entire exercise. You will be exhaling through your mouth around your tongue; try pursing your lips slightly if this seems awkward.

1. Exhale completely through your mouth, making a whoosh sound.
2. Close your mouth and inhale quietly through your nose to a mental count of four.
3. Hold your breath for a count of seven.
4. Exhale completely through your mouth, making a whoosh sound to a count of eight.
5. This is one breath. Now inhale again and repeat the cycle three more times for a total of four breaths.

Note that you always inhale quietly through your nose and exhale audibly through your mouth. The tip of your tongue stays in position the whole time. Exhalation takes twice as long as inhalation. The absolute time you spend on each phase is not important but the ratio of 4:7:8 is. If you have trouble holding your breath, speed the exercise up, but keep to the ratio of 4:7:8 for the three phases.

With practice you can slow it all down and get used to inhaling and exhaling more and more deeply. Practice at least twice a day, or more if possible. You cannot do it too frequently. Do not do more than four breaths at one time for the first month of practice. Later, if you wish, you can extend it to eight breaths. If you feel a little lightheaded when you first breathe this way, do not be concerned - it will pass.

We will be using the 4:7:8 breathing technique extensively in our Ascension meditations, so the sooner you get this down pat, the sooner you can begin the Ascension meditations!

Breathing for when life throws you a curve ball

We all have hurdles and challenges thrown at us during life. Sometimes, it comes like a kick in the guts! Maybe you just got dumped, maybe you lost your job, or didn't get the job you thought you deserved. Maybe they ran out of your favourite ice-cream (just kidding)! The point is, sometimes things happen just to test our reaction. Sometimes, we need to stop, breathe, and initiate the "Wise Mind" before we allow the kneejerk reaction to take over.

If you need a pick-me-up or are feeling a bit anxious, try the following breathing exercise; it can help to bring energy and clarity to your mind. The first time, do it for just 15 seconds, increasing the duration by five seconds every time until you can complete one full minute. Always breathe normally between exercises:

1. Sit upright with your back straight, eyes closed, and shoulders relaxed.
2. Place the tip of your tongue against the bony ridge behind and above your upper teeth.
3. Breathe rapidly through your nose, in and out, with your mouth slightly closed.
4. Keep your inhale and exhale short and equal. Your chest should be almost mechanical in its movements – rapid, like air is pumping through it.
5. Try to inhale and exhale three times per second, if you can, keeping your breath audible.

Ideally, you will feel the muscular effects of this breathing exercise at the base of your neck (just above the collarbone) and at the diaphragm. Put your hands on these areas to get a sense of the movements.

This should re-centre you after the body blow you just had. Now you can re-examine the "why" did this happen reaction. You can also rechoose the "what next" move. Try to lift above the situation and look at the bigger picture.

There are three types of rejection or hurdles in your life – 1: The Universe (your Higher Self) is testing you. 2: You imposed your Will (Ego) over the master plan. 3: A negative, jealous, spiteful, close minded, fear based individual has selected you for special punishment.

Solution: 1: Accept and Allow. 2. Accept and Allow. 3. Fight, then Accept and Allow.

Breathing for life

Breathing exercises are a wonderfully effective way to reduce stress, regulate mood, and feel energised. One way to promote deeper breathing and better health is by exhaling completely. Try it: take a deep breath, let it out effortlessly, and then squeeze out a little more. Doing this regularly will help build up the muscles between your ribs, and your exhalations will naturally become deeper and longer. Start by practicing this exhalation exercise consciously, and eventually it will become a healthy, unconscious habit.

Enlightenment through Breath

In Buddhist and yogic traditions, people have reached an enlightened state by doing nothing more than paying attention to the rising and falling of their breath. What easier way could there be to reach such a state? Especially since breathing – following the ebb and flow of your breath – is an intrinsic part of meditation. By paying attention to your breath, you will rapidly change your state of consciousness, begin to relax, and slowly detach from ordinary awareness. Try to focus on the point between your in breath and out breath that is dimensionless, and glimpse the elements of enlightenment in that space.

Pranic Breathing for Meditation

Prior to starting any meditation, you need to relax your body. To do this we still breathe in through the nose, and out through the mouth as previously described. But this time, as we breathe in, force your stomach out. As you exhale, force your stomach in. This is known as "circular" or "pranic" breathing. By forcing our stomach out, it allows more breathe in. By pushing the stomach in on the exhale, it allows us to drain the lungs completely.

We also do some visualisation during this breathing. As you breathe in, visualise a brilliant white light going in. As you breathe out, visualise a grey/black smoke like substance going out. As you purge the negative vibration from your body, (usually after about four breaths), you will see white light going in, and white light going out. You are now ready to begin the meditation, and your breathing returns to normal.

During the meditation description, I will reference this breathing as Pranic Breathing X4. X4 means four breaths. One breath means one inhale, and one complete exhale.

Visualisation Techniques

Part of all the meditations we will do in the Ascension Process require clear visualisations. I have found over the years of running meditation classes that, on the one hand, about 25% of people have difficulty at first with visualisation. Others, on the other hand, take to it like a duck to water. Effectively, this visualisation is carried out by the Pineal Gland, or the "mind's eye." If you have not done the Pineal Gland Activation at this point, and you are having trouble with visualisation, I suggest you do so now. If you still have problems, I have devised a couple of techniques that have always proved successful in the past.

- **Candle Gazing**: Light a small candle, and place it on a table in front of you. Make sure the lights are off. Now sit and gaze at the candle flame. Allow your eyes to relax, and just watch – DO NOT STARE. After about 2 minutes, close your eyes, and try to visualise the candle flame as you remember it. Open your eyes, look at the flame, close your eyes, visualise the flame. Do this over and over until you can start to clearly see the flame in your mind's eye.

- **The Pencil Test**: Similar to the candle flame, this time we will use an ordinary pencil or pen. Hold it up in front of you and carefully scan it from top to bottom. Look for every scratch, divot, writing on it, and the colours of the labels, details etc. Again, after about 2 minutes of this, close your eyes and try tosee it with your mind's eye. Repeat the open/close eyes part of the exercise. When you can easily see it, move to the next phase. Rotate the pencil and see all sides of it. When you are ready, visualise the pencil in mid-air, rotating and seeing every detail on it, on all sides.

- **Walk the House**: Close your eyes, and imagine you are walking around your house, or even place of work. Visualise walking through the front door, then visiting each room. You can even go one step further and open cupboards and the pantry, and see what is inside. Finally, you may like to walk out of the house and up the road. See if you can visualise your neighbour's houses, street signs, and the local stray dog! If you can do the House Walk, then you are more than ready to do the Ascension Guided Meditations.

Guided Meditations

A Guided Meditation is simply when a voice, either pre-recorded, or a person in the room, "talks" you through the meditation. There are CD's you can buy, free YouTube videos, and even smartphone apps with guided meditations. Guided Meditations are perfect for beginners, but they are also very useful for experts, particularly if you are participating in a group or a global meditation. You just visualise whatever the voice is telling you to visualise. However, most of the time you will be meditating alone, with no one to guide you. So, it is this scenario I will focus on next.

14

BASIC MEDITATION TEMPLATE

"You have power over your mind --not outside events. Realize this, and you will find strength." ~ MARCUS AURELIUS

rarely, if ever, use pre-recoded guided meditations. But then again, I have been doing this for a long time, so I do not really need it. It is my personal preference to burn incense and play background music whenever I meditate. You do not have to do this if you don't want to. I try to meditate in the same room, around the same time each day, as it becomes a trigger to get me into the right frame of mind. Again, this is a personal choice.

I prefer to sit up straight, bare feet on the floor. You may choose to sit cross-legged, or maybe lie down. Socks on is Ok. I find if I lie down I fall asleep! But do what is good for you.

I sometimes meditate with a crystal to either boost my meditation or to re-charge/re-program the crystal. I find if I hold it in my hand, even a small tumble stone, it becomes too hot to handle by about halfway through the meditation. So, instead, I just place it on my lap. Again, this is a personal choice.

Finally, I always have a glass/bowl of clean, chemical-fluoride free water sitting in front of me (on the floor is ok). During every meditation, I take a moment to "charge" this water with whatever I need. For example, healing, energy, higher Spiritual vibration. Whatever you want. Then, immediately after the meditation I drink the water. This helps to "ground" me.

Intro Meditation Procedure

Incense

My favourite incense is **Spiritual Guide** by Padmini Products India. I also use **Precious Chandan Incense** by Hem. Both are readily available in "New Age" shops and online. There are literally hundreds of different incenses to choose from, so find what works well for you.

Music

The music I use regularly is: **Cherubin - Floating Gently** by Anugama & Sebastiano. In other meditations I use **Extasias** by Robert Lafond and Chakra **Meditation Music** by Merlin's Magic. Steven Halpern's **Music for Sound Healing** is also a regular. There are many others, so find something you like.

1. Fill your glass of water and place in front of where you will be sitting.
2. Light the incense stick.
3. Start the music.
4. Sit down, back straight, close your eyes, and start Pranic Breathing X4. As you exhale, allow your shoulders to drop and your body to relax.
5. Now switch all of your attention to your right foot. Imagine it is glowing white like a ball of light. Now do the same thing for the left foot. Allow the light to surround your feet, and with both your feet, gently flex and relax the muscles.
6. Draw the white light up into your calves – again, gently flex and relax the muscle. Now bring the light up into your thighs and buttocks – flex and relax. Your whole lower body is now a bright white light and already you are feeling relaxed.
7. Now draw the light up into your abdomen and chest – flex and relax. Draw the light down your arms and into your fingertips. Feel your fingers tingle as the light completely fills them. Give them a little wiggle, and with your hands, flex and relax.
8. Bring your focus to the base of your neck. Turn your head in big, slow circles, three times in any direction. Now visualise all the negative energy in your body leaving via the base of your neck. See it leave like dark, wispy smoke. As it does, your body feels lighter and lighter.

9. Finally, draw the light up into your head. Try to feel it tingling at the very top. Imagine now you are standing in a full length mirror; see yourself standing in a column of pure white light.

10. We are now ready to begin our task.

[In this part, you will do the purpose of your meditation e.g. Chakra cleansing, Ascension meditation etc.]

Conclusion – Grounding

The conclusion is designed to "ground" the person meditating. During deep meditation a person's Astral Body can drift out of the physical body. So, to make sure it is back in, we do a simple grounding exercise. If someone is not grounded they may fall off balance when they get up to walk. They will be vague and dreamy. They may also get a head ache. This can last for several hours if nothing is done. It is a good idea to have a drink of water immediately after the meditation. For group meditations, I always have a large punch bowl of water in the middle of the room. During the meditation I get everyone to focus light (Pink=Love; Green=healing; Blue=peace/harmony etc.) into the water. So, at the end, everyone has a drink from it and receives the energies. This helps to ground them.

Grounding Visualisations

11. *I will Say, "Our work is done. It is now time to return to your light door. As you stand in front of your door, feel your feet firmly on the ground. Give your toes a little wriggle. Walk through the light door, and as you do, take a deep breath, exhale and open your eyes. You are home."*

12. ***Alternative:*** *I will say, "Turn around and you will see a large tree. Go up to it and place your hands on the bark. Now hug the trunk. Feel its strength. Your feet begin to go into the ground, just like the roots of the trees. Feel the solid ground all around your legs. Give your toes a little wriggle. Visualise a door of light in front of you. Walk through the light door, and as you do, take a deep breath, exhale and open your eyes. You are home."*

13. *Just take a minute to get your bearings. Have a drink of water if you have some. Well done!*

Most Common Mistakes with Meditation:

- Don't Slouch – keep the spine straight while meditating.
- Remove watches and jewellery! Or at least remember to psychically insulate yourself from their effect. Earrings are fine, but facial rings may cause problems.
- Problems with visualising – go back to **Visualisation Techniques**.
- Can't stop a chatty mind – go back to focusing on your breath. Focus on the breath in and the breath out. This should re-centre you then you can pick up where you left off.
- Practice! – maintaining a regular practice is essential to learning meditation correctly.

Let's put it all together! What follows is a basic **Chakra Cleansing Meditation** you can perform daily.

BASIC CHARKRA CLEANSING MEDITATION

---

1. Begin with Pranic Breathing X4. Now you are ready.
2. Visualise yourself standing on a beach at dawn, just near the water's edge. The sun is starting to rise above the waves, and you can feel a gentle, cool breeze on your cheeks.
3. Start to wriggle your toes and feet into the sand. Feel your legs grow longer and go deeper into the earth. Your feet are deep in the earth and you can feel a warmth in your feet.
4. Draw this energy slowly up your legs…into your thighs, now into your abdomen – the energy is filling your body with a brilliant white light: it goes into your chest, shoulders and down your arms. Your fingers begin to tingle. Now focus the energy to the base of your neck. Visualise all the negative energy you have built up begin to leave your body here. See it leaving like wispy smoke…
5. Now draw the energy up into your head and feel the tingling at the very top of your head.
6. Take a moment to pulse the energy through your being by keeping your eyes closed; but look up, then down very quickly. Do this three times. You should feel a high energy burst, or butterflies in your tummy.

7. We will now begin to clean our Chakras.

8. Focus on the Base Chakra – see a swirling vortex of brilliant red – the vortex protrudes from the front and back about 1/2 foot, or 15 centimetres. Floating down from the sky comes a red silk cloth, spinning and twirling around. Allow the red cloth to enter your base chakra from the front and pull it back and forth with your silk cloth to clean the chakra out. With each pull through, visualise small, black blockages being vaporised away.

9. When you are ready, focus on the orange Sacral Chakra just below your belly button. Just as we did before with the red cloth, now we see an orange cloth. Use it to go in and out, and clean the Sacral Chakra. When you feel you have removed the black spots, vaporise the cloth.

10. Now focus on the Yellow, Solar Plexus Chakra. Use a yellow, silk cloth and clean the chakra inside and out. Don't forget that the chakra extends out from your body about 15 centimetres, or ½ foot, front and back.

11. Move up to the Green, Heart Chakra. Follow the same process.

12. Next is the Electric Blue for the Throat Chakra – use the blue cloth as before. You may need to give this an extra good clean – visualise the chakra bursting with blue light. We often hold back from saying things to friends or family members, so you will need to clean them out good and proper.

13. Now you can move up to the Third Eye – visualise deep Indigo front and back. Pull the indigo cloth back and forth, and focus on opening your third eye.

14. Finally, move up to the Crown Chakra at the top of your head.

15. See the Violet light shoot straight up into the sky. Clean with the cloth.

16. Now visualise a pipe going from your Crown Chakra, right through your body, and exiting at your Base Chakra. Draw the Divine White light down the pipe, and as it draws down it fills your body and chakras with the beautiful white light.

17. All your chakras are now glistening pure white.

18. Use this time to ask the Universe for guidance, or help, or simply say thank you.

19. For a really big request, visualise your request as clearly and as simple as you can. Try not to complicate the image. When you can see the image, or your request, enclose it in a pink bubble.

20. Using your mind, push the pink bubble up and away...watch it as it goes higher, and eventually out of view.

21. Release your request to the Universe. You may need to repeat this every day until you get an answer.

22. Now it is time to return. Focus back on your feet...feel them shrinking back to normal size.

23. When you feel your feet flat back on the sand, turn around, and see a doorway of Light. Take a deep breath, and exhale and open your eyes at the same time.

This meditation, along with all the others in the Annex, are available on my YouTube Channel, with music and with myself doing the narration. Go to the **Playlist** called "*Ascension - A Step by Step Guide - Book Files*" to listen to them.

15

YOGA, TAI CHI, AND QI GONG

"Married to a soul and a mind, the body provides us with carnal pleasures and serves to reflect our overall spiritual and mental condition like a polished mirror... To the extent that we can discover our own, unique balance, we are whole... and once whole, we can truly dance like the free spirits we are. Qigong (Chi Kung) calls us to the dance floor of life."

~GARRI GARRIPOLI, QIGONG: ESSENCE OF THE HEALING DANCE

Yoga, Tai Chi, Qi Gong – they're not like other workouts. While a long swim or jog might leave us drained, ancient mind-body practices such as Yoga, Tai Chi, or Qi Gong have the power to do just the opposite: They produce more energy than they consume. When we practice Yoga, Tai Chi, or Qi Gong, we feel calm, invigorated, and clear-headed. We experience a sense of renewal on all levels.

What is Yoga?

Yoga, at this moment in time, is the most popular of the three mind-body practices in the West. It is an Indian art (for lack of a better word, some may say it's a "discipline"). It means yoke, and it is very old and intertwined with Hinduism – a religion. When Yoga is mentioned in the

West it usually means **Hatha Yoga** – the most commonly practiced yoga in the West. This is much less than what Yoga means in India. The West has stripped Yoga of just about everything spiritual, religious, and shamanistic, and this is the kind of Yoga which is most likely taught in your local Yoga studio. So, what has been left after this process of stripping?

Basically an elaborate form of gymnastics combined with breathing that may, or may not, include a bit of chanting and a bit of sitting down quietly. Originally Yoga was Shamanism, as was all religion. Later as Indian Shamanism was turned by the government into the state religion of Hinduism, Yoga became the ascetic discipline which goes with the religion.

Even the stripped down version of Yoga can still aid you in your Ascension process. I would strongly recommend you seek out the spiritual aspects of Yoga, particularly relating to the chakras and the aura. It can also help with astral travel, deep meditation, and it has amazing powers of healing and levitation.

What is Tai Chi?

Tai Chi (pronounced Tie Chee) is the second most popular Eastern practise followed in the West. It started out as one Chinese family's Internal Martial Arts form in the 1700s. It grew in popularity rapidly, and more families started making their own forms.

When **Mao Zedong** seized power over China, resulting in that country being forced into Communism, the new Government decided to make its own form of Tai Chi. The government took as a basis the Yang family's Tai Chi form and also called it Yang – causing much grief to the Yang family.

The Yang family had already modified the original (Chen) Tai Chi very much, and it had become much less combat-oriented. When people in the West say Tai Chi they normally mean Yang Tai Chi – either government or family.

Currently Tai Chi in the West is no longer practiced for combat purposes and is done solely for its health benefits and enjoyment. As Internal Martial Arts are largely based on Qi Gong, and as the Martial Arts part was stripped from Tai Chi, what remains of Tai Chi is an elaborate, long form of Qi Gong.

What is Qi Gong

qi
energy

gōng
cultivation

Qi Gong (pronounced Chee-goong) is the least known and most mysterious of the three Eastern arts. Qi means energy/life force, and Gong means to work with the purpose of cultivation. So, Qi Gong literally means life force cultivation (harvesting energy in order to live longer). In fact, people that practise Qi Gong daily, do so because they firmly believe it can extend their life way past 100 years. The word Qi Gong translates almost exactly into the Indian word **Pranayama**, but Pranayama deals only with breath. It is just one part of Yoga, while Qi Gong is the cumulative term for Taoist (Daoist) physical, mental and breathing exercises, much like Yoga is for Hinduism.

Qi Gong's roots, like those of Yoga, are found in Shamanism. Before there was Taoism, there was Chinese Shamanism. When Chinese Shamanism was institutionalised and became the religion of Taoism, certain exercises and practices of the Shamans became Qi Gong. From there on, Qi Gong was developed, spread, and protected by Taoists. Nowadays, there are thousands of types of Qi Gong, and they mostly consist of gentle physical, breathing, and mental exercises. Qi Gong is the main pillar of Traditional Chinese Medicine, which is mostly famous for its acupuncture and herbalism in the West.

What are the benefits?

People have been practicing these healing postures for thousands of years, but it's only recently that scientists have begun to demonstrate how they affect our brains. In fact, two recent studies have added to the growing body of evidence that Tai Chi does more than condition our bodies. This research further substantiates the connection between physical fitness and cognitive health.

In substantiating the link between the health of body and mind, the research reminds us that ancient mind-body exercises such as yoga and Tai Chi can benefit us on multiple levels: Physical, mental, emotional, and psycho-spiritual. By deepening the mind-body connection with mindful breathing, stretches, postures and meditation, these ancient practices encourage our innate healing capacities, allowing them to flourish.

Brain Size Matters

Recently, investigators at the **University of South Florida** and **Fudan University in Shanghai** asked what happens to the brain when seniors practice Tai Chi. Published in the *Journal of Alzheimer's Disease*, the study found that participants who practiced Tai Chi showed improved memory and other cognitive abilities and even experienced increased brain volume. The research also showed similar results for those who participated in spirited discussions.

Why is brain volume important? A number of studies have indicated a relationship between dementia and declining brain size. Other studies have shown that aerobic exercise stimulates proteins that help the brain grow. Whether Tai Chi directly affects our brains the same way will require more investigation.

Another study by scientists at the **Oregon Research Institute** and published in the *New England Journal of Medicine,* found that Parkinson's Disease patients who practiced Tai Chi had fewer falls, improved balance and posture and could walk better.

Finding Balance

The beauty of these ancient exercises is that, in addition to being good for our brains, they're great for our bodies. In fact, I would make the case that they are better for you than most Western, conventional approaches to exercise.

We have been conditioned to believe that more is always better; that in order to benefit, we must work harder. However, this runs counter to what we know about the human body. Extreme forms of exercise stress our bodies and minds and take a considerable toll over time. As in all things, beneficial exercise requires balance. While we need to take time to work the body, we also need plenty of time to allow it to rest. Extreme workouts often don't factor in that all-important respite. As a result, our bodies endure increased wear and tear because they don't have the opportunity to remove accumulated lactic acid and other exercise by-products.

This is not to say that we shouldn't embrace strenuous workouts. Rather, we shouldn't embrace **only** strenuous workouts. Why go in one direction when we can take a multi-pronged approach?

Yoga, Tai Chi and Qi Gong provide strength, flexibility, conditioning and mental well-being. In addition, numerous studies have shown these practices lower the risk of hypertension, heart disease, diabetes, and cancer, while improving quality of life.

Another important mind-body practice is meditation. Regular meditation, even just 20 minutes a day, can improve overall health, with particular benefits for cardiovascular health, inflammation, and immune responses. Meditation practice is also shown to be as effective as antidepressants – if not more so – for anxiety, depression and other emotional issues.

Finally, we should never neglect our diets. Organic foods emphasizing lean protein, leafy and cruciferous vegetables, and whole grains, plenty of filtered water and, of course, high quality nutritional supplements, all play an important role in overall health. By integrating these practices, we can enhance longevity and bring calming counterpoints to our busy lives.

Of course, our aim is to give ourselves the best chance of Ascending when the time comes. Will these practices benefit you with your Ascension? Absolutely. You do not need to do all three. Just pick one, and stick to it. I find all of them to be very beneficial, but I must admit traditional Qi Gong is my favourite. I think I am drawn to the mysticism of it. But that is a totally subjective opinion. Find which one works best for you. During the Ascension Process Daily Planner, I have included time to conduct these practices as I feel they could be the difference between Ascending or not.

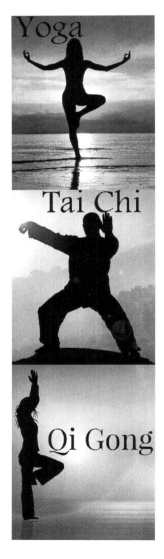

16

THE RAINBOW DIET

"I've always believed in a rainbow diet. As many colors and foods as you can eat, the better..." ~ CHRISTIE BRINKLEY

The vast spectrum of natural colour in fresh produce is astounding! Colour also happens to be a very useful indicator (and constant reminder) of the many magical health benefits of fresh plant-based foods. The deep greens, vibrant reds, deep purples, bright oranges, and yellows that we see in common and widely available foods provide far more than just "a rainbow" of colourful visual stimulation.

A rainbow diet is a very good diet for those on the Ascension Process. Indeed, as we have already learnt, different colours vibrate at different frequencies, and the colours in our foods are no different. It is no coincidence that fruit and vegetables resonate at the same frequency as our Chakras. Cooked meat on the other hand has the colour of dark browns/greys/reds etc. These colours in our auras indicate sickness, poor health, mental disorders, and sometimes entity attachment.

I am not here to tell you, you must become a vegetarian or vegan. Frankly, I do not care what people eat. That is their business and free will. All I am doing is pointing out that some foods resonate with our auras and chakras, and some do not. So, if you want to Ascend, you need to harmonise with the things that resonate with our energy centres. In my experience, that is the Rainbow Diet!

Eat a rainbow every day!

Whilst there's no one particular food or nutrient that gives us everything we need, likewise, no one colour provides all the available nutritional power either. Every colour found in food, whether it's green, red, purple, blue, yellow, and even white, reveals something nutritionally quite unique. By choosing a variety of colour in the diet, preferably at each meal, we can all be sure of enjoying a rich and varied spectrum of nutrients. For those who find nutritional science intimidating, or worse a "turn-off," eating by the colours is not only more appealing, it's easy as ABC. Often the best advice to give is simply to "*eat the rainbow*" every day!

Red (Root/base Chakra)

Strawberries, raspberries, and tomatoes immediately come to mind when thinking about red foods. All are super-nutritious, as is the great winter red fruit, the pomegranate, with its sweet, sour, and tangy flavours. Nutritionists love the pomegranate too, but more so because of its superfood powers! The rich red juice of the pomegranate is a powerful anti-inflammatory and is a concentrated source of antioxidants, B vitamins, vitamin C, and minerals too.

Strawberries and other red berries, including cranberries are known rich sources of ellagitannins, polyphenols that the body uses to convert to ellagic acid. Ellagic acid has been widely studied in the laboratory, and scientists think it may play a key role in preventing cancer. Another red gem is the little cherry!

Cherries come around later in the year and for a relatively short period of time, so make the most of them when they do appear. Their deep red colour again reveals the many amazing antioxidant pigments. These anthocyanin chemicals found in cherries are particularly effective in reducing pain and inflammation, just like pomegranate juice. Cherry juice and pomegranate juice are both commercially produced nowadays (look for 100% juice) and a perfect way to get your daily antioxidant hit!

Cherry juice has been found to help reduce post-exercise muscle soreness, and in turn, helping with muscle recovery. Cherries are also a great food if you, or someone you know, suffers with gout. Interestingly, cherries have also been found to contain melatonin, which is actually a hormone. Melatonin is produced by the pineal gland in the brain and regulates the body's internal clock, or sleep-wake cycle, as well as your connection to the Spirit world. It has other roles too, and research has shown that people who have heart attacks have low melatonin levels. It also plays an important role in the immune system.

Tomatoes are worth picking out amongst the red food group, partly because they are one of the best food sources of well-known antioxidant called lycopene. Lycopene is one of nature's most powerful antioxidants, and in fact you'll find it in most red foods, as well as those foods with a pink or pink-red hue. Think of watermelon, red or pink grapefruits, and you are looking at some lycopene! Cooked tomatoes have very high levels of lycopene, and have been found to effectively prevent prostate cancer as well as be helpful to maintain good cardiovascular health.

An excellent way of ensuring a quality dose of lycopene is by using lots of tomato puree or rich tomato sauces in your cooking! Remember, however, that raw, ripe, and juicy red tomatoes will have higher levels of other useful nutrients that have not been lost via cooking, so ensure you are getting these into your diet too. Lycopene may also slow the hardening of arteries and the growth of other cancer-related tumours.

Beetroot is begging for a mention of its own, with its deep red (almost purple) colour. There has been some significant and very interesting research of late, with regards to beetroots, particularly beetroot juice. Science has revealed the effectiveness of beetroot juice on lowering blood pressure, as well as improving exercise endurance and stamina. This is due to the juice being especially high in nitrates, compounds that convert to nitric oxide in the body.

Nitric oxide has several metabolic effects, such as dilating blood vessels (hence its blood pressure lowering effects) and helping deliver oxygen to working muscles. These and other findings of the health benefits of beetroot juice are also potentially relevant to those with heart disease, breathing complications, or modern-day metabolic diseases.

New research from **University of Exeter** in the UK suggests that a simple beetroot juice could be a very worthy contender to take the crown as a top sports drink. Certainly beetroot juice is much healthier, compared with many of the sugar loaded sports and energy drinks on the market.

According to the findings published in the *Journal of Applied Physiology*, drinking half a litre of beetroot juice every day improved exercise endurance by 16 per cent, compared with when they drank a blackcurrant cordial. The boost in nitric oxide after drinking beetroot juice makes exercise less tiring. Beetroots are also a good source of the B vitamin, folic acid. Folic acid is critically involved in normal red cell production, so all in all, don't be afraid to go for beetroot!

Orange and Yellow (Sacral and Solar Plexus Chakras)

The words that spring to mind when orange or yellow foods come into view are heart, protection, and immunity. Vitamin C is certainly visible with yellow and orange foods. In this department, we have grapefruit, cantaloupe melon, persimmons or Sharon fruits, summer and winter squashes, yellow peppers, corn, and carrots; all these are wonderful immune system boosters.

Fresh oranges as we know are rich in vitamin C, but so too are lemons, grapefruits, yellow peppers, and persimmons too. Grapefruits that have pink and red hues also contain lycopene, a star "antioxidant" of the red food group. Cantaloupe melons incidentally, are not only deliciously sweet fruits, they're rich super-rich in polyphenol antioxidants. These polyphenols are known to help regulate the formation of nitric oxide, a key chemical, or gas, produced in many cells of the body from the amino acid arginine. Sufficient production of nitric oxide prevents heart attacks, and ensures good blood circulation and blood flow.

Melons are also great sources of vitamin C and beta-carotene, or pro-vitamin A that is stored in the liver, and later converted to Vitamin A.

Vitamin A is essential for healthy eyes and vision, as well as being a key "immune" supportive nutrient. Carrots also contain significant amounts of Vitamin C, as well as B6, and even iron. Let's not forget squash and sweet potatoes, as these great winter and summer vegetables are excellent sources of the mineral potassium (important for regulating blood pressure), beta carotene, and many other minerals.

Peppers

- Sweet peppers from green, to yellow, to orange and red, beautifully illustrate how nutrient concentrations change with the colours.
- Yellow peppers typically contain more of the lutein and zeaxanthin carotenoids than green peppers.
- Red peppers will usually have more lycopene and astaxanthin, two other important carotenoids.
- Orange peppers will deliver more alpha, beta, and gamma-carotene
- Purple peppers will provide more anthocyanin flavonoids – most notably found in blueberries, blackberries and the new "super" Acai berry. Since all of these nutrients can make important contributions to your health, make sure you get into the habit of mixing and matching your use of sweet peppers in salads – go raw, stir-fry, steam-fry, or chargrill.

Greens (Heart Chakra)

In the nutritional sense, green is worth becoming a favourite colour! It signifies energy, vibrancy, and cleansing! Green veggies, and fruits too, such as watercress, spinach, chard, kale, courgettes, celery, dark seaweeds, rich green lettuces, kiwi fruits, limes, gooseberries, cucumbers and asparagus possess some of the most crucial nutrients for health, energy production, detoxification, rejuvenation and longevity.

The dark leafy greens such as broccoli, watercress, lettuce, spinach, rocket etc. are particularly crucial foods to try to get into the diet on a daily basis. These are rich in chlorophyll (similar in chemical structure to iron), many B vitamins, minerals, and fibre for an overall healthy body and blood system. Leafy greens are very alkalising too, helping to buffer the typically acidic western diet that commonly underpins most states of disease.

Lutein is a particular plant antioxidant found in kale, chard, and romaine lettuce helps to protect the eyes and ensure our long-term visual health. Broccoli is a well-loved and widely available vegetable, and is actually a great source of vitamin C (as are Brussels sprouts!). Vitamin C is an effective antioxidant that reduces disease risk, boosts the immune system, improves iron absorption, and promotes wound healing too.

Green vegetables in general are excellent sources of vitamin A, and vitamin K too (known to be vitally important in building bone density), as well as many of the B vitamins (such as B6 and folic acid), potassium, carotenoids and even omega-3 fatty acids. Green vegetables are also what you might term "low calorie, high nutrient" foods, so they can help significantly with weight loss too. Try replacing your starchy carbs (potatoes, bread and pasta) with a selection of green vegetables, and you might find losing weight a whole lot easier!

Greens and green vegetables are also valuable protein sources, especially when eaten in the raw state. "Raw" means that the food enzymes stay intact, and enzymes are made of amino acids – yes protein! Any well-informed and healthy vegetarian will include plenty of green vegetables in their diet every day, and vegans have to rely fairly heavily on these foods for calcium, iron, and magnesium too.

Blue and Purple (Throat and Third Eye Chakras)

Blueberries, black berries, grapes, aubergine, plums, and figs are some of the purple foods we can include in our diets, and for great reason too! You will find some of the highest levels of anthocyanidins and proanthocyanidin pigments in these foods – potent antioxidants found in the fruit, bark, leaves, and seeds of plants. They provide flavour and astringency as well as powerful health benefits. Proanthocyanidin-rich grape seed extract for example has been found to have preventive actions on diseases such as atherosclerosis, gastric ulcer, large bowel cancer, cataracts and diabetes.

One the easiest ways to get daily berry goodness year-round, is to buy frozen summer berries from your local supermarket. By all means choose fresh whenever you can, but fresh are not always available, or affordable. So, make the use of frozen, and throw them into smoothies, or onto cereals or into porridge. Of course you can just enjoy a big bowl full, with some cool natural yogurt, and a sprinkling of raw seeds – a perfect breakfast, or pudding.

Fresh plums and figs make excellent low sugar, low GI snacks, as well as being easy to carry or keep in the car. Both plums and figs also happen to be excellent sources of vitamin A, calcium, magnesium, iron, potassium, Vitamin C, and fibre. Blueberries are rich in antioxidants and other phytochemicals, but are also a significant source of the trace mineral manganese, and Vitamin K too. Grapes have been positively linked to fighting cancer, heart disease, degenerative nerve disease, and other ailments. Aubergines are a good soup or stew ingredient, and famously known as a key food in ratatouille, a dish in which you can use plenty of tomato puree and get your lycopene too!

Aubergines are very low in calories, yet rich sources of potassium and calcium. Blueberries are often singled out as little nutritional powerhouses, which they are! Anthocyanins are the pigments responsible for the purple tint of these fruits, and purple veggies too, and are known for their antioxidant qualities. In addition to anthocyanins cancer-fighting potential, these plant chemicals also support the vascular system.

White (Crown and Divine Light)

Just because a food appears to have no colour, doesn't necessarily mean "no nutrition"! Vibrant colour certainly isn't an exclusive indicator of phytochemical content. Whilst some phytochemical pigments do give amazing hues, others are in fact, colourless. Colourless pigments are found in foods such as cabbage, mushrooms, and onion. Most of the pigments we find in these and other foods are collectively called flavonoids. Flavonoids are powerful food chemicals, and counteract the free-radical formation, and resultant damage to the body's cells. When free-radical damage is not controlled, it can cause significant cellular changes, which can lead to cancer or other disease states.

Rainbow diets are a great way to get all of the nutrition you need, as well as making your meals exciting and delicious all at the same time!

Consider Changing your Diet

There are over 4,000 different plant chemicals in foods that present us with a spectrum of colours to create a truly healthy and balanced "rainbow diet" of wholefoods. Nutrition today, and what is now known about healthy eating, extends far beyond the vitamins and minerals we learned about in school or college.

To perform the Ascension activation you must be vibrating at a very high frequency. Only eating fruit and veg, then juices, then water, then nothing, can achieve this. Furthermore, I would recommend starting your Rainbow diet at least four weeks before you start the Ascension Process. If you are already a Vegan, then this does not apply to you.

17

LIVING ON AIR AND LIGHT ALONE

*"Why do we watch the sunrise? Why do we
concentrate on it? In order to learn to mobilize all our
thoughts, all our desires, and all our energies, and to
direct them toward the realization of the highest ideal…
He lives in such freedom that he expands the field of
his consciousness to include the entire human race, to
which he sends the abundance of light and love that
pour forth from him."*

~ OMRAAM MIKHAËL AÏVANHOV

On the closing parts of the Ascension Process, you will survive purely on sunlight and breath alone. This is not so much a requirement as it is a natural phenomenon. Indeed, by the time you have raised your vibration to such a high rate, your body will no longer be able to tolerate or digest solid food, not even water! As amazing as this sounds, it is really possible, and there are documented cases.

However, over the years, there have also been several out and out charlatans that have claimed to have lived for years on breath and light alone. So, who is correct? In order for you to feel comfortable about this process, we need to delve into it a bit further.

Ayurveda

Ayurveda medicine is a system of medicine with historical roots in the Indian subcontinent. Globalised and modernised practices derived from Ayurveda traditions are offered as a type of complementary or alternative medicine. In the Western world, Ayurveda therapies and practices (which are various) have been integrated in general wellness applications and, in some cases, in medical use. It is from the ancient teachings of Ayurveda medicine that we get *Inedia*.

Breatharianism

Inedia (Latin for "fasting"), or *breatharianism*, is the belief that it is possible for a person to live without consuming food. Breatharians claim that food and, in some cases, water, are not necessary for survival, and that humans can be sustained solely by **prana**, the vital life force in Hinduism. According to Ayurveda, sunlight is one of the main sources of prana, and some practitioners believe that it is possible for a person to survive on sunlight alone. The terms breatharianism or inedia may also refer to this philosophy when it is practiced as a lifestyle in place of the usual diet.

Breatharianism is considered a lethal pseudoscience by scientists and medical professionals, and several adherents of these practices have died from starvation and dehydration. Though it is common knowledge that humans require sustenance to survive, breatharianism continues. Why?

Some breatharians have submitted themselves to medical testing, including a hospital's observation of Indian mystic **Prahlad Jani** appearing to survive without food or water for 15 days, and an Israeli breatharian appearing to survive for eight days on a television current affairs style program. In a handful of documented cases, individuals attempting breatharian fasting have died. Among the claims in support of Inedia, investigated by the **Indian Rationalist Association**, all were found to be fraudulent.In other cases, people have attempted to survive on sunlight alone, only to abandon the effort after losing a large percentage of their body weight and falling ill.

Modern Breatharianism

The physician and occultist **Paracelsus** (1493–1541) was described as having lived "*several years by taking only one half scruple of Solar Quintessence,*" in the 1670 Rosicrucian text *Comte de Gabalis*. In this book, it is also stated that, "*Paracelsus affirms that He has seen many of the Sages fast twenty years without eating anything whatsoever.*" This information was later seized upon by charlatans like the next fellow.

1980 – The Kook

Breatharianism is the American movement founded by **Wiley Brooks** in the early 1980s that believes humans can live just fine by replacing food with both sun and the passive inhalation of cosmic micro-dust. It moved slightly in from the fringe in 2014 when **Valeria "The Human Barbie" Lukyanova** revealed herself to be one of Breatharianism's followers.

For obvious reasons, the sun and dust diet is fast becoming a trend in pro-anorexia communities and Lukyanova's viral endorsement is leading the resurgence. To be clear, if you try to live off of light and air, common sense says you will die.

Brooks was first introduced to the public in 1980 when appearing on the TV show *That's Incredible!* Brooks, now 80 years old in 2017, stopped teaching about 10 years ago so he could:

> "*devote 100% of his time on solving the problem as to why he needed to eat some type of food to keep his physical body alive and allow his light body to manifest completely.*"

In 2014, he conducted an interview with *Vice*. In this interview, he claimed he was **John the Baptist** in a past life, even though years earlier he said he was once **Jesus Christ**, a contemporary of John the Baptist. When this was pointed out, he said it was because he was really **God**, so he could pull this off. He also claimed that he was already in the fifth dimension as he was conducting the phone interview, even though it would be physically impossible.

Brooks claims to have found "*four major deterrents*" which prevented him from living without food: "people pollution", "food pollution", "air pollution," and "electro pollution."

In 1983, he was observed leaving a Santa Cruz **7-Eleven** with a Slurpee, a hot dog, and Twinkies. He told **Colors Magazine** in 2003 that he periodically breaks his fasting with a cheeseburger and a diet cola, explaining that when he's surrounded by junk culture and junk food, consuming them adds balance. He confirmed this again in 2014 when he stated that he advocates people only eat double quarter-pounder with cheese meals and drink diet Coke because they're the only things that are not radioactive.

The idea of separate but interconnected 5D and 3D worlds is a major part of Wiley Brooks' ideology, and Wiley Brooks encourages his followers to only eat these special (McDonalds) 5D foods, as well as meditate on a set of magical 5D words.

Brooks' institute has charged varying fees to prospective clients who wished to learn how to live without food. The fees have ranged from US$100,000 with an initial deposit of $10,000, to one billion dollars, to be paid via bank wire transfer with a preliminary deposit of $100,000, for a session called "Immortality workshop." After the immortality workshop, Wiley offers an elixir of life (a bottle of spring water) for the bargain price of just $10,000.

A payment plan is also offered. These charges have typically been presented as limited time offers exclusively for billionaires who wish to extend their lives way past the normal human age range. You can read the full transcript of his 2014 Vice interview here:(Mccasker, 2014)

1990 – The Naïve

Jasmuheen (born Ellen Greve) was a prominent advocate of Wiley's breatharianism in the 1990s. I know this story well because it played out in the city where I was living at the time. She said,

> *"I can go for months and months without having anything at all other than a cup of tea. My body runs on a different kind of nourishment."*

In 1999, she volunteered to be monitored closely by the Australian television program **60 Minutes** for one week without eating to demonstrate her methods. Interviewers found her house stocked with food; Jasmuheen claimed the food was for her husband and daughter.

After just 48 hours into the test, Jasmuheen's health began to deteriorate. She stated that she found it difficult because the hotel room in which she was confined was located near a busy road, causing stress and pollution that prevented absorption of required nutrients from the air.

> *"I asked for fresh air. Seventy percent of my nutrients come from fresh air. I couldn't even breathe," she said.*

Thus, the test was moved to a mountainside retreat where her condition continued to deteriorate. After Jasmuheen had fasted for four days, **Dr Beres Wenck**, president of the Queensland branch of the **Australian Medical Association**, urged her to stop the test.

According to Dr. Wenck, Jasmuheen's pupils were dilated, her speech was slow, and she was *"quite dehydrated, probably over 10%, getting up to 11%."* Towards the end of the test, he said,

> *"Her pulse is about double what it was when she started. The risks if she goes any further are kidney failure. 60 Minutes would be culpable if they encouraged her to continue. She should stop now."*

The test was stopped. Dr. Wenck said,

> *"Unfortunately there are a few people who may believe what she says, and I'm sure it's only a few, but I think it's quite irresponsible for somebody to be trying to encourage others to do something that is so detrimental to their health."*

Jasmuheen challenged the results of the program, saying, *"Look, 6,000 people have done this around the world without any problem."*

Ellen Greve AKA "Jasmuheen" was awarded the ***Bent Spoon Award*** by **Australian Sceptic's Society** in 2000 (*"presented to the perpetrator of the most preposterous piece of paranormal or pseudoscientific piffle"*). She also won the embarrassing 2000 **Ig Nobel Prize** for Literature for her book, ***Pranic Nourishment – Living on Light***.

Jasmuheen claims that her beliefs are based on the writings and "*more recent channelled material*" from **St. Germain**. She stated that some people's DNA has expanded from 2 to 12 strands, to "*absorb more hydrogen.*" When offered $30,000 to prove her claim with a blood test, she said that she didn't understand the relevance as she was not referring to herself.

In the documentary **No Way to Heaven**, the Swiss chemist **Michael Werner** claims to have lived for several years without food following the directions in Jasmuheen's book. The documentary also describes two attempts at scientific verification of his claims. As of 2012, four deaths had been directly linked to breatharianism as a result of Jasmuheen's publications. Jasmuheen has denied any responsibility for the deaths.

1995 The Liar

Hira Ratan Manek (born 12 September 1937) claims that since 18 June 1995 he has lived on water and occasionally tea, coffee, and buttermilk. Manek states that Sungazing is the key to his health, citing yogis, ancient Egyptians, Aztecs, Maya and Native Americans as practitioners of the art. He claims that he stared at the sun for 10 seconds per day, until the combined time reached 44 minutes. After this, he says you no longer need to gaze at the sun to gain its benefits.

While he and his proponents state that medical experts have confirmed his ability to draw sustenance by gazing at the sun, no such documented evidence has been forthcoming.

In 2011, during the filming of the documentary **Eat the Sun**, Hira Ratan Manek was caught on camera eating a huge meal in a San Francisco restaurant.

2003 The Master

Prahlad Jani is an Indian sadhu who says he has lived without food and water for more than 70 years. His claims were investigated by doctors at **Sterling Hospital**, Ahmedabad, Gujarat in 2003 and 2010. The study concluded that Prahlad Jani was able to survive under observation for two weeks without either food or water, and had passed no urine or stool, with no need for dialysis.

Interviews with the researchers speak of strict observation and relate that round-the-clock observation was ensured by multiple CCTV cameras. Jani was subjected to multiple medical tests, and his only contact with any form of fluid was during bathing and gargling, with the fluid spat out measured by the doctors. The research team could not comment on his claim of having been able to survive in this way for decades.

The case has attracted criticism, both after the 2003 tests and the recent 2010 tests. Sanal Edamaruku, president of the **Indian Rationalist Association**, criticized the 2010 experiment for allowing Jani to move out of a certain CCTV camera's field of view, meet devotees, and leave the sealed test room to sunbathe. Edamaruku stated that the regular gargling and bathing activities were not sufficiently monitored, and accused Jani of having had some "influential protectors" who denied Edamaruku permission to inspect the project during its operation. So far, their criticisms have been unsubstantiated.

2006 – The Monk

In 2006, a **Discovery Channel** documentary titled *The Boy with Divine Powers*, reported that **Ram Bahadur Bomjon**, a young Nepalese Buddhist monk neither moved, ate nor drank anything during 96 hours of filming. Bomjon lives as an ascetic in a remote area of Nepal. He appears to go for periods of time without ingesting either food or water. One such period was chronicled in the documentary. To date, no one has been able to disprove his claims.

2013 The Iron Will

In late September of 2013, **Ray Maor** appeared in a documentary produced by the Israeli television investigative show called **The Real Face**. The show is hosted by **Amnon Levy**, a very popular TV personality in Israel.

Israeli practitioner of Inedia, Ray Maor, appeared to survive without food or water for eight days and eight nights. According to the documentary, he was restricted to a small villa and placed under constant video surveillance, with medical supervision that included daily blood testing. The documentary claimed Maor was in good spirits throughout the experiment, lost 9kg/20 lbs after eight days, blood tests showed no change before, during, or after the experiment, and Cardiologist **Ilan Kitsis** from Tel Aviv **Sourasky Medical Center** was "baffled."

My take on Ray's Eight Days

For the first three days Ray reported feeling fine, however after four days, he began to feel weak, similar to Jasmuheen's test. But unlike Jasmuheen who tried to blame her failure on everyone and everything else, Ray began to meditate and exerciseusing *Phalon Gong* and Tai Chi. However, he only performed these tasks sporadically, so it was no surprise to me that boredom set in.

When you get bored, you begin to focus on how hungry you are. Indeed, when there is no food preparation and eating involved during your daily routine, you have a lot of extra time on your hands. In fact, it could be as much as an extra four to six hours per day. Thus, it is very important to keep your mind active.

After the experiment, Ray lost 9kg/20 lbs. He openly regretted not drinking water, and vowed he would never go without water again. I do not know if he stuck to that vow. He also claimed he had regained all his weight loss five days later. This is not surprising since our bodies are made up of 75% water, so the weight he lost was just the weight of the water. By starting to drink again, his body rehydrated and, therefore, regained the weight.

Another important fact is that after your fast, if you do not Ascend on the first attempt, you must take at least three hours before you drink a glass of water. It was claimed an Australian woman had died when, after fasting, she gulped down a glass of water in less than 60 seconds. I was unable to substantiate this story, but I have no reason to doubt it.

Ray claims there are about 10,000 Breatharians worldwide, and they all say a little prayer before they take their first sip of water after a long fast. Even though they did not recite the prayer on camera, I have put one together based on different things Ray was saying prior to taking his first drink:

> *"Holly water, special water, tasty water. Water that is part of us. After oxygen, you are the most important thing for my body. Special water that is becoming my cells, I drink you with love and intention. "*

In my opinion, Ray achieved this amazing feat through iron Will alone. He did not raise his vibration sufficiently to last eight days, as is evident with his "regrets," boredom and weight loss. This was not his first time fasting, and you would be amazed at what your body can endure when well trained. As interesting as Ray's experiment was, I was not impressed. To me, this was the outcome of several years practising. I have no doubt it was his longest attempt at the time.

You can watch the entire TV show with English subtitles on Ray's website (see Maor, 2013).

Why do so many people fail?

Breatharianism and sun gazing are very controversial topics. This is mainly due to the many charlatans. Indeed, what these people try todo is live a normal, everyday life, although not eat. That is a recipe for disaster! If you stop eating right now, you will die. End of story.

As we have seen, these dodgy, pseudo-science, New Age cults mix a little bit of truth, with a whole lot of bunk. Their whole purpose is to make money, not raise their vibration.

Indeed, the only way to survive without eating on the 3rd Dimension is to raise your vibration to such a high frequency that your body metamorphosises into a "Light" body. As such, you no longer require typical nourishment, nor crave it.

It is possible to practise both sun gazing and fasting leading up to your Ascension Process, however I see this as a complete waste of time. If you do not raise your vibration, then you will only damage your eyes, and drop like a rock from dehydration. Of course, if you want to give it a go, then by all means try, but I will not explain how to go about these practises here. That is a journey you will need to partake on your own.

As for doing these things during the Ascension Process, there is nothing to learn. At this point, you will instinctively give up food and water. You will have no cravings, no thirst, no hunger pangs, and definitely no loss of weight. By practicing Yoga, Tai Chi or Qi Gong, performing daily meditations and doing mind activities like puzzles, cross words, art, crafts, problem solving etc., you will also ward off boredom. In fact, you only need to practise Mindfulness and centre yourself to not become bored.

If you reach eight weeks and have still not instinctively given up food and water, then I would strongly recommend you stop immediately. You can always try again at a later time.

18

SACRED GEOMETRY & THE MERKABA

"Geometry is a science explained by Pythagoras and demonstrated by him. It is the science of God and its formulas are illustrative of the fact of the very energy of life that can be focused in the angle, in the pyramid, in the octagon, in the cell structure that is also geometric... Thus, beauty and mathematics, proportion and the golden ratio serve to enhance the message of the Word itself." ~ THE ASCENDED MASTER PAUL THE VENETIAN THROUGH THE MESSENGER ELIZABETH CLARE PROPHET, DECEMBER 29, 1983. PUBLISHED IN PEARLS OF WISDOM, VOL. 27, NO. 3.

The theory that the 3rd Dimensional reality as we consciously experience it is not real has had deep roots in indigenous shamanistic belief systems for many millennia. They believe that we exist in a dream or illusion. In our modern western culture, we refer to our virtual reality experience as a matrix, grid, simulation, and hologram. There are those trying to prove the hologram exists and others who are trying to break us out of it. Theories about reality being a simulation are increasing.

Time is an illusion, therefore so is everything else. The universe is a consciousness hologram. Our 3rd Dimensional reality is a projected illusion within the hologram. It is a virtual experiment created in linear time to study emotions. Our hologram is composed of grids, created by a source consciousness brought into awareness by electromagnetic energy at the physical level. The hologram is created and linked through a web, or grid matrixes based on the patterns of Sacred Geometry.

Just as a house is built with bricks and mortar, our reality has been constructed with 3D mathematical geometry and electromagnetic energy. The hologram had a beginning and it has an end. As consciousness evolves, obsolete parts of the hologram collapse. As the grids collapse, everything within the hologram will end as it fades to black. Thus, once the Earth Ascends, the planet in the 3rd Dimension will no longer exist. In order to work with, and "hack" the matrix, we need to understand the building blocks – Sacred geometry.

Sacred geometry involves sacred universal patterns used in the design of everything in our reality, most often seen in sacred architecture and sacred art. The basic belief is that geometry and mathematical ratios, harmonics, and proportion are also found in music, light, and cosmology. This value system is seen as widespread, even in prehistory - thus, it may just be that it is a cultural universal of the human condition.

Sacred geometry is considered foundational to building sacred structures such as temples, mosques, megaliths, monuments and churches; additionally, sacred spaces such as altars, temenoi and tabernacles; meeting places such as sacred groves, village greens and holy wells and the creation of religious art, as well as iconography and using "divine" proportions. Alternatively, sacred geometry based arts may be ephemeral, such as visualization, sand painting and medicine wheels.

Sacred geometry may be understood as a worldview of pattern recognition, a complex system of religious symbols and structures involving space, time, and form. According to this view, the basic patterns of existence are perceived as sacred. By connecting with these, a believer contemplates the Great Mysteries, and the Great Design. By studying the nature of these patterns, forms and relationships, and their connections, insight may be gained into the mysteries – the laws and lore of the Universe.

As stated, Reality is a consciousness hologram set in linear time to experience and record human emotions. Reality is science and math. The term "sacred geometry" is often used by archaeologists, anthropologists, geometricians, and metaphysicians to encompass the religious, philosophical, and spiritual beliefs that have sprung up around this geometry in various cultures during the course of the human biogenetic experiment.

The Golden Ratio

The golden ratio (symbol is the Greek letter "phi") is also known as the Golden Mean. It is a special number approximately equal to 1.618. It appears many times in geometry, art, architecture and other areas. In fact, it appears in almost every surviving megalith like the Great Pyramid of Giza, the ancient Mayan buildings in Cuzco, Peru, and even at Easter Island in the Pacific.

The Golden Mean occurs all over the natural world as well. In the shapes of plants, snail shells, astrology, and in the proportions of the human form as well as great art. The Golden Mean appears to be a constant in the universe. By dividing the half perimeter by the total height, we get The Golden Mean squared. And The Golden Mean occurs again and again in the Great Pyramid and all of the other megalith sites so far mentioned.

Greek letter "phi"

The Path of the Soul

We are soul sparks of light having a physical experience; our consciousness spirals down through the patterns of the golden ratio, now about to reverse the spiral (spin) and return to source consciousness and Light. To understand reality is to focus on the patterns that have repeated throughout time, as if on a higher octave with each programmed experience for the souls. Science and science fiction are merging in the twenty first century when all becomes clear; and the nature of reality, as based on a sacred geometric design, is understood. It's really not that complicated.

You are probably thinking by now, what has all this got to do with Ascension? Well, everything! You see, when we get to the main Ascension meditation, we will be using sacred geometry to help us spiral back up to the Light. Specifically, we will be using the Star Tetrahedron.

The Star Tetrahedron

Two, three sided pyramids interlocked make the Star Tetrahedron.

In order to understand exactly what significance the Star Tetrahedron plays in our reality, we must first have a general understanding of its creation.

The Star Tetrahedron is a pattern found in Sacred Geometry. To summarise, Sacred Geometry is an amazing and complex system of sacred universal patterns that are found in the design of everything from the architecture of sacred spaces such as temples, monuments, and altars, to music and art, such as Labyrinths and Mandalas.

The Star Tetrahedron, also called a *Double Tetrahedron*, is made up of two interlocking Tetrahedrons. A Tetrahedron is the first and simplest of the five **Platonic Solid shapes**. Each face is an identical triangle, each side is equal, and the angles are the same. These two interlocking Tetrahedrons form a three dimensional **Star of David**.

The Star Tetrahedron is the geometric and energetic representation of the human body, of heaven and earth, male and female. It is also called the **MERKABA**.

The MERKABA

The Egyptian word, MERKABA, is actually three words combined to give it a whole new meaning. The word can be broken down in order to understand the concept more clearly.

- "**Mer**" is translated into the word "Light."
- "**Ka**" refers to the spirit or soul and
- "**Ba**" (in this reality) refers to the physical being or body.

So, roughly translated, it means **Light Body**. It is pronounced "Mer – Kah-BAH" – NOT "Merka-bar"

And so the entire world in ancient Egypt referred to the rotating light that would take the spirit and the body from one world and reality to another. In the modern world, we refer to these worlds and realities as dimensions and portals. The ancient African Zulu meaning of the MERKABA is "*space-time-dimension vehicle.*"

The MERKABA represents the shape of our energy system in upper dimensions. By meditating on the MERKABA, you can more easily connect with your Higher Self. This can help to align your spiritual, mental, emotional, and physical bodies.

The MERKABAis a tool that helps humans reach their full potential. It is a crystalline energy field that is comprised of a counter rotating Star Tetrahedron that aligns the mind, body, and heart together. This energy field created from sacred geometry extends around the body for a distance of 17 meters/55 feet.

These geometric energy fields normally spin around our bodies at close to the speed of light, but for most of us they have slowed down or stopped spinning entirely due to a lack of attention and use. Indeed, your MERKABA is dormant and non-functional, waiting for the right moment to be activated. If you have been seeing 11:11 or other duplicate numbers regularly, then your time has come!

When the spirit that inhabits the body 'remembers' that it is there and begins to change certain aspects of itself, an incredible transformation begins to grow.

When this field is reactivated and spinning properly it looks just like the structure of a galaxy. The MERKABA enables us to experience expanded awareness, connects us with elevated potentials of consciousness, and restores access to and memory of the infinite possibilities of our being. When the MERKABA meditation is performed correctly, the MERKABA fluidly integrates our feminine (intuitive, receptive) and masculine (active, dynamic) aspects of our mind and Spirit.

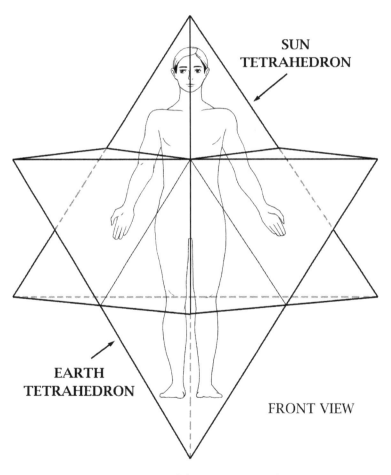

A representation of the MERKABA standing

A representation of the MERKABA sitting

The MERKABA is a Living Field

The MERKABA is a living field, not a purely mechanical field of energy. As it is living, it responds to human thought and feeling, which is a way to connect to the field. The 'computer' that guides the MERKABA is the human mind and heart. The possibilities are endless.

As stated, it is a crystalline energy field that is comprised of specific sacred geometric shapes that align the mind, body, and heart together. In addition, when activated, the MERKABA field can become alive. When this happens, an electromagnetic change occurs which results in a disc of energy that comes out from a tiny place near the base of the spine and quickly expands to about 8-10 metres/27–30 feet in radius around the body. The disc can easily be perceived by scientific means.

Metaphysical Aspects of the MERKABA/Star Tetrahedron

The MERKABA Star Tetrahedron is an amazing and powerful tool, especially during these current times of shifts and transitions. It can assist in the connection between the physical and ethereal bodies, allow us to see the psychological patterns and programs that may limit us, and is a constant reminder to remember our true, loving and divine nature. By meditating on the MERKABA Star Tetrahedron we are able to merge with Source, the Divine, All that is. Indeed, think of it as a vehicle that will allow you to travel to the higher 4th and 5th Dimensions. Because it is constructed by the same "bricks and mortar" as the holographic Universe, it is able to move freely through the dimensions.

I have developed a unique method of using the MERKABA as a tool for Ascension. Previously, people only used the MERKABA meditation to activate their MERKABA. I have taken this one step further. Using our breathing and visualising techniques, we will be able to ignite the etheric fire, turning it into the **SAHU**, or Immortal Energy Body – your Light Body! This will in turn activate your 12 strand DNA. With your 12 strand DNA activated, this will then trigger your Ascension. The MERKABA will take us to the 5th Dimension!

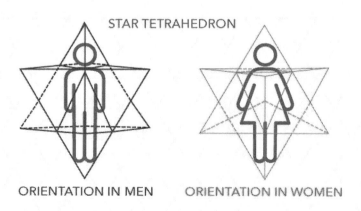

STAR TETRAHEDRON

ORIENTATION IN MEN   ORIENTATION IN WOMEN

Other Uses of the **MERKABA**

You can acquire then hold a MERKABA Star Tetrahedron when in meditation or prayer. Using the Star Tetrahedron in this way reminds us that we are not limited to this single physical body, but are multidimensional beings with no limits. The Star Tetrahedron allows us to keep this type of awareness within our consciousness as we go about our day.

Many MERKABA Star Tetrahedrons come in the form of pendants, which are perfect to maintain the energy field in this state of awareness. MERKABA Star Tetrahedrons are also available in a variety of crystals and minerals, which allows you to choose one that will work for the issues you would like to concentrate on.

- **Green Aventurine** Star Tetrahedron to specifically clear and heal Heart issues.
- **Rose Quartz** Star Tetrahedron to bring Divine, Universal Love into the physical field. It also is a wonderful reminder of our true nature.
- **White Jasper** or Yin/Yang combination (white/black) Star Tetrahedron to connect with Universal energies.
- **Bloodstone** or **Moss Agate** Star Tetrahedrons would assist in healing, either for an individual or a group. Place a MERKABA Star Tetrahedron in the middle of a healing circle for a balance of healing energies.

The MERKABA Star Tetrahedron is a powerful and unique tool with amazing energy vibrations. There are in-depth courses you can do, like the **Flower of Life** course for those that want to know more. If you opt for self-study, this is definitely a piece you want to work with. Its uses are limitless, just another reminder that we, too, are limitless in nature.

Your MERKABA looks like you are sitting in a small, light filled UFO floating in mid-air. Nothing can get in, and nothing can get out. You can see out, but no one or nothing can see you inside. You are totally safe. Use this time now to edit your subconscious. You can purge negative vibrations, severe attachments, and communicate with your Guides. Your MERKABA can also be used as a UFO to travel to any point on the Earth, or inter-dimensionally. Direction and speed are controlled by your thoughts.

The Activated MERKABA appears on 3D Earth as a UFO

19

ASCENSION DAILY PLANNER

"The price of success is hard work, dedication to the job at hand, and the determination that whether we win or lose, we have applied the best of ourselves to the task at hand." ~ VINCE LOMBARDI

scension simply means transferring from the 3rd dimension to the 5th dimension, body and all. Unlike death, where you leave the body behind, with Ascension, we take our body with us. However, to accomplish this, your body must transform into a body of Light.

To achieve this, you must purge all negative vibration from your Being, as well as release all attachment to anyone or anything in your life. To do this, you must complete multiple, daily meditations, for about 6-8 weeks. It is best done in isolation, in nature.

Why Isolation is best

I believe to get the most out of this program you need to take yourself out of your day to day life. In fact, I would recommend camping, or finding a little cabin in the mountains, by yourself, away from all civilisation. No cell phones, no computers, and no TV.

The reason I recommend being by yourself is because you will spend long hours purging negative vibration from your Being. In these early days, when you are still vulnerable, think about this: You just spent all day working on yourself. You are in peace and at one.

Suddenly, the kids come home from school, or your wife/husband just got home from work. They had a crap day, a fight with the boss, then had to deal with a traffic jam all the way home. Their energy is spiked in frustration, anger, and hostility. Your teenage girl/boy is spiked in self-hate, angst, and an entitlement (brat) mentality.

Remember back to Chapter 6, *The Bio-Psychological Effects of Ascension*. There, I spoke about "entrainment." This is where your aura will start to vibrate in sympathy with a stronger energy. In other words, all that brilliant work you spent all day performing, has just been wiped out in the first 20 minutes of everyone getting home.

Obviously, if you live alone you do not have this problem. But you will still be tempted to answer the phone, go to work, go on social media, or go to the shopping mall etc. That is why I believe your best chance is to completely isolate yourself. Bring all your food, water, and equipment with you.

If you are in a very close and energetically aligned partnership with someone, it may be beneficial to work together in the early stages, however I still believe it is impossible for two people to advance at exactly the same rate. As per human nature, this alone will create either fear (of being left behind), or jealously (why are they advancing and I am not), or unworthiness (I know I am moving ahead, but it is not fair to leave them behind). Thus, I say again, I believe your best chance of success is to do this alone, in isolation.

WARNING: Always consult medical advice from a doctor before making any radical changes to your diet.

Food and Water

You will be required to start on a vegan style diet, followed by juicing, then pure water, then finally sunlight. In other words, you must give up eating meat, drinking alcohol, smoking and taking drugs of any description, legal or otherwise. No processed food, no junk food, or dairy. This is critical. If you do not change your diet, then there is no point continuing.

If you are not used to a vegan diet right now, then don't expect to start one on day one without unwanted side effects. Indeed, in order to hit the ground running, I recommend starting your new diet 2-4 weeks prior to starting the Ascension Process. This gives your body, and mind, time to re-adjust.

As for juicing – there are juicers and then there are juicers. Do some research. Find one that keeps as much of the nutrients and good stuff as possible. The top of the line juicers are very expensive, but there are middle of the road juicers that are just as good. My personal preference is still the **Oscar Neo**, the original horizontal cold-press juicer. It is a total food processor, so you can make nut butters, sorbet, pasta, and what they call "living juice" which can be stored in a refrigerator for up to 48 hours and not lose any of the goodness. It retails for around $400-$500 (in 2017) and is great value for money. If you cannot afford an electric juicer, then you can use an old school, handheld one.

You will need to work out how much fruit and vegetables you will need for your solid diet, then for your juicing diet. By the time you start the juicing diet, your Aura and subtle bodies may be aligned and strong enough for you to go to the local market to buy fresh produce. You will have to make that decision yourself. By the way, "green juices" include any vegetables, so beetroot, peppers, corn etc. are Ok, even though they are not "green."

After juicing, you will just consume pure, clean water. It must not contain fluoride, chlorine or any other additive. Bottled spring water is fine, and is what I would recommend.

Finally, for the last couple of weeks, you will exist on sunlight and breath only (Refer to Chapter 17 for a look at the role of living on breath and sunlight in the final stages of Ascension).

Forgiveness

Day one, you will start on Forgiveness. This includes forgiving others. Make a long, honest list of every person that irritates you, challenges you, upsets you, or that you just have a problem with. Stop holding grudges.

Most people have made poor choices in their lives at some point. This is because they have allowed fear to do the thinking for them. Indeed, usually they have done this because they are in a state of scarcity. They believe that their life is measured by what they own, or what status they have in community or among their peers. They believe these things will change them into the person they want to be. They think this way because they are disconnected from The Source (God).

To make matters worse, our current society encourages this mind set. Society reinforces this notion that there is a "pile" and you must claw your way to the top of it. But the truth is there is no "pile." The pile is a fiction.

Life is not fair – pure and simple. Therefore, you cannot judge people by what they have done. Their actions are a product of this distorted and disconnected system. I realise people will find it very difficult to forgive child molesters and murderers, for example. Yes, there are some people who are just plain bad, and they are this way owing to something innate, rather than as a product of society. But I can assure you, in Spirit there is no good or bad, there just "Is."

Break out of Limited Consciousness

As abhorrent as child molestation is in our society, these individuals are most likely younger souls expressing (thus, learning) this very negative trait, which is that of Power and Domination. Therefore, it is not up to us to judge those people. Believe it or not, there is a very good chance you were a paedophile, rapist, murderer – the list goes on – in previous lives. The reason you find them distasteful now is because you have learnt that lesson.

So, does that mean I accept child molestation and murderers? Absolutely not. As an older soul, I am teaching the younger souls right from wrong. Therefore, I openly support the capture and incarceration of all criminals. I am in a state of mind where I can oppose certain behaviours, but I can also show compassion for those younger souls in learning. Having compassion and supporting their actions are two different things. If a three year old child took some lipstick and drew on the wall, would you go crazy and scream and yell, belt them within an inch of their life, and banish them to a dark closet? I hope you would not. I would tell the child (calmly) that they should not do that. I would then show them how I clean the wall, and let them help. I would give them some drawing paper and crayons and draw a picture with them. As crazy as it may sound, this is the same approach we need to take toward every criminal in our society. Not to mollycoddle them – rather, to show them adult compassion.

Allow Compassion to Dominate Your Thinking

Part of Forgiveness is allowing Compassion to dominate your thinking. Try to view the world from outside your body. See people as if you were an outside observer, taking notes. Do not allow your emotion into this process, instead use the Wise Mind.

When you have gone through your list of people to forgive, you then work on Nations, institutions and organisations. For example, you do not support your country's role in wars – forgive the country. You do not like New World Order groups like Planned Parenthood – forgive them. You do not like organisations like the Catholic Church – forgive them.

Forgiving Yourself

Finally, you need to forgive yourself. This is the hardest one of all. Start by forgiving your body. Remember, you are not your body. And your body is not you. Pick every fault YOU perceive, and learn to love it. Own it.

This body was chosen by you before you got here. It was chosen so as to offer you the best chance of doing your Lessons (see the 12 Primary Life Lessons). Like an old war horse or a brand new sports car each have lovable traits. Maybe it is a reliable old truck, or a golf buggy – whatever! The point is your body has served you dutifully for your life so far. It has allowed you to interact in the 3D Holographic Universe you currently inhabit. You have been partners in this experiment, so thank it, and love it.

Next, forgive You. The "real" you. NO, not your mind – that is part of the brain. Yes, your eternal soul is what I am talking about. The part that survives after death. The part of you that is forever.

I am sure there are times when you feel life sucks, or wonder why are you here, or why would you pick such a crappy life etc. The fact is you need to remind yourself that you chose this life, your body, your family, friends, partners, children – everybody and everything – in a place of perfect harmony, of perfect Love, and of perfect Trust. Yes, you made these choices on the Spirit Plane where negativity does not exist. Now you are trying to figure out the why, in a land of almost constant negative vibrations, electro-magnetic interference, toxic food, water and air. Do you really think you know better than your Soul? Let it go. Accept and Allow.

As trivial as these exercises may seem now, it is crucial in the big picture. The single biggest failure people have for not igniting their Ascension Process is failing to forgive at some level. You must radiate nothing but Pure, Unconditional Love to Ascend.
I strongly recommend reading *How to Forgive Someone Who Has Hurt You: In 15 Steps* by Dr. Wayne W. Dyer (Dr. Wayne W. Dyer, 2010)

Forgiveness

Predictors of Forgiveness

Increased Likelihood of Forgiveness →

Selfish Apathetic	Personality	Selfless Empathetic
Over Benefitted	Relationship Quality	Heavily Invested
Discovery through 3rd party / Serious Offense	Nature of Transgression	Unsolicited partner discovery / Trivial Offense
Viewed as intentional / malicious	Social-Cognitive Variables	No responsibility attribution

Source: McCullough et al. (1998)

Detachment

Detachment from the 3rd Dimension is one of the most difficult things to do when you are in the 3rd Dimension. It is like asking a fish to live outside the water. Your brain has evolved, and is hard wired to form, strong bonds with family and peers. Scientists believe this behaviour evolved to solicit mutual empathy. In other words, you scratch my back, and I will scratch yours. As a consequence of this hard-wired binding, humans have projected this attribute onto other organisms, like pets, and also inanimate objects, like cars, jewellery, clothing, houses etc.

So, is it even possible to detach? In short, yes, but it is usually only achieved by Old Souls in their last life. However, due to the Shift, the opportunity is available to any Soul Age that puts in the effort.

How do I know if I have detached?

This is a simple test. Answer these questions honestly:

- Imagine right now, you just found out every member of your family, and every friend you have, as moved to a new country. You will never see them again, and you will never hear from them again. In fact, there will not even be a farewell – they have already gone. How does this sit with you right here and now?

- You just returned to your home to find it has disappeared. Everything you own is gone. You have no money to buy new clothes, furniture, or food. How does this sit with you right here and now?
- You wake up in the morning, and your pet cat/dog/etc. is gone. You will never see them again. How does this sit with you right here and now?
- Go to the local shopping centre car park. Leave your keys in the ignition and walk away. Leave your car there and never return. How does this sit with you right here and now?
- Grab everything you have accumulated over the years – books, clothes, jewellery, music, computers, smart phones, TV's, the coffee maker, photo albums, art work, musical instruments, your bed – everything – and put it on the sidewalk. How does this sit with you right here and now?

Can you do any of these things without pangs of sentimentality, fear, regret, or stress? It is normal to feel these things right here and now. That is part of your evolution and conditioning.

What we are attempting to do is hack this conditioning. To do that, we have to raise our vibration so high that we realise that material things are just stuff. Stuff can always be replaced, and stuff is inanimate, so it is not real. People and pets are never gone; we are always connected, even if they are in Spirit. The point is you have to get to a point where this is no longer a belief – but a knowing.

The best way to tackle the attachment issue is to use concentric circles. Make the furthest out circle the whole planet then each circle gets closer and closer to you, so the things that are very dear to you are in the circles closer to yours. Eventually you are left with the last circle – the one you are in. Release and detach one circle at a time. Draw it on a piece of paper to see how attached you are right now to certain things.

This may seem impossible right now, and for most people it is. They have become slaves to their stuff and their fake relationships. But know this, if you raise your vibration, you begin to vibrate higher than the material world, and higher than the people that are around you. You are the fish that was lifted out of the water, but you learnt to grow wings and lungs and to transform into an eagle.

Working Hours

Another point that may prove difficult for some of our younger Ascenders is the working hours (just kidding). It is very important that you attune your body back to the natural rhythms. Therefore, you will rise with the sun, and your work will continue until just after sunset. You can read, study, or do nothing, from sunset to about 10pm, if you want. Or maybe you can sleep as soon as the sun goes down. It is your choice. But remember, by tuning to the Earth's rhythms, you will naturally resonate with the Schumann's Resonance.

Meditation Explanations

In the daily planner that follows, I list meditations that are required to do each day, in a set order. They are:

- *Aura Cleansing Meditation:* Performed each night. This helps to make sure you are ready for the next day, and to get a good night's sleep.

- *Ascension Meditation 1 - (Physical) Whole Body Alignment:* This is a Chakra balancing and cleansing routine.

- *Ascension Meditations 2 - (Emotional) Forgiveness Meditation:* This is part of you forgiving everyone, and everything, including yourself. You will see numbers in brackets e.g. (2) or (3). This means you do the same base meditation, but substitute the people, or the things, or yourself. For example, (1) is you, (2) is parents, (3) is siblings etc. Remember to make a thorough list before you begin the Ascension process. You do not want to be doing this in the middle, as it can upset your balance.

- *Ascension Meditations 3 - (Mental) Release Fear:* This is to let go of phobias, fears, ill feelings, guilt, etc. Any Fear based thoughts. Again, write a long and honest list and concentrate on a different area each day, then recycle through the list again.

- *Ascension Meditations 4 - (Spiritual) Cosmic Consciousness:* This is designed to expand your consciousness and to open your Third Eye and pineal gland. It is during this meditation you can expect to get psychic messages, and to communicate with your Guides.

- *(Crossover Physical/Spiritual) Life Lessons Healing:* These are your top three life lessons from the survey in Chapter 12. Cycle through each one. For example, Lesson I is your top rated lesson, Lesson II is the second, and Lesson III is the third.

- *MERKABA Practice Meditation I:*(Basic) this is preparing you for the more complex MERKABA Activation Meditation. You need to do this blind-folded, so to speak, before you move onto the second practice.

- *MERKABA Practice Meditation II:*(Intermediate) this is more advanced than the first practice; and again, you need to be able to perform it at will before moving onto the more complex MERKABA Activation Meditation.

- *MERKABA Activation Meditation:*(Advanced) Designed to activate your own MERKABA. This is a prerequisite for the final meditation. Unless you can do this meditation perfectly and at will, then there is no point attempting the final Ascension meditation.

- **Ascension Activation Meditation:** (Highly advanced)this is the final meditation designed to raise your vibration and activate your 12 strand DNA. This, in turn, will spark your Ascension. It has been written as such that you can do it in small chunks, until you learn the complete meditation.

Daily Routine

What follows is my suggested daily routine for a six week program. The idea is to get you into an identical, daily routine so it becomes second nature. That way, you don't have to waste time each day wondering what you should do. You do not have to follow it exactly, but you doneed to incorporate the daily meditations from the program into your daily routine.

Morning Routine

- Rise at 6AM
- Stretch, arms in the air, chest out and say *"Thank you. Thank you. Thank you."* Feel nothing but Love and Gratitude for being alive. Drink 1 glass of pure water.
- Dress and prepare for either a 20 minute jog, or 40 minute brisk walk. Whichever is easiest for you. After your run/walk, drink another glass of pure water.
- Shower or bathe.
- Conduct **Meditation 1** for 20 mins.
- Drink water after meditation.
- Prepare breakfastas per diet guide, drink water with breakfast.
- Clean or tidy your place of residence. Wash your running clothes if you need to. Do general housework/tidy.
- Conduct **Meditation 2** for 1 hrs.
- Spare time – engage in mind expanding activities. Reading, writing, puzzles, painting, drawing, building (kits), jigsaw puzzles, listening to music, Yoga, Tai Chi, Qi Gong etc. Anything that is productive and keeps you in the "mindfulness" mode.

Mid-Morning Routine 10AM – 12PM

- Prepare morning tea – a piece of fruit or whatever you like within the dietary guide for this week. It is ok to drink herbal tea or Chinese green tea.

- Conduct **Meditation 3** for 1-2 hrs.
- Drink water.
- Write in a journal what you are feeling, what changes you are experiencing. Did you see something in your meditation?

Lunch Routine 12PM – 1PM

- Prepare lunchas per diet guide. Drink water with lunch.
- Use spare time to go for a short, leisurely walk. Observe nature, the sky, the ground, the sound of the birds. Sit under a tree for a time, close your eyes, and just listen and feel. This is designed to entrain your brain waves with the alpha waves of the Schumann's Resonance.

Mid-Afternoon Routine 1PM – 3PM

- Drink a glass of water.
- Conduct **Meditation 4** for 1hr.
- Write in a journal what you are feeling, what changes you are experiencing. Did you see something in your meditation?

Late-Afternoon Routine 3PM – 5PM

- Prepare afternoon tea – a piece of fruit or whatever you like within the dietary guide for this week. It is ok to drink herbal tea or Chinese green tea.
- Spare time – engage in mind expanding activities. Reading, writing, puzzles, painting, drawing, building (kits), jigsaw puzzles, listening to music, Yoga, Tai Chi, Qi Gong etc. Anything that is productive and keeps you in the "mindfulness" mode.
- Conduct **Meditation 5** for1-2 hrs.
- Write in a journal what you are feeling, what changes you are experiencing. Did you see something in your meditation?

Evening Routine 5PM – 7PM

- Prepare your evening meal as per diet guide. Drink water with meal.
- Conduct **Meditation 6** for 20 mins.
- Practice aura viewing, energy work, and divination etc. for 1hr.
- Write in a journal how your day went. Did you meet your objectives? Do you need to improve on something? Don't forget to be grateful for this experience. Thank your body for getting you through the day. Thank your Higher Self for guiding you through the day. Know that you did the best you could do under the circumstances. There is no pass or failure – there is just "Is."
- Prepare for bed – if you need to, set your alarm for 6AM. Tomorrow is a new day!

WARNING: Always consult medical advice from a doctor before making any radical changes to your diet.

WEEK 1 - DIET: VEGAN	
Day	**Meditations**
1	1. (Physical) Whole Body Alignment	2. (Emotional) Forgiveness (1)	3. (Mental) Release Fear	4. (Spiritual) Cosmic Consciousness	5. MERKABA practice I	6. Aura Cleansing
2	1. (Physical) Whole Body Alignment	2. (Emotional) Forgiveness (2)	3. (Mental) Release Fear	4. (Spiritual) Life Lesson I	5. MERKABA practice I	6. Aura Cleansing
3	1. (Physical) Whole Body Alignment	2. (Emotional) Forgiveness (3)	3. (Mental) Release Fear	4. (Spiritual) Life Lesson II	5. MERKABA practice I	6. Aura Cleansing
4	1. (Physical) Whole Body Alignment	2. (Emotional) Forgiveness (4)	3. (Mental) Release Fear	4. (Spiritual) Life Lesson III	5. MERKABA practice I	6. Aura Cleansing
5	1. (Physical) Whole Body Alignment	2. (Emotional) Forgiveness (1)	3. (Mental) Release Fear	4. (Spiritual) Life Lesson I	5. MERKABA practice I	6. Aura Cleansing
6	1. (Physical) Whole Body Alignment	2. (Emotional) Forgiveness (2)	3. (Mental) Release Fear	4. (Spiritual) Cosmic Consciousness	5. MERKABA practice I	6. Aura Cleansing
7	1. (Physical) Whole Body Alignment	2. (Emotional) Forgiveness (3)	3. (Mental) Release Fear	4. (Spiritual) Cosmic Consciousness	5. MERKABA practice I	6. Aura Cleansing

WEEK2 - DIET: VEGAN	
Day	**Meditations**
1	1. (Physical) Whole Body Alignment | 2. (Emotional) Forgiveness (1) | 3. (Mental) Release Fear | 4. (Spiritual) Cosmic Consciousness | 5. MERKABA practice I | 6. Aura Cleansing
2	1. (Physical) Whole Body Alignment | 2. (Emotional) Forgiveness (2) | 3. (Mental) Release Fear | 4. (Spiritual) Life Lesson I | 5. MERKABA practice I | 6. Aura Cleansing
3	1. (Physical) Whole Body Alignment | 2. (Emotional) Forgiveness (3) | 3. (Mental) Release Fear | 4. (Spiritual) Life Lesson II | 5. MERKABA practice I | 6. Aura Cleansing
4	1. (Physical) Whole Body Alignment | 2. (Emotional) Forgiveness (4) | 3. (Mental) Release Fear | 4. (Spiritual) Life Lesson III | 5. MERKABA practice I | 6. Aura Cleansing
5	1. (Physical) Whole Body Alignment | 2. (Emotional) Forgiveness (1) | 3. (Mental) Release Fear | 4. (Spiritual) Life Lesson I | 5 MERKABA practice I | 6. Aura Cleansing
6	1. (Physical) Whole Body Alignment | 2. (Emotional) Forgiveness (2) | 3. (Mental) Release Fear | 4. (Spiritual) Cosmic Consciousness | 5. MERKABA practice I 6. Aura Cleansing
7	1. (Physical) Whole Body Alignment | 2. (Emotional) Forgiveness (3) | 3. (Mental) Release Fear | 4. (Spiritual) Cosmic Consciousness | 5. MERKABA practice I | 6. Aura Cleansing

WEEK3 - DIET: GREEN JUICES	
Day	**Meditations**
1	1. (Physical) Whole Body Alignment | 2. (Emotional) Forgiveness (1) | 3. (Mental) Release Fear | 4. (Spiritual) Cosmic Consciousness | 5. MERKABA practice II | 6. Aura Cleansing
2	1. (Physical) Whole Body Alignment | 2. (Emotional) Forgiveness (2) | 3. (Mental) Release Fear | 4. (Spiritual) Life Lesson I | 5. MERKABA practice II | 6. Aura Cleansing
3	1. (Physical) Whole Body Alignment | 2. (Emotional) Forgiveness (3) | 3. (Mental) Release Fear | 4. (Spiritual) Life Lesson II | 5. MERKABA practice II | 6. Aura Cleansing
4	1. (Physical) Whole Body Alignment | 2. (Emotional) Forgiveness (4) | 3. (Mental) Release Fear | 4. (Spiritual) Life Lesson III | 5. MERKABA practice II | 6. Aura Cleansing
5	1. (Physical) Whole Body Alignment | 2. (Emotional) Forgiveness (1) | 3. (Mental) Release Fear | 4. (Spiritual) Life Lesson I | 5. MERKABA practice II | 6. Aura Cleansing
6	1. (Physical) Whole Body Alignment | 2. (Emotional) Forgiveness (2) | 3. (Mental) Release Fear | 4. (Spiritual) Cosmic Consciousness | 5. MERKABA practice II | 6. Aura Cleansing
7	1. (Physical) Whole Body Alignment | 2. (Emotional) Forgiveness (3) | 3. (Mental) Release Fear | 4. (Spiritual) Cosmic Consciousness | 5. MERKABA practice II | 6. Aura Cleansing

WEEK 4 – DIET: FRUIT JUICES	
Day	**Meditations**
1	1. (Physical) Whole Body Alignment| 2. (Emotional) Forgiveness (1) | 3. (Mental) Release Fear| 4. (Spiritual) Cosmic Consciousness| 5. MERKABA Activation II| 6. Aura Cleansing
2	1. (Physical) Whole Body Alignment| 2. (Emotional) Forgiveness (2) | 3. (Mental) Release Fear| 4. (Spiritual) Life Lesson I| 5. MERKABA Activation II| 6. Aura Cleansing
3	1. (Physical) Whole Body Alignment| 2. (Emotional) Forgiveness (3) | 3. (Mental) Release Fear| 4. (Spiritual) Life Lesson II| 5. MERKABA Activation II| 6. Aura Cleansing
4	1. (Physical) Whole Body Alignment| 2. (Emotional) Forgiveness (4) | 3. (Mental) Release Fear| 4. (Spiritual) Life Lesson III| 5. MERKABA Activation II| 6. Aura Cleansing
5	1. (Physical) Whole Body Alignment| 2. (Emotional) Forgiveness (1) | 3. (Mental) Release Fear| 4. (Spiritual) Life Lesson I| 5. MERKABA Activation II| 6. Aura Cleansing
6	1. (Physical) Whole Body Alignment| 2. (Emotional) Forgiveness (2) | 3. (Mental) Release Fear| 4. (Spiritual) Cosmic Consciousness| 5. MERKABA Activation II| 6. Aura Cleansing
7	1. (Physical) Whole Body Alignment| 2. (Emotional) Forgiveness (3) | 3. (Mental) Release Fear| 4. (Spiritual) Cosmic Consciousness| 5. MERKABA Activation II| 6. Aura Cleansing

WEEK 5 – DIET: FRUIT JUICES	
Day	**Meditations**
1	1. (Physical) Whole Body Alignment| 2. (Mental) Release Fear| 3. (Spiritual) Cosmic Consciousness| 4. MERKABA Activation| 5. Aura Cleansing
2	1. (Physical) Whole Body Alignment| 2. (Mental) Release Fear| 3. (Spiritual) Cosmic Consciousness| 4. MERKABA Activation| 5. Aura Cleansing
3	1. (Physical) Whole Body Alignment| 2. (Mental) Release Fear| 3. (Spiritual) Cosmic Consciousness| 4. MERKABA Activation| 5. Aura Cleansing
4	1. (Physical) Whole Body Alignment| 2. (Mental) Release Fear| 3. (Spiritual) Cosmic Consciousness| 4. MERKABA Activation| 5. Aura Cleansing
5	1. (Physical) Whole Body Alignment| 2. (Mental) Release Fear| 3. (Spiritual) Cosmic Consciousness| 4. MERKABA Activation| 5. Aura Cleansing
6	1. (Physical) Whole Body Alignment| 2. (Mental) Release Fear| 3. (Spiritual) Cosmic Consciousness| 4. MERKABA Activation| 5. Aura Cleansing
7	1. (Physical) Whole Body Alignment| 2. (Mental) Release Fear| 3. (Spiritual) Cosmic Consciousness| 4. MERKABA Activation| 5. Aura Cleansing

WARNING: If you have not prepared for this section properly you could die! Conduct at own risk.

WEEK 6 – DIET: WATER/SUNLIGHT/BREATH	
Day	**Meditations**
1	1. (Physical) Whole Body Alignment | 2. MERKABA Activation 3. (Mental) Release Fear | 4. ASCENSION Activation
2	1. (Physical) Whole Body Alignment | 2. MERKABA Activation 3. (Mental) Release Fear | 4. ASCENSION Activation
3	1. (Physical) Whole Body Alignment | 2. MERKABA Activation 3. (Mental) Release Fear | 4. ASCENSION Activation
4	1. (Physical) Whole Body Alignment | 2. MERKABA Activation 3. (Mental) Release Fear | 4. ASCENSION Activation
5	1. (Physical) Whole Body Alignment | 2. MERKABA Activation 3. (Mental) Release Fear | 4. ASCENSION Activation
6	1. (Physical) Whole Body Alignment | 2. MERKABA Activation 3. (Mental) Release Fear | 4. ASCENSION Activation
7	1. (Physical) Whole Body Alignment | 2. MERKABA Activation 3. (Mental) Release Fear | 4. ASCENSION Activation

Continue for a further two weeks if required, and if you are feeling healthy. If after eight weeks you cannot ignite your Ascension activation, then changes are required. Change your diet in reverse – go back to fruit juice, green juice, vegan etc. over a period of two weeks.

One of the main reasons for not being able to ignite your Ascension activation is the Forgiveness part of the program. The other is detachment. Both are hurdles that are difficult to overcome on the first attempt. You need to be brutally honest with yourself. Study the **Predictors of Forgiveness** chart. But do not see this as a failure – it is far from that. You have just gone through a process that 1 in 10,000 wouldn't even attempt. You are awesome and in an elite group of finishers. Learn from this and try, and try, again.

20

BRINGING IT ALL TOGETHER

"When you rise in the morning, give thanks for the light, for your life, for your strength. Give thanks for your food and for the joy of living. If you see no reason to give thanks, the fault lies in yourself." ~ TECUMSEH

I must be honest, very few people will undergo this training and Ascend. I know this because of the comments I get from many people after they find out how much work they have to put in. They say things like, *"Oh, well, looks like I won't be going anywhere…"* or *"Oh, I may as well just die and keep reincarnating, because I will never be able to do all that."* Yes, it is very disappointing from my point of view. What they are really telling me is, *"I couldn't be bothered changing…I would rather watch TV than to take responsibility for my own life"*. Look, I am not judging these people. But think of it like this:

You have a very dear and wealthy friend who you have known since your childhood. They have just built a multi-million dollar house, and have invited you for a house warming. It's been raining all week, and when you arrive after a long, slow drive in terrible weather, you notice the front yard has not been finished, so it is just one big mud puddle. There is no way to get into the house without going through the mud. So, you resign yourself – after all, you just spent two hours in a grid lock, raining cats and dogs, so you're damned if you are going to turn around and go back home.

Thus, you grit your teeth and start the hard slog through the mud. Halfway to the house, you lose both your shoes to suction. Two steps later, there go your socks. Could this day get any worse? You are soaking wet, cold, the wind is driving the rain into your face, and you can see no end to this torture.

Finally, you make it to the front porch. The light is on. You can hear music, people are laughing, and the smell of food cooking and an open fire has you mesmerised. You just remembered you forgot to eat lunch today because you had that "important" job to do for work – that just had to be done or the world would stop turning, or so you thought at the time. It is now that you realise you are dripping wet, covered in mud from head to toe, wearing no shoes, and the bottom of your jeans are filthy. You can see through the window that there is a beautiful, thick, cream coloured carpet. Do you really want to walk in anyway and ruin the carpet? No, that would be very rude. Now, you have a choice. You ask, do I sit here cold and shivering and feel sorry for myself, or do I get up and find a solution.

Thankfully, you decide to go around the side of the house. There, under cover and on the concrete, is a hose. Well at least you can wash your feet, and the bottom of your jeans.

Just as you start to clean up, your host appears out of nowhere – holding a towel, fresh clothes, and a brand new pair of shoes. Your host smiles broadly and tells you how after it had been raining all week, and the landscaping could not be finalised, they thought they better prepare a plan B.

After you wash and dry off, your host takes you around the back to the discrete changing room, next to the pool. You realise after you put on the new clothes that fit perfectly how refreshed you actually feel from the involuntary shower. You are now led into the house through the back door. As soon as you enter, you feel the warmth of an open fire, smell your favourite food cooking, and see that all your best friends are there – wearing exactly the same outfit as you! Right down to the shoes! Everyone just bursts into laughter.

A couple of hours later, you have finished the most delicious meal you have ever had, and now everyone is lying around on the soft and luxurious sofas in front of the fireplace. People are talking, telling their stories, and laughing a lot. In the background, you can hear angelic music playing, tempting you to sleep. It is at this point that you realise that this was the best party you have ever been to. You suddenly don't care about losing your shoes in the mud, the drive to get here, the wet and cold hardship.

All at once, nothing matters any more. Everyone realises that their clothes do not define them – it is what is inside that makes the night so right for everyone. This night was always meant to be, exactly how it played out. The only variables were your choices. You could have gone home. You could still be on the front porch brewing pneumonia. Instead, you chose to keep going forward – to find a way into the party. And aren't you glad you did. Oh, and look! The host just came into the room with a tray full of homemade chocolates. Could it get any better!

The moral of this story is simple. You cannot get into the 5th Dimension until you are totally "clean," and free from negative vibration. Once there, however, you will wonder why you did not put the effort in sooner.

It is all about your choices

I have spent a lifetime advising people how to turn their life around and move forward. During that time, the number one fear is "change". Especially when it comes to changing themselves. People would rather stumble though life, with one train wreck after another, rather than accept responsibility and initiate change. Truly mind boggling to me, but it is so common.

Indeed, I often hear people tell me, "*I have been like this for too long. I can't change now.*" NONSENSE I say! Imagine you wrote a note on a piece of paper that said, "*I don't like the colour red.*" You folded it up, put it in a sealed envelope, and kept it in a drawer for 20 years. All this time. You avoided anything red. Balloons, sweets, clothes, pizza (because it has red tomatoes sauce). Imagine all the good things you have denied yourself over a silly, childhood choice – to not like red. Now, in your adult life, your car has just packed it in, and you have no money to buy a new one. So, you buy a ticket in a raffle for a new car. Much to your shock and horror, you have won the car. It is a top of the line car, perfect for you – a dream come true. But there is one problem - it is red. You have no choice but to accept the car as is – red. Now, what do you do?

Do you sell it and buy another car? Or, much simpler, do you change your choice about not liking red? Yes, let's do that. Now remember, you left that note in your dresser drawer. You find it, and open the envelope. In your little, child writing you see the words after 20 years –"*I don't like the colour red.*"

You pick up a pen, cross out the words,"*I don't like the colour red,*" and in your big, adult writing you say, "*I LOVE the colour red!!!*" You reseal the envelope, and put it back in the drawer. Problem solved, and not very hard, was it?

Overwrite your subconscious

In the previous story, the note you wrote was something you saved to your subconscious – as a child, or it might happen at any time or stage of life. As adults, we too are capable of saving limiting beliefs to our subconscious. Just because you wrote it, does not mean you can't change it – any time. Indeed, it is as simple as opening a Word document you created 10 years ago, or opening a sticky note you handwrote two days ago. You can change, and "save", the new message.

I have explained all of this previously in a video that is part of your Ascension training. In the Daily Planner, I have called it **(Mental) Release Fear** meditation. I keep harping on about this because it is so critical to change your consciousness if you want to Ascend. Nothing you have done in your past can stop you if you change your consciousness today. The past cannot be changed, and the future never comes. All that matters is NOW. Living in the now, and living from the Heart.

Living from the Heart

What we mean by Living from the Heart is, quite simply, your Heart Chakra – expanding your Heart Chakra. If every choice you make comes from the Heart, if every action comes from the Heart, and if every word and thought comes from the Heart, then there is nothing left except Love. Love is the ONLY thing that will get you into the 5th Dimension.

Many New Agers have invented (literally) a fallacy that all you have to do to Ascend is to do Yoga at the gym with the girlfriends (or boys) once a week, drink Chia Lattes, be Vegan and non-Vegan 60/40 (yep, look it up!). Their version of meditation is to close their eyes and fantasise about living in "their" perfect world, filled with luxury, exotic locations, and being treated like a five star celebrity. All the time they buy into this fallacy without actually putting in any real effort, or changing their consciousness. When they hear my methods, they poo-poo it, and say that it is ridiculous and that how could anyone do all that etc. It's that not wanting to change or take responsibility for their own lives thing. I don't mean to pick on the New Agers. They are generally 6th and 7th level Young Souls, and sometimes up to 3rd level Mature Souls. The point is, they are doing exactly what is appropriate for their soul age. However, it does frustrate me that the very people who claim to be spiritual, are anything but.

What is Being Spiritual?

Being spiritual simply means this: Your actions determine how "spiritual" you are. There is only one real test – how do you respond to a challenge or trigger? Do you have a melt down? Do you rant and rave and scream? Do you blame everybodyelse because it is "never" your fault; everybody else is an idiot? How about this, do you just wallow in self-pity and depression? Maybe you drink yourself stupid or take drugs to "cope." All of these things are the opposite of living a Spiritual life.

Being Spiritual means you **Accept and Allow**. If you Accept and Allow, then you are most probably living from the Heart. In fact, before you incarnated onto the Earth, you left strict instructions with your Higher Self to keep throwing challenges at you until you learnt the lessons you came here to learn. So, if you learn to Accept and Allow, less and less challenges get thrown at you. I am not saying you will have smooth sailing all the time, but I am saying you will have an extremely smooth and peaceful life, with just the odd bump in the road. For those who accept and allow, life is a journey opposed to the trainwreck most people's lives are at the moment. Indeed, when a bump does occur, what makes you different is how you respond to it. You Accept and Allow. You ask, *"Why has this happened. What have I done to bring this experience about? What can I do to correct it?"*

If you are constantly resisting change, then you should examine why. Be brutally honest with yourself. I know many people who complain about a problem in their life, like their weight, for example. I give tips and suggestions. But for every suggestion, they have a counter argument, telling me why they cannot do it.

Indeed, for every tip I have, they have a counter argument that it cannot be done. This is classic resistance to change. Why are they resisting? Only they can answer that, and until they do, their life and situation will not change.

The worst thing you can ever do is to blame someone else. The "*they made me do it*" excuse is nonsense. Unless someone put a gun to your head, then they didn't make you do anything. You did, through your poor choices.

Indeed, it is all about choices. Fear based choices always lead to failure, hardship, pain, and misery – always, at some level. Choices made from Love, no matter how hard they seem at the time, always end in clearance and closure. You are not responsible for how another person feels. I don't mean this gives you licence to treat people like crap. Always be aware of how you treat others. What I am talking about, for example, is if say you are in a terrible relationship. Maybe you tried to fix it for years, but it is just not working out. Then you need to make a choice. Fear will keep you in that relationship. Love will see you end the relationship. And if the other person goes to water or becomes aggressive, or depressive (which is just aggression turned inward), then that is *their* choice.

As much as they say, "*you made me feel like this*," just remember, you did not make them feel anything – they did. You are not in control of their emotions – they are. That was *their* response, their choice – not yours. All you can do is leave them, in Love and compassion; but stay strong, firm and follow through. I know how difficult it can be, but it is the best thing for the both of you, whether they will admit it at the time or not.

Always show gratitude, and be grateful for the things in your life. Always show compassion for those that genuinely deserve it (including animals and nature). To live from the Heart means to always speak the truth. When a man lies, he murders some part of the world.

Ultimately, I think being Spiritual breaks down into three simple things:

- Live in balance in all things
- Accept and Allow
- Live from the Heart

It's a lot to take in, I know!

How to eat an elephant.

I like to ask people thequestion, *"How do you eat an elephant?"* The answer I give is, *"One mouthful at a time."*

It is normal to feel overwhelmed by all of this information, especially if it is new to you. But remember the lessons. When you feel overwhelmed – stop; breathe; relax. Always centre yourself when you get flustered. That is your first step. Next, learn to breathe. Then meditate. Then do more complex meditations. Really work on visualisations. Your mind is the most powerful thing in the Universe – and I really do mean that. Once you figure that out, there will be no holding you back. So, simply take this information one day at a time. If you make the conscious decision to spend X amount of time per day or week on these things, then your journey has begun. Maybe start with something as simple as this: today, I will look someone directly in the eyes and smile. A genuine, warm smile. I seek nothing in return. Whatever the outcome, Accept and Allow. If I succeed with this task today, tomorrow I will try for two people, and so on, and so on.

Accept and Allow

Accept the outcome. Accept the decision that was made, out of your control. Accept responsibility for the problems in your life. Accept that you are imperfect in an imperfect world – we all are.

Allow the outcome. Allow other people to make choices that you may not agree with. You can voice your opinion, but then let it go – allow. Allow yourself to Love yourself. If you are lonely and seeking a mate then learn to love yourself first. Most people think that, if only I could get someone to love me, then I could love myself. If both sides think this, it's no wonder most relationships fail. Don't try to change people – allow them to be themselves. If you don't like it – leave. It is all about choice.

Try not to have expectations. Our expectations never live up to reality. Instead, just accept and allow and let things play out as they should, without expectations. By the way, if you are looking for a short-cut, or easy way to Ascend, then what I have offered here is it! Yes, it used to be a lot harder, a lot harder indeed.

In closing, even if you do not Ascend or go through the process, but you do take on some of the information in this book, then you have put yourself on the Spiritual path which will one day, in this life or in the next, prepare you for Ascension. I wish you all the best on your journey, and I hope to see you on the other side!

A woman photographed the UFO that created this Star Tetrahedron Crop Circle in Wiltshire, UK, – July 21, 2014. The UFO appeared as a ball of light. I believe the UFO was a MERKABA.

ANNEX 19.1.1

AURA CLEANSING MEDITATION

Perform *Intro Meditation Procedure* (from page 146).

1. Visualise yourself standing in a tropical rainforest. Before you is a beautiful waterfall flowing into a small pond.

2. Start to walk into the water and under the waterfall.

3. The waterfall is gentle like a shower. The water in the pond is only knee deep.

4. Begin to shower in the waterfall. Feel the dirt and grime begin to wash away from your body.

5. Focus your attention on your Etheric body. This is the layer closest to your body. It is the first layer and most dense of all. It is where the physical body is formed. See it as a thin, electric blue/white light all around your body.

6. The waterfall now changes to the colour to match the **Etheric Body**. See the blue/white light of the water completely wash over, and through you. As it does, this layer begins to glow. Say the words, "*My body is my temple. It serves me graciously in my journey.*"

7. When you are ready, focus your attention to the second layer, the **Emotional body**. The Emotional body is where healing of our emotions occurs and we develop self-love. Visualise the waterfall colour change to a vibrant pink. Bathe in the pink light. See your body begin to glow pink. Look for any dark energy spots, and wash them away. Say the words, "*I love myself, I forgive myself, I am grateful for myself*".

8. Now focus on the third layer, the **Mental body**. It comprises the mental aspect, thoughts, and beliefs. Healing this aura layer creates positive thought forms. The waterfall changes to a vibrant yellow colour. Wash the yellow light all over you – look for dark spots and wash them clean.

Say the words, "*My beliefs do not define me. I am open to the winds of change.*"

9. When you are ready, focus your attention on your fourth layer – the **Astral body**. The Astral body is on the astral plane and contains the records of all our past. All of your childhood experience, conception, pre-conception, as well as your past life experiences, and your future plans for this life. Visualise the waterfall change to indigo – a deep blue/purple colour. Tilt your face up so the water is hitting you directly into your **Third Eye Chakra**. Feel the water enter every little fold and crevice and completely clean everything out. See your body glowing the indigo colour. Say the words, "*All of my experiences made me the awesome Being I am today. I am open and willing to the Universal mysteries.*"

10. Now raise your consciousness to your fifth layer, the **Spiritual body**. The Spiritual body is located on the Spiritual plane and encompasses your will and your purpose in life, in this physical form, becoming your own authority and your own sense of truth. See the waterfall change to a beautiful, violet colour. The violet also sparkles with gold. Allow it to rain all over you. Feel it on your head, through your hair, penetrating deep into your brain. Say the words, "*Truth is my word. I live to be honest*".

11. Focus on the sixth layer – the **Celestial body**. This layer is also located on the spiritual plane and this is the layer of divine love and unconditional love for all of creation. The waterfall changes to a vibrant dark blue colour with sparkles of silver, like the deep oceans of the world. Allow the dark blue water to wash all over your body. Say the words, "*I am Love.*"

12. When you are ready, focus on the last layer – the seventh layer known as the **Ketheric body**. Being the last of the seven layers, it vibrates at the highest frequency. It is also located on the spiritual plane. This is the layer of divine wisdom, divine perfection, and oneness with the universe. The waterfall changes to a sparkling, golden colour. It rains down a dazzling, golden light. Allow it to expand out of your body in every direction. Say the words, "*I AM all that is, was, and will ever be!*"

Grounding

❙ *Now say, "My work is done. It is now time to return."*

Turn around and see a doorway of Light, and feel your feet firmly on the ground. Give your toes a little wriggle. Walk through the light door, and as you do, take a deep breath, exhale and open your eyes. You are home.

ANNEX 19.2.1

ASCENSION MEDITATION 1 (PHYSICAL): WHOLE BODY ALIGNMENT

1. Perform **Intro Meditation Procedure**(from page 146).
2. Visualise being on a mountain top. The sun is shining, the sky is blue, and it is nice and warm. All around you is lush green grass and wild flowers of every colour.
3. In front of you is your cosmic juicer! It looks like a blender or juicer that you would normally see, however to turn it on you simply put your hands on either side of it. Think "On," and see your hands glow with white light. To turn it off you just remove your hands. We are going to mix up some wonderful, Spiritual juices to help us open and balance our Chakras.

Let's start at the top:

4. CROWN CHAKRA

Located at the top of the head. This chakra links you with the universal consciousness. The highest chakra, it represents our ability to be fully connected spiritually: Inner and outer beauty, our connection to spirituality and pure bliss. Use sunshine. Fill the juicer up with sunshine, turn it on, and watch it spin. When you are ready, open the juicer, and pour the contents into a tall glass. Now drink it. It is cool and soothing.

5. THIRD EYE CHAKRA

Located between the eyes. This is higher intelligence and psychic power. Our ability to focus on and see the big picture. The Third Eye Chakra represents our ability to use intuition, imagination, wisdom, and our ability to think and make decisions. Drop some dark purple grapes and Lavender flowers into your juicer. Mix them up, and pour them into your glass. Drink it, and feel your third Eye expanding.

6. THROAT CHAKRA

Located at the throat. This is the chakra of creativity, self-expression and the search for truth. The Throat Chakra represents our ability to communicate and express ourselves. Mix up some Blueberries, and blue flower petals. Drink it down, and feel your Throat Chakra expand.

7. HEART CHAKRA

Located at the heart. This is the link to your Higher Self, to love, joy, and inner peace. The Heart Chakra represents our ability to love – the quality of our love, our past loves, and our future loves. Simply opening up our hearts to others is the best healing exercise to open up the Heart Chakra. Let's mix up some Leafy vegetables, spinach, Green tea and a squeeze of lime. Drink it down; as you do, feel your Heart Chakra expand.

8. SOLAR PLEXUS CHAKRA

Located at the solar plexus. This is the chakra of sense of identity, self-expression, self-worth, self-confidence, self-esteem, and intellect. The Solar Plexus Chakra allows for our ability to be confident and in control of our lives. Drop in a banana, some corn, a yellow pepper, and a squeeze of lemon juice. Top it off with some chamomile tea. Give it an extra-long mix then drink it up. As you do, feel your Solar Plexus Chakra expand.

9. SACRAL CHAKRA

Located just below the belly button. This is the chakra of physical health and energy. Sense of abundance, well-being, pleasure, sexuality, are associated with this energy centre. The Sacral Chakra is our connection and ability to accept others and new experiences. Mix in some Oranges and tangerines. Mix them up, pour it out. Drink it up. Feel your Sacral Chakra expand.

10. ROOT CHAKRA

Located at the genitals. This is the animal or base nature that monitors sexuality, reproduction, and survival, such as financial independence, money, and food. The Root Chakra represents our foundation and feeling of being grounded. This one needs to be a little bit hot! So mix up some red chillies, Red apples, strawberries, and Red Pepper. Drink it up. Feel your Root Chakra warm up then expand.

11. Take a moment now to allow your chakras to settle.
12. Now visualise a beam of pure white light coming straight down from the heavens, into your Crown and down the centre of your body, exiting out at the Base Chakra and going into the heart of the Earth.
13. Feel it going through you like a rod. Try very hard to feel your subtle bodies. Do they feel in alignment? Make small changes to the subtle bodies to align them with your physical body. Use the centre rod as your reference point.
14. When you feel your subtle bodies are aligned with your physical body, begin to float high into the air. You can look down and see the planet below you. There is no fear, just floating bliss.
15. The white light now exits from your Base Chakra, down and out to the other side of the planet, and loops around the Earth, back into your Root Chakra. You have now created a closed loop between your aligned Chakras, the Earth, and the Cosmos.
16. You have now successfully created a Rainbow Bridge between the Source and the Earth. There is nothing you cannot achieve in this moment. As above, so below – as below, so above. You are at one with all Creation.
17. Take a moment to absorb the new rainbow energies.

18. Grounding

Begin to lower yourself down, down, down and back onto the ground, back to our mountain top. Bend down and pick a flower – smell it, put it in your hair or in your pocket. In front of you is a doorway of light. Walk through the doorway; wriggle your fingers and toes. Take a deep breath, exhale, and open your eyes. Have a drink of fresh, clean water.

That concludes the Physical Ascension Meditation.

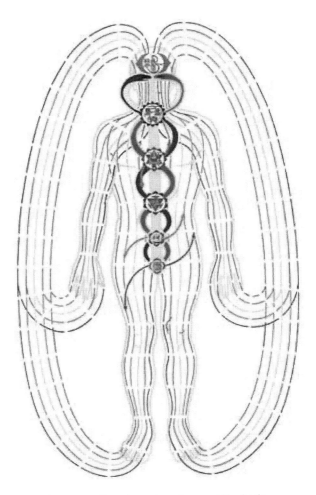

The energy flow through and around the body

ANNEX 19.2.2

ASCENSION MEDITATION 2 (EMOTIONAL): FOR-GIVENESS MEDITATION

*Y*ou should have created a list of everyone in your life that you have ever had a significant dealing with. It could include parents, siblings, ex-lovers, mates, children, bosses, work colleagues, landlords, teachers, or anyone. You can also include countries, organisations, and religions.

1. Perform Intro Meditation Procedure (from page 146).
2. Visualise yourself in a cool, quiet place of your choice. You may choose a temple, a pyramid, or even a favourite room. Somewhere that feels comfortable and secure.
3. Sit in the centre of your sacred space, and illuminate yourself with light. Visualise a column of bright, white light coming straight down on top of you and surrounding you.
4. When you are feeling relaxed and at peace, visualise a doorway to outside.
5. Stand up and walk outside, through the doorway. You can feel the cool touch of the green grass under your feet. There is beauty and peace all around you. In the distance you hear the gentle running of a stream.
6. The sunshine is bright and covers you in warmth and love. Walk towards the stream and see the clarity of the water.
7. Bend down and feel its cool touch. Enter the water and bathe yourself in its healing waters – let it carry away the dross and the darkness of this world. Let it take away your pain, your heartache, and all things that will tie you to this world. Allow your negative emotions to float gently away.
8. As you step out of the water you feel invigorated, light, and at peace.
9. In front of you is a large mountaintop that reaches high into the clear sky. At the very peak is a small, open air temple. There is the place where we would like to be right now.

10. Using your will alone, ascend to the top of the mountain, and into the small, circular stone temple. In the centre is a full size mirror.

11. Visualize yourself in front of the mirror and hug yourself. Look at yourself with love. You might imagine that you are looking at your child self. Forgive your child self of any transgressions. Returning to your adult form, forgive and forget your flaws in loving acceptance. Say to yourself,

> *"I forgive you for all the times you let me down. I know we agreed beforehand to experience all of these things together in order to learn. Thank you for your willingness and courage. I love and appreciate you for all that you are."*

12. Allow the love from Spirit to flow throughout your body into every organ, nerve, bone, and cell. Allow this high frequency energy to nurture your body from inside out, replacing any dents or resistance with joy and light.

13. Take some time to do this. Relax and enjoy the feeling of renewed energy and well-being. Know that this inner peace is a gift you can give to yourself at any time. By doing so, you gain a powerful ally in your Ascension Process.

14. We are now going to focus our forgiveness and healing on the other people in your life. The mirror has been replaced by a plinth. It is a small column with a flat, square platform on top.

15. One at a time, visualise the people from your list standing in mini form on top of the plinth. See them like a hologram. Project pink light from your Heart Chakra. Tell them that you forgive them for any harm that you have ever felt that they have done to you. Remember that it was all done by prior agreement, even if you don't remember it. Thank them for fulfilling their part of the bargain. Tell them that you love them, and forgive them. Again, visualise a beautiful pink light coming directly out of your Heart Chakra. This light will dissolve any animosity, and set you both free from any heavy emotional entanglement. When you feel complete with one person, move on to the next, repeating the procedure.

16. Finally, we will perform a Universal Forgiveness. Say to yourself,

> *"I forgive anyone I think has harmed me in this life, or any lifetime, anywhere, on any plane of existence. I forgive all debt, and erase all Karma. I choose Light for myself, and for all my selves. It is done!"*

17. When you are ready, return to the riverbank where we started. Turn around and you will see a large tree. Go up to it and place your hands on the bark. Now hug the trunk. Feel its strength. Your feet begin to go into the ground just like the roots of the trees. Feel the solid ground all around your legs. Give your toes a little wriggle. Visualise a door of light in front of you. Walk through the front door, and as you do, take a deep breath, exhale and open your eyes. You are home.Just take a minute to get your bearings. Have a drink of water.

FEELING LIKE A LION,
EVERYTHING IS RAWRSOME

ANNEX 19.2.3

ASCENSION MEDITATION 3
(MENTAL): RELEASE FEAR

1. Perform Intro Meditation Procedure(from page 146).

2. Visualise yourself standing, floating in Space. In front of you is the Universal Light Elevator.

3. We are going to take the Universal Light Elevator up to the 5th dimension. When you step inside, the walls are made of glass, and you can see space and the stars outside.

4. Above the door are the typical floor numbers. Watch them as they count up to the 5th level. Feel yourself rising ever upwards. The elevator stops, and the doors open.

5. Step out and roam around freely. Communicate with whomever you meet. These will be high frequency projections of your own Spirit. They can teach your human mind what your Spirit, or Higher-Self, already knows.

6. When you are ready, imagine yourself seated in front of a computer. If you are not comfortable with a computer, imagine a filing cabinet. Turn on your "Sub-conscious" computer or open the top draw of your filing cabinet. Call up the menu of files you have stored in your sub-conscious, and choose the one you want. Remember, we want to use this opportunity to eliminate or correct any behaviours that no longer serve us. This can include correcting any fears, shyness, anxiety, illness, allergy, coping mechanisms, addictions or anything else you may think of. It can even include how you react in a given situation or relationship. The idea is to clean out our sub-conscious and remove any limiting programmes.

7. When you find the file you want to change, open it up. Delete or over-type the current information with any new information you want to install. If you want to delete the file all together, then open it, remove the text and type *"I no longer require this file."* After you make your changes, save the file and close it. Take some time now to correct your files. You can always come back and do more at another time.

8. The "save" position is this: Cross your legs, ankle over ankle, and your forearm over forearm, with fingers interlocked, arms bent up to rest on your chest.

9. This is the "Save" position. Hold this position and visualise yourself clicking the save button. Now visualise an intense laser beam of white light streaming straight from the Mind of God down into the top of your head and all around your body. In this Light is all the love, wisdom, and power of the Divine frequencies. It is warm, nurturing, and serene.

10. It is now time to return to the elevator and come back down to the physical plane. Watch the floor numbers descend, and feel yourself moving downward. The doors open and you step out. You are now back in the room where you started. Take a deep breath, exhale, and open your eyes. Have a drink of fresh, clean water.

ANNEX 19.2.4

ASCENSION MEDITATION 4 (SPIRITUAL): COSMIC CONSCIOUSNESS

1. Perform Intro Meditation Procedure(from page 146).
2. Visualise your physical body surrounded by a brilliant white light.
3. Imagine shrinking this light from body size down to a tiny cell within your body.
4. By thought, shrink it further to atomic size. Within the atom, you can see the electrons and neutrons circling around nucleus. Be aware of the space that fills the atom. From the nucleus to the outer edge of the atom is the length of a football field! See the endless orderly motion. How beautiful it is! How perfect it is!
5. Imagine this inner space expanding and expanding, and gradually becoming outer space.
6. The same orderly patterns and cycles are functioning.
7. See the planets circling around the Sun, the solar system spiralling around in the Milky Way Galaxy, and the galaxy floating around the cosmos.
8. See its perfection. Feel its orderly, intelligent movement. Know you are part of this cosmic whole. Relax your fears and resistance. Float along with the stars in their graceful dance. Know all is well and in balance. Finish by just floating in space.
9. When you are ready, return to your normal consciousness.
10. You are now back in the room where you started. Take a deep breath, exhale, and open your eyes. Have a drink of fresh, clean water.

ANNEX 19.2.5

ASCENSION MEDITATION 5 (PHYSICAL/SPIRITUAL): LIFE LESSONS HEALING

t is important to first complete the Life Lesson Survey in **Chapter 11**. Once you determine your top three Life Lessons, it is a case of reading, and rereading the descriptions for each of your three main lessons. Your third on the list may already be partially completed, so that is why I would include it, – it may be the easiest to start with. I would recommend rereading these descriptions with a pencil in your hand. As you read through, circle words or statements that ring true to you. When you have finished, write down these circled words or statements on a piece of paper. From these words, build up a picture. Try to put them into scenarios in your own life. For the meditation, you will need to insert these scenarios, but this time, using your Wise Mind, stand outside of the situation, and advise. Imagine you are advising someone else on how they can perfect these lessons.

Make no mistake, this is the hardest task you are required to complete for the Ascension Process. In effect, what once took about 25 lives to perfect one life lesson, we are now trying to do in six weeks! Sounds crazy, right! No it is not – remember back to **ASCENSION MEDITATIONS 3: (MENTAL) RELEASE FEAR**. That is when we change the "files" in our sub-conscious. This is the same principle. The only difference is, for this meditation, we need to access the fifth layer of your *aura*, the **Spiritual body**, rather than your sub-conscious. Remember back, the Spiritual body is located on the Spiritual plane and encompasses your will, your purpose in life, in this physical form, becoming your own authority and your own sense of truth.

Only do one Life Lesson per meditation. Do one per day and recycle them. It will take many meditations on each of your Life Lessons to perfect them. When you can do these and feel that it has become second nature, or if you feel you are doing them in your sleep, then you may have finally completed that lesson.

The Meditation

1. Perform Intro Meditation Procedure (from page 146).

2. Visualise yourself floating in the sky, high above the Earth. Using your mind, draw in the clouds from all around you. The clouds first appear pure white, and fluffy.

3. As the clouds are drawn in they begin to slowly circle around you. They change to a violet colour. They start to spin faster and faster. You are in the centre of the clouds, so you do not feel any wind or movement. You feel warm and secure as the clouds spin faster and faster.

4. The clouds are an intense violet colour. They are spinning so fast now that they appear as a solid wall. You are sitting in the eye of this storm feeling totally at peace.

5. In front of you appears a screen. In this screen you can project your own scenarios. Start by placing yourself in the picture, but with your consciousness remaining outside. Watch yourself go through different interactions based on your life lessons. Now advise yourself on how to better deal with certain situations. Take as long as you like to play out, advise on and correct any of your scenarios.

6. When you are ready, dismiss the screen.

7. Watch now as the clouds start to slow down. They go from being a solid wall to spinning again, now slower and slower. Eventually all the clouds go back into the Earth's atmosphere, and you are left floating in a clear, blue sky.

8. You can look down and see your house. Fly down and land in front of your door.

9. Put your hand on your door, take a deep breath, exhale, and open your eyes.

10. Have a drink of fresh, clean water.

ANNEX 19.3.1

MERKABA PRACTICE MEDITATION 1

*T*his is a simplified version of the Merkaba Activation Meditation. I strongly advise you do this meditation daily until you can do it without listening to the guided voice or without reading it.

The actual Merkaba Activation Meditation is much more complex, thus the sooner you can master this version, the sooner you can start on the Activation Meditation. This meditation is not designed to activate your Merkaba. What it will do is get you prepared. Think of this as warming up an engine before you take the car out on the road. It is getting you ready for the real thing.

You can view a simple animation, narrated by **Tuesday May Thomas**, and animated by **Jaime Velasquez. TITLE: *MERKABA Practise Meditation 1***. See ANNEX 19.5.1 for video links.

The Meditation:

Perform ***Intro Meditation Procedure*** (from page 146).

1. Take a long, slow breath in and out, and relax.
2. To begin, bring your first finger and thumb to touch.
3. Inhale – breathe light into the Sun Tetrahedron.
4. Send your light filled exhalation into the Earth Tetrahedron.
5. Hold your breath at the end of the exhale.
6. Roll your eyes upward to the Third Eye, and then straight down to the Earth.
7. Thumb and second finger touch.
8. Inhale – breathe light into the Sun Tetrahedron.
9. Exhale into the Earth Tetrahedron.
10. Hold your breath at the end of the exhale.

11. Roll your eyes upward to the Third Eye, and then straight down to the Earth.
12. Thumb and third finger touch.
13. Inhale third breath into the Sun Tetrahedron.
14. Exhale into the Earth Tetrahedron.
15. Hold your breath at the end of the exhale.
16. Roll your eyes up, and straight down.
17. Thumb and pinkie finger touch.
18. Inhale the fourth breath into the Sun Tetrahedron.
19. Exhale into the Earth Tetrahedron.
20. Hold your breath at the end of the exhale.
21. Roll your eyes up, and straight down.
22. Thumb and first finger touch.
23. Inhale the fifth breath into the Sun Tetrahedron.
24. Exhale into the Earth Tetrahedron.
25. Hold your breath at the end of the exhale.
26. Roll your eyes up, and straight down.
27. Thumb and second finger touch.
28. Inhale sixth breath into the Sun Tetrahedron.
29. Exhale into the Earth Tetrahedron.
30. Hold your breath at the end of the exhale.
31. Roll your eyes upward, and straight down to the Earth.
32. Thumb and first two fingers touch.
33. Inhale – breathe life force into the crystalline tube that houses the spine. Visualise a small, light-filled sphere in your solar plexus.
34. Exhale – imagine this sphere growing in size.
35. Inhale breath eight. See the sphere growing larger in all directions.
36. Exhale. See it reaching its largest size at the end of your exhale.
37. Breath nine, inhale. Visualise this sphere becoming luminous and bright.
38. Exhale – see the sphere become brighter, and brighter still.
39. As you inhale for breath 10, see this sphere shine with golden light.
40. Exhale through the mouth, and visualise the sphere growing to surround your entire body.
41. Inhale for breath 11, see this golden sphere surround you.
42. Exhale, continue to fill the sphere with golden light.
43. As you inhale for breath 12, imagine breathing in from the top of your

head and the base of your spine. Draw the inhale into the centre of your body.

44. Exhale into the centre.

45. Inhale for breath 13, breathing steadily.

46. Exhale, and change your hand positions. Palms face up, resting in one another on your lap, with tips of thumbs touching.

47. Inhale for breath 14. Move your awareness to the centre of your sphere, and move your sphere up to the Heart centre.

48. Exhale, relaxing at the heart.

49. Inhale of breath 15. This sets up the spin of rotating Tetrahedrons to an equal speed. Blow out through the mouth audibly.

50. Inhale of breath 16, blowing out through the mouth again. Visualise your sphere growing outwards.

51. Inhale of breath 17, sets the spin state to 9/10ths the speed of light.

52. Exhale, blow out through the mouth, and relax in this higher state.

53. Perform Grounding Procedure to finish.

ANNEX 19.3.2

MERKABA PRACTICE MEDITATION 2

O nce you are comfortable with the previous practise meditation, you can move on to this one. It is more advanced, but still not as complex as the final MERKABA Activation Meditation.

That said, this is a powerful meditation that may indeed lead you to activating your MERKABA Light Body. Again, practise the meditation as many times per day as you like. The more familiar you become, the greater your chances are of successfully completing the Ascension Process.

The video for this meditation has been perfectly animated by **Nelumbo Institute True Self Inquiry**. See ANNEX 19.5.1 for links to videos. They hold workshops (restarting, ayahuasca on the beach and othereventsin Portugal, travelling also to Italy, UK, Ireland, Poland and other countries. You can contact them at **www.nelumbo.pl**.) It should help you immensely with your visualisations. The narration was originally done in Russian, however this is an English version. Unfortunately, the narrator pronounces MERKABA wrong! Oh well.

TITLE: *MERKABA Practise Meditation 2.* See ANNEX 19.5.1 for video links.

Perform ***Intro Meditation Procedure*** (from page146).

First Mudra

The first Mudra, the first breath.

1. Imagine that around your body there are two, joint Tetrahedrons, which together form the Star Tetrahedron.
2. The upper Tetrahedron is the Sun Tetrahedron; exhale.
3. The lower Tetrahedron is the Earth Tetrahedron.
4. Exhaling, let the air out of your body, thus clearing the body and mind of negative energy.

The Second Mudra, the second breath.

Second Mudra

5. Inhale, for five to eight seconds.
6. The air is filling your midriff and your chest.
7. Exhalation. Exhaling, you let the air out of your body, thus clearing another electrical circuit, together with your body and mind.

The Third Mudra, the third breath.

Third Mudra

8. All the time, your awareness is placed in your Heart. Again, steadily, you are filling your body with air.
9. Exhalation. Exhaling, you are clearing another electrical circuit of your body.

The Fourth Mudra, the fourth breath.

Fourth Mudra

10. You are slowing filling your stomach with air.
11. Exhalation. With the same pace, you are exhaling the air, and you are disposing of all contamination. All the time, your awareness is residing in your Heart.

The Fifth Mudra, the fifth breath.

Fifth Mudra (same as first)

12. Take a deep breath. Your midriff and your chest are filling with air.
13. Exhalation. Contamination is leaving your body and mind.

The Sixth Mudra. The sixth breath.

Sixth Mudra (same as second)

14. Inhale the air, deep into your belly. Your chest is filling in with air.
15. Exhalation. With the same pace, you are disposing of the contamination from the sixth electrical circuit.

The Seventh Mudra. The seventh breath.

Seventh - Thirteenth Mudra

16. Through the Pranic tube, through the top of your head and from below, and through the Sacral Chakra,two powerful streams of energy are flowing in. They become united into a sphere, which is growing while you take another three breaths.

The Eighth Breath.

17. The air is flowing through your body, and the energy keeps flowing through the Pranic tube.

18. The sphere in your stomach keeps growing, and at the end of this breath, it is filling the whole stomach.

The Ninth Breath.

19. The air keeps flowing through your body, and the energy keeps flowing through the Pranic tube. While you are exhaling, the sphere is becoming brighter and brighter.

The Tenth Breath.

20. At the moment of absolute concentration, see how the ball is flashing, and how it is changing its quality and its colour.

21. Exhalation. Make a small opening in your mouth, and exhale the air under pressure.

22. The golden sphere is expanding to the size of the sphere of Leonardo. It contains your whole body.

The Eleventh Breath.

23. Relax. Feel how the Star Tetrahedron is surrounding you. Feel the stream of prana flowing through your body. Breathe calmly, filling the golden sphere with prana.

The Twelfth Breath.

24. The prana of the sphere is now being maintained, visualised, and reinforced.

The Thirteenth Breath.

25. Don't forget that your awareness is still residing in your Heart. If you have forgotten, summon it back to your Heart, now. Relax.

The Fourteenth Breath. Relaxation Mudra.

Relaxation Mudra either postion is fine

26. Use the energy of your mind to move the sphere, which is now at the level of your Solar Plexus, to the level of your Heart Chakra. It is a great, qualitative change, which transfers your consciousness from the third to fourth dimension.

The Fifteenth Breath.

27. Inhaling, you are filling your stomach and your chest with air. Steady pace; you are activating the engine of the MERKABA Light Body.

28. The Tetrahedrons are swirling around your body. The Male Tetrahedron to the left, the Female Tetrahedron to the right. The Neutral Tetrahedron stays motionless.

The Sixteenth Breath.

29. Feel how from the place where the first primeval cells of your body are placed at your tailbone, there is a disc of 18 metres/60 ft. in diameter sliding out. Now, your MERKABA Light Body is linking with the whole field of sacred geometry.

The Seventeenth Breath.

30. 9/10ths the speed of light – feel and see how both the male and female Tetrahedrons are swirling at the speed of 9/10ths the speed of light. Your MERKABA Light Body has reached its full potential.

31. Feel how this powerful source of energy is surrounding you. Feel that you can safely stay within it, as if you were at home.

32. Only in an absolutely pure state of mind, with the awareness that is constantly residing in your Heart, and linked with the cosmos and Mother Earth, are you able to program your MERKABA Light Body.

33. Feel that you are part of something infinitely great, and that eventually, it is you who are infinitely great.

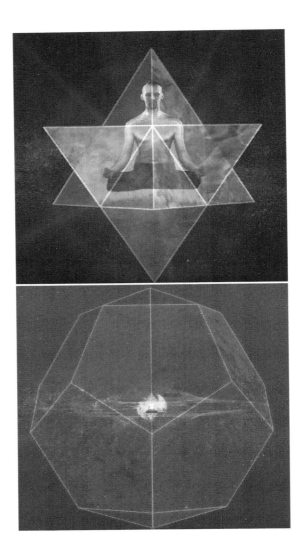

ANNEX 19.3.3

MERKABA ACTIVATION MEDITATION

The Remembrance and Reactivation of 'Spherical Breathing' and the Human Mer•Ka•Ba

As originally taught by Drunvalo Melchizedek

A Note from Drunvalo Melchizedek

> *"Emotional healing is essential" if you really wish to find enlightenment in this world. There is NO way around this. Once you begin to find out about the higher worlds, you, yourself, will stop your own growth past a certain point until this emotional healing has taken place. I am sorry, but that is the way it is. You can't do this meditation or any other kind of mediation to any real degree of success if your emotional body is out of balance. It is only when a person is in a relatively healthy emotional balance, can they successfully function through the Mer-Ka-BA. What you are about to see (hear), from my point of view, is probably the most important information I can give you. You can know everything about the Mer-Ka-BA and how to create the rotating fields. You can know the Sidhis and know everything else on the creation of the Mer-Ka-BA and how it works ... but without making a connection with the Higher Self, you would not have the wisdom (that) would be necessary to use the Mer-Ka-BA." – Drunvalo 1993*

Most Common Mistakes with Meditation:

- Don't Slouch – Keep the spine straight while meditating.
- Don't allow the fingers to touch each other during the first 6 Mudras. Don't rest your hands and fingers in such a way that they come in contact with clothing or the body in the first 6 Mudras.

- Remove watches and jewellery! – Or at least remember to psychically insulate yourself from their effect.
- Understand the difference between tetrahedrons and 'star-tetrahedrons' – There is confusion between the use of tetrahedron and star tetrahedron. When using the MerKaBa, never spin a tetrahedron, instead only spin star-tetrahedrons, which are composed of conjoined Earth-pointing and Sun-pointing tetrahedrons.
- Spinning the Tetrahedrons – Don't spin the Sun and Earth Tetrahedrons separately or in opposite directions. This can create electrical and physical problems in the body.
- Practice! – Maintaining a regular practice is essential to learning the meditation correctly.
- Love. Don't forget that the fields are pure love. Don't allow the practice to become overly mechanical, or habitualised to the point where you are not connected to Love.
- Superimpose the Tetrahedrons correctly. Never forget that the star tetrahedrons are superimposed. Do not view them separately and/or away from the body.

The Mer•Ka•Ba is a field of light generated from the spinning of specific geometric forms that simultaneously affects one's spirit and body. It is a vehicle that can aid mind, body, and spirit to access and experience other planes of reality or potentials of life. In fact, the Mer•Ka•Ba is even much more than this. Those who have taken the **Flower of Life** workshop and have learned the Mer•Ka•Ba meditation have stated that they have learned more about themselves, connected with their higher selves, and moved to new levels of awareness.

The Mer•Ka•Ba is a tool that helps humans reach their full potential. The Mer•Ka•Ba is a crystalline energy field that is comprised of specific sacred geometries that align the mind, body, and heart together. This energy field created from sacred geometry extends around the body for a distance of 55 feet (17 m). These geometric energy fields normally spin around our bodies at close to the speed of light, but for most of us they have slowed down or stopped spinning entirely due to a lack of attention and use. When this field is reactivated and spinning properly, it is called a Mer•Ka•Ba.

A fully activated Mer•Ka•Ba looks just like the structure of a galaxy. The Mer•Ka•Ba enables us to experience expanded awareness, connects us with elevated potentials of consciousness, and restores access and memory of the infinite possibilities of our being. When the Mer•Ka•Ba meditation is performed correctly, the Mer•Ka•Ba fluidly integrates our feminine (intuitive, receptive) and masculine (active, dynamic) aspects of our mind and spirit.

Recreating the Mer•Ka•Ba:

There are seventeen breaths to reactivating the Mer•Ka•Ba; each breath consists of breathing in (and then out) in one motion. The first six breaths of this meditation cleanse and balance the eight electrical circuits of your Star-tetrahedral Mer•Ka•Ba. It will also help you to remember the shape of the Star tetrahedron around your physical body. The next seven breaths re-establish the 'Spherical Breathing ' and Pranic flow within your physical body, which leads you to intake Prana in the correct way. The Fourteenth breath changes the balance of the Prana within your body and also focuses on opening your 'Heart Chakra' (which will in time transform your Mer•Ka•Ba experience and your perception of 3rd and 4th dimensional awareness). The last three breaths of this process are the breaths that actually activate the Mer•Ka•Ba by recreating the counter-rotating fields around your physical body.

The instructions for each individual breath are broken down into various sections to help you study the process:

Heart: (what you will need to have opened to be able to be 'feeling/sensing')

Mudra: (what mudra or hand positions you will need to use)

Body: (what you will need to physically do with your body)

Mind: (what you will need to think/see/visualise or sense)

Breath: (what you will need to do with your breathing)

As part of your preparation to do your Mer•Ka•Ba meditation is to set the intention that your 'Higher Self' oversees every aspect of what you are about to do in this meditation, and that your Higher Self takes you as far as it is appropriate at this time.

Part I - The First Six Breaths:

(Balancing of the polarities, and the cleansing of your electrical system)

First Breath, Inhale:

Heart: It is important to open your heart and to feel love for all life during every breath of this meditation. This is the **key aspect to the meditation**. If the feeling of love is missing from the meditation then very little will happen. Feeling love may not be an easy thing to do in the beginning stages. A suggestion to help you develop this ability may be to begin by thinking of something you love. This will create the feeling within.

Nature can be a good thing to think about because it stimulates an unconditional feeling rather than thinking of a person or an object. A place you love, or the way something makes you feel, like looking into the stars at night, are all things that will help you to remember the feeling of love in your heart. 'Unconditional love' means loving something without any conditions.

Mudra: At the moment of inhalation, place your hands in the 'first mudra' position, with your palms facing up and your thumb and first finger touching at the tips. Remember to have them touching lightly, and do not allow anything to interfere with the circuit by having your other fingers touch each other or any other object.

First Mudra

Mind: Become aware of the 'Sun' tetrahedron (the apex pointing up to the sky/sun). The pointed side faces front for males, and flat side faces front for females. See and visualise the tetrahedron filled with a brilliant white light. See the tetrahedron around you. If you cannot visualise it then 'sense' or 'feel' it around you.

Breath: With empty lungs, begin to inhale, breathing only through your nostrils. Breathe in deeply and slowly stretch the duration of the inhale for approximately seven seconds. As you begin breathing, push out on your stomach (thus filling the lower part of your lungs) and then continue to breathe in, pushing out your chest (so your chest lifts up, thus filling the upper part of your lungs).

First Breath, Exhale:

Heart: Begin when you feel love in your Heart.
Mudra: Keep the same mudra.
Mind: Become aware of the 'Earth' tetrahedron (the apex facing down and pointing to the Earth). The flat side faces front for males, and the pointed side faces front for females. See this tetrahedron filled with a brilliant white light.

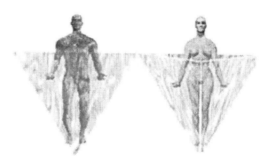

Earth Tetrahedron

Breath: As you finish inhaling, begin to exhale without any pause. Exhale through the nostrils deeply, and slowly stretch the duration of the exhale for approximately seven seconds. Exhale whilst pulling the chest in, followed by pulling in the stomach. There should now be no air left in your lungs. Now that the air is out of your lungs, relax and hold your breath for five seconds. (Please note that while these instructions break down everything step-by-step, the actual process of the 'inhale' and 'exhale' is one flowing motion with no breaks or pauses during the flow.)

Mind: 'Pulse'– Be aware of the flat equilateral triangle at the top of the 'Earth' tetrahedron located in the horizontal plane that passes through your chest at the base of the sternum (top of the Solar Plexus). In a flash, and with a pulse like motion, send that triangular plane down through the 'Earth' tetrahedron. The triangular plane gets smaller as it goes down and pushes all the densely charged energy of the mudra/ electrical circuit out of the apex of the 'Earth' tetrahedron. A light will shoot out of the apex toward the centre of the Earth.

This mind exercise is performed simultaneously with the following Body movements:

Body: Move your eyes slightly toward each other, (slightly crossing your eyes). Now bring them up to the top of their sockets, or, in other words, look up (approx. 45 angle). This motion of looking up with your eyes crossed should not be extreme. You will feel a tingling sensation between your eyes in the area of your "third" eye. Now look down (without moving your head) to the lowest point you can (as fast as you can). You may feel an electrical sensation move down your spine. The Mind and the Body must co-ordinate the above mental exercise with the eye movements. The eyes look down from their uppermost position at the same time as the mind sees the triangular horizontal plane of the 'Earth' tetrahedron move down to its apex.

This combined exercise will clean out the densely charged thoughts and feelings that through time have entered into your electrical system. It will specifically clean out the part of your system that is associated with the 'mudra' you are using at the time. Each mudra deals with a different part of your tetrahedral/chakra system. Immediately upon pulsing the energy down your spine, change mudras to the next one and begin the entire cycle over again.

The next five breaths are a repeat of the first breath, with the following mudra changes:

Second Breath: Thumb and second finger together.

Second Mudra

Third Breath: Thumb and third finger together.

Third Mudra

Fourth Breath: Thumb and little finger together.

Fourth Mudra

Fifth Breath: Thumb and first finger together, (same as first mudra)

Fifth Mudra (same as first)

Sixth Breath: Thumb and second finger together (same as second mudra)

Sixth Mudra (same as second)

Part II - The Next Seven Breaths:

(Recreating the 'Spherical Breathing' within your body)

At this point, an entirely new breathing pattern begins. You do not need to visualize the star tetrahedron at this time. You only need to visualize and work with the prana tube that runs vertically through the entire star tetrahedron, from the apex of the 'Sun' tetrahedron above your head, to the apex of the 'Earth' tetrahedron below your feet.

The tube extends from one hand length above your head to one hand length below your feet. The diameter of your tube will be the size of the hole formed by touching your thumb and middle finger together. In appearance, the tube looks like a glass fluorescent tube running straight through your body with a crystalline tip at each end that fits into the apex of each tetrahedron.

Seventh Breath, Inhale:

Heart: Feel love in your heart.

Seventh - Thirteenth Mudra

Mudra: For the next seven breaths, use the same mudra for both inhale and exhale. The thumb, the first and second fingers touching together, palms up.

Mind: Visualize or sense the tube running through your body. The instant you begin the seventh breath, inhale, see the brilliant white light of prana moving up from the bottom of the star tetrahedron to behind the navel, and at the same time, down the tube from the top of the star tetrahedron to behind the navel. This movement is almost instantaneous. The point where these two light beams meet is within you at the navel level. The moment the two beams of prana meet, (which is just as the inhale begins), a sphere of white light/prana (about the diameter of a grapefruit or your own closed fist) is formed at the meeting point centred on the tube. It all happens in an instant. As you continue to take the inhale of the seventh breath, the sphere of prana begins to concentrate and grow slowly.

Breath: Deep rhythmic yogic breathing, seven seconds in, and seven seconds out. There is no holding of the breath from now on. The flow of prana from the two poles will not stop or change in any way when you go from inhale to exhale. It will be a continuous flow that will not stop for as long as you breathe in this manner.

Seventh Breath, Exhale:

Heart: Feel love in your heart.
Mudra: Keep the same mudra.
Mind: The prana sphere centred at the navel continues to grow. By the end of the full exhale, the prana sphere will be approximately eight or nine inches in diameter.

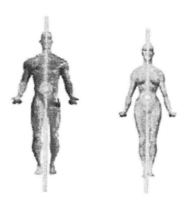

Prana Sphere 1

Breath: Do not force the air out of your lungs. When your lungs empty naturally, immediately begin the next breath, thus keeping a flowing motion.

Eighth Breath, Inhale:

Heart: Feel love in your heart.
Mudra: Keep the same mudra.
Mind: The prana sphere continues to concentrate life force energy and continues to grow in size
Breath: Deep rhythmic yogic breathing.

Eighth Breath, Exhale:

Heart: Feel love in your heart.
Mudra: Keep the same mudra.
Mind: The prana sphere continues to grow in size and will reach maximum size at the end of this breath. The maximum size is different for each person. If you put your longest finger in the centre of your navel, the line on your wrist defining your hand will show you the radius of the maximum size of this sphere for you. This sphere of prana cannot grow any larger.

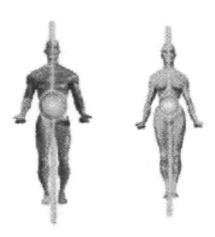

Prana Sphere 2

Breath: Deep rhythmic breath. Feel the flow.

Ninth Breath, Inhale:

Heart: Feel love in your heart.
Mudra: Keep the same mudra.
Mind: As the prana sphere cannot grow any larger, the prana begins to concentrate within the sphere. The sphere becomes brighter and brighter.
Breath: Deep rhythmic breath. Feel the flow.

Ninth Breath, Exhale:

Heart: Feel love in your heart.
Mudra: Keep the same mudra.
Mind: See the sphere getting brighter and brighter.
Breath: Deep rhythmic breath. Feel the flow.

Tenth Breath, Inhale:

Heart: Feel love in your Heart.
Mudra: Keep the same mudra.
Mind: As you breathe in the tenth breath, the sphere of light in your stomach area will reach maximum concentration. Approximately halfway into the inhalation, at the moment of maximum possible concentration, the sphere will "ignite," changing the colour and quality. The electric colour of prana will tum into the brilliant light of the sun. The sphere will become a golden sun of "brilliant light." As you complete the tenth breath, inhale. This new golden sphere of brilliant light will rapidly reach a new and higher concentration. At the moment you reach full inhalation of the tenth breath, the golden sphere of light in your body is ready for another transformation.
Breath: Deep rhythmic breath. Feel the flow.

Tenth Breath, Exhale:

Heart: Feel love in your heart.

Mudra: Keep the same mudra.

Mind: At the moment of exhale, the outer layer of the sphere of golden light bulges to expand. In one second, combined with the breath talked about below, the sphere expands quickly to the diameter of the 'sphere of Leonardo' (Christ sphere), which is the diameter of the distance between the longest fingertips of your extended arms. Your body is now completely enclosed within a large sphere of brilliant golden light, and you have now returned to the ancient form of spherical breathing. However, at this point, the sphere is not stable, so you must now breathe three more times to stabilize the sphere.

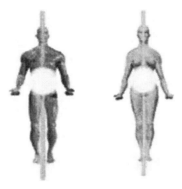

Prana Sphere 3

Breath: Forced Breath. At the moment of exhale, make a small hole with your lips and blow out with pressure. As you feel the sphere begin to bulge, within the first second of this exhale, rapidly push out all of your breath. The sphere will expand at this moment.

Eleventh, Twelfth and Thirteenth Breath, Inhale and Exhale:

Heart: Feel love in your heart.

Muda: Keep the same mudra

Mind: Relax and just feel the flow of the prana flowing from the two poles, meeting at the navel sphere and expanding out to the larger 'Christ' sphere.

Sphere of Leonardo

Breath: Deep rhythmic yogic breathing. At the end of the thirteenth breath you have stabilised the large 'Christ' sphere and are ready for the important fourteenth breath. It is important to note here that the original small sphere is still there inside the larger sphere. In fact, the small sphere is actually brighter and more concentrated than the larger one. It is from this inner sphere that prana is drawn for various purposes, such as healing.

Part III -The Fourteenth Breath:

(Opening the 'Universal Heart Centre', tuning to 4th dimensional awareness)

Fourteenth Breath, Inhale, and Exhale:

Heart: Feel love within your heart centre.

Mudra: Change the mudra to the 'relaxing mudra '. This mudra is different for males and females. Males place the left palm on top of the right palm and females will place the right palm on top of the left palm. Let the thumbs lightly touch each other. It is a mudra that relaxes. This mudra will be used for the rest of the meditation.

*If this Mudra feels more comfortable with your hands in the opposite position, then feel free to change hand positions. The goal is to feel more relaxed and comfortable.

Male, 14th Breath Mudra:

Female, 14th Breath Mudra:

Mind: As you begin to inhale, using your intent and your mind, raise the point where the two beams of prana meet at the navel to about 2 inches (5 cm) above the base of the sternum, (the 4th dimensional chakra). The entire large 'Christ' sphere, along with the original small sphere (which is still contained within the large sphere), is now at the new meeting point within the tube, at the 'Universal Heart Centre'.

Breathing from this new point within the tube (and with an open heart) will inevitably change your awareness from 3rd to 4th dimensional prana conscious-breathing–from Earth consciousness to 'Christ Consciousness'. It may take a while, but it is inevitable.

Christ sphere

Breath: Deep rhythmic yogic breathing. If you decide to remain at breath 14 without moving on to the Mer•Ka•Ba, then shift to a shallow breath, (continue breathing using your stomach). In other words, breathe rhythmically but in a comfortable manner where your attention is more on the flow of energy moving through the tube meeting at the sternum and expanding out to the large sphere. At this point, don't think, just breathe, and feel the flow. Feel your connection to all life through the Universal Heart Centre. Remember your intimate connection with God (the Universe).

Part IV -The MER• KA• BA:

(Activating the Mer•Ka•Ba - The Vehicle for Ascension)

Fifteenth Breath, Inhale:

Heart: Feel unconditional love for all life.

Mind: Be aware of the whole star tetrahedron. Each whole star tetrahedron is comprised of one 'Sun' tetrahedron and one 'Earth' tetrahedron. These two, the 'Sun' and 'Earth' tetrahedrons together, form the whole star tetrahedron (The three dimensional Star of David).

There are three of these whole star tetrahedrons around your human body, and they are super-imposed over each other. Each whole star tetrahedron is exactly the same size, dimension, and exists on the same axis. Each whole star tetrahedron has a polarity of its own: Male, Female, and Neutral.

The first whole star tetrahedron is neutral in nature. It is literally the body itself and it is locked in place at the base of the spine. In this meditation it does NOT change its orientation and does rotate in any way. As with the other whole star tetrahedrons, it is placed around the human body according to the gender of the male or female performing the meditation.

The second whole star tetrahedron is male in nature. It is electrical, and is literally the human mind. It rotates counter-clockwise relative to your body looking outward (It rotates toward your left side, beginning from a point in front of you).

The third whole star tetrahedron is female in nature. It is magnetic, and is literally the human emotional body. It rotates clockwise relative to your body looking out. It rotates toward your right side, beginning from a point in front of you.

On the inhale of the fifteenth breath, as you are inhaling, set the intention in your mind to rotate the star tetrahedrons at "Equal Speed." This will start the two whole star tetrahedrons spinning (in opposite directions to each other) at equal speeds to each other. This means there will be a complete rotation of the mind (male) star tetrahedron, for every complete rotation of the emotional (female) star tetrahedron. If one set goes around 10 times, the other set will also go around 10 times; only, in the opposite direction.

Breath: Deep rhythmic yogic breath again, followed by forced breath, but only for the next three breaths. After that, return to shallow rhythmic breathing.

Fifteenth Breath, Exhale:

Mind: The two sets of star tetrahedrons take off spinning. In an instant, they will be moving at exactly one-third the speed of light at their outer tips. You probably will not be able to see this because of the tremendous speed, but you can feel it. What you have just done is to start the "motor" of the Mer•Ka•Ba. You will not go anywhere, or have an experience. It is just like starting the motor of a car, but keeping the transmission in neutral.

Breath: Make a small hole with your lips just like you did for breath number ten. Blow out in the same manner, and as you do, feel the two sets of star tetrahedrons take off spinning.

Sixteenth Breath, Inhale:

Heart: Feel unconditional love for all life.

Mind: As you begin to inhale, set the intention in your mind for, "34-Left: 21-Right." This is the code to your mind to spin the two sets of star tetrahedrons at a ratio of 34 times to 21 times, meaning that every time the 'mind' (male) star tetrahedron spins to the left 34 times, the 'emotional' (female) star tetrahedron will have spun to the right 21 times. As the two sets speed up, the ratio will remain constant (This is connected to the Fibonacci sequence).

Breath: Deep rhythmic yogic breath.

Sixteenth Breath, Exhale:

Unstable Mer-Ka-Ba

Mind: As you let out your breath, the two sets of star tetrahedrons take off from their setting at 'one-third the speed of light' to 'two-thirds the speed of light' in an instant. As they approach 'two-thirds the speed of light', a phenomenon takes place. A rotating disk about 55 feet (17m) in diameter pops out around the physical body, the centre being at the level of the base of the spine. The sphere of energy that is centred around the two sets of star tetrahedrons forms with the rotating disk to create a shape around the human body that looks like a "flying saucer". This rotating energy matrix is called the Mer•Ka•Ba. However, at this point the field is not stable. If you could see or sense the Mer•Ka•Ba around you at this point, you will know it to be unstable, as it will be slowly wobbling. Therefore, the next breath is necessary. Please note that you must complete breath seventeen immediately after breath sixteen. Do not wait or meditate at this point because your fields are not stable yet.

    Breath: Same as breath number fifteen. Make a small hole in the lips, and blow out with pressure. It is at this point that the speed increases. As you feel the speed increasing, let all your breath out with force. This action will cause the higher speed to be fully activated and the Mer•Ka•Ba to be formed.

Seventeenth Breath, Inhale:

Mer-Ka-Ba Activation Phase 1

Heart: Remember, unconditional love for all life must be felt throughout all of this meditation or very little results will be experienced.

Mind: As you breathe in, set the intention in your mind for "nine-tenths the speed of light". This code will tell your mind to increase the speed of the Mer•Ka•Ba to 'nine-tenths the speed of light', which will stabilize the rotating field of energy. It will also do something else. The 3rd dimensional universe that we live in is tuned to 9/10 the speed of light. Every electron in your body is rotating around every atom in your body at 9/10 the speed of light. The Mer•Ka•Ba will attune you to 9/10 the speed of light. This is the reason this particular speed is selected.

Breath: Deep rhythmic yogic breath.

Seventeenth Breath, Exhale:

Phase 2 Stable and Activated Mer-Ka-Ba

Mind: The speed increases to 9/10ths the speed of light and stabilizes the Mer•Ka•Ba.

Breath: Same as breaths fifteen and sixteen. Make a small hole in your lips, and blow out with pressure. As you feel the speed take off, let all your breath out with force. You are now in your stable, and 3rd dimensionally tuned Mer•Ka•Ba. With the help of your 'Higher Self', you will understand what this really means.

After you are finished with the breathing exercise, at either breath fourteen or breath seventeen, technically speaking you can immediately get up and return to your everyday life. If you do, try to remember your breathing and the flow through your body as long as you can.

However, it would be desirable to remain in the meditation for a while longer, perhaps fifteen minutes to an hour. While you are in this meditative state, your thoughts and emotions are amplified tremendously. This is a great time for positive affirmations, programming, and the setting of intent. Talk to your Higher Self to discover the possibilities of this special meditative time.

Below is an abbreviated version of this meditation. As you become more familiar with the meditation you may find it useful to follow the phrases in the abbreviated instructions to simplify your thoughts during the meditation. You can also use it for quick reference.

Abbreviated Instructions for the Mer•Ka•Ba Meditation

17 Breaths (Short Version)

Breath	Mudra	Action
Breath 1	Thumb & Index Finger	Inhale: Sun Tetrahedron Exhale: Earth Tetrahedron. Hold your Breath -Eyes In and Up...Pulse.
Breath 2	Thumb & Middle Finger	Inhale: Sun Tetrahedron Exhale: Earth Tetrahedron. Hold your Breath - Eyes In and Up ...Pulse.
Breath 3	Thumb & Ring Finger	Inhale: Sun Tetrahedron Exhale: Earth Tetrahedron. Hold your Breath - Eyes In and Up...Pulse.
Breath 4	Thumb & Little Finger	Inhale: Sun Tetrahedron Exhale: Earth Tetrahedron. Hold your Breath - Eyes In and Up...Pulse.
Breath 5	Thumb & Index Finger	Inhale: Sun Tetrahedron Exhale: Earth Tetrahedron. Hold your Breath - Eyes In and Up...Pulse.
Breath 6	Thumb & Middle Finger	Inhale: Sun Tetrahedron Exhale: Earth Tetrahedron. Hold your Breath - Eyes In and Up...Pulse.

Breath 7	Thumb, Index & Middle Finger	Inhale: Prana coming in through both sides of your tube, meeting at navel. Exhale: Prana Sphere forming at navel, grapefruit size.
Breath 8	Thumb, Index & Middle Finger	Inhale: The Prana Sphere is growing larger. Exhale: It reaches maximum size.
Breath 9	Thumb, Index & Middle Finger	Inhale: Prana Sphere will grow brighter. Exhale: Continues to grow brighter.
Breath 10	Thumb, Index & Middle Finger	Inhale: Prana Sphere ignites and becomes like a sun. Exhale: Blow out forcefully and with the Power Breath into a golden sphere that surrounds the body. Small sphere at navel still present.
Breath 11	Thumb, Index & Middle Finger	Inhale/Exhale: Prana comes in and radiates out to large sphere, which stabilizes it.
Breath 12	Thumb, Index & Middle Finger	Inhale/Exhale: Prana comes in and radiates out to large sphere, which stabilizes it.
Breath 13	Thumb, Index & Middle Finger	Inhale/Exhale: Prana comes in and radiates out to Large sphere, which stabilizes it.
Breath 14	Hands together, palms upward	Inhale: Place your hands together as small Prana sphere moves up to Universal Heart Centre. Exhale: Prana continues to come in the tube, meeting at the Universal Heart Centre.

Continue rhythmic breathing with Prana, meeting at Universal Heart Centre. You have now initiated Christ Spherical Breathing, breathing from the 4th Dimension. This is an unlimited source of Unconditional Love from Father Sky above and Mother Earth below.

In preparation for Activating your Mer•Ka•Ba through Breaths 15-17, envision yourself within your three superimposed Star Tetrahedrons:

- One star remains stationary and represents the physical body.
- A 2nd star spins left or counter-clockwise and represents male, electric, mental body.
- A 3rd star spins right or clockwise and represents female, magnetic, emotional energy plane.

Breath	Mudra	Action
Breath 15	Hands together, palms upward	Inhale: Equal Speed Exhale: Blow forcefully out with forced exhalation.
Breath 16	Hands together, palms upward	Inhale: 34:21 - 2/3 Speed of Light Exhale: Blow forcefully out with forced exhalation.
Breath 17	Hands together, palms upward	Inhale: 9/10 Speed of Light Exhale: Blow forcefully out with forced exhalation.

ANNEX 19.4.1

ASCENSION ACTIVATION MEDITATION

BY DANNY SEARLE

*T*he *Ascension Activation Meditation* is not one you can just do. I included 144 breaths, instead of the MERKABA Activationof 17 breaths. That is because we also need to activate our 12 strand DNA.

By the time you are ready to do the *Ascension Activation Meditation*, your breathing, visualisations, and mudras should come as second nature. You really need to be able to do these functions without thinking, but still maintain Love, because you will need your concentration for the more important aspects – like 12 strand DNA activation!

So, it really is a case of practise, practise, and practise! I cannot overstate that enough. This is not a game, and it is not for the curious mind. It is for the committed, disciplined student that is working toward becoming a Master. Unless you can give 100% to the training for the final *Ascension Activation Meditation*, then I doubt you will get much out of it.

For those that do persist, it will be the most powerful meditation you have ever performed! This meditation alone will raise your vibration to such high levels that you will change both physically and spiritually. Your very fabric will change. Your aura will expand. Your psychic abilities will increase. Your healing abilities will be enhanced.

Breaths

The Four (4) breaths =

- **Breath 1: Mudra 1** - thumb and index finger touching. Inhale/exhale;
- **Breath 2: Mudra 2** - thumb and middle finger touching. Inhale/exhale;
- **Breath 3: Mudra 3** - thumb and third finger touching. Inhale/exhale
- **Breath 4: Mudra 4** - thumb and pinkie finger touching. Inhale/exhale.

The Meditation

Steps:

1. Visualise an energy centre placed about a 60 cm/1 foot beneath you. This is the **Earth Chakra**. Visualise it as a bright, dark green, 3 sided pyramid – a Tetrahedron, spinning clockwise. As you breathe in, the energy centre expands, and as you breathe out, it contracts and condenses. With each breath and exhale it grows in size and intensity. 4 breaths.

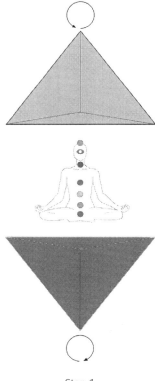

Step 1

2. Spiral this energy up your body counter-clockwise to the top **Sun tetrahedron** (4 breaths). The Sun tetrahedron is placed about a 30 cm/1 ft. above your head. Visualise it as a bright yellow/gold inverted three sided pyramid, rotating counter-clockwise. As you breathe in, the energy centre expands, and as you breathe out, it contracts and condenses. With each breath and exhale it grows in size and intensity. 4 breaths.

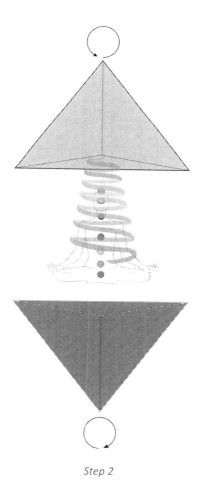

Step 2

3. Spiral this energy down clockwise (4 breaths) to the **Root Chakra**. Visualise a bright red energy centre. 4 breaths.

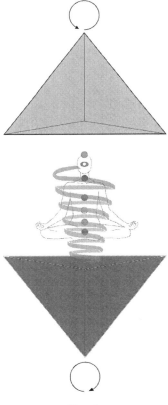

Step 3

4. Spiral this energy up your body counter-clockwise (4 breaths) to the **Crown Chakra**. Visualise a bright violet energy centre. 4 breaths.

5. Spiral this energy down clockwise (4 breaths) to the **Sacral Chakra**. Visualise a bright orange energy centre. 4 breaths.

6. Spiral this energy up your body counter-clockwise (4 breaths) to the **Third Eye Chakra**. Visualise a bright indigo energy centre. 4 breaths.

7. Spiral this energy down clockwise (4 breaths) to the **Solar plexus Chakra**. Visualise a bright yellow energy centre. 4 breaths.

8. Spiral this energy down clockwise (4 breaths) to the **Throat Chakra**. Visualise a bright blue energy centre. 4 breaths.

9. Spiral this energy down clockwise (4 breaths) to the **Heart Chakra**. Visualise a bright green energy centre. 4 breaths.

10. 4 more breaths in the **Heart Chakra**.

TOTAL 36 BREATHS – Return to normal breathing for 60 seconds.

CONTINUE:

11. 4 more breaths in the Heart Chakra.
12. Focus consciousness to the **Solar plexus Chakra** for 4 breaths.
13. Focus consciousness to the **Throat Chakra** for 4 breaths.
14. Focus consciousness to the **Sacral Chakra** for 4 breaths.
15. Focus consciousness to the **Third Eye Chakra** for 4 breaths.
16. Focus consciousness to the **Base Chakra** for 4 breaths.
17. Focus consciousness to the **Crown Chakra** for 4 breaths.
18. Focus consciousness to the **Earth tetrahedron** for 4 breaths.
19. Focus consciousness to the **Sun tetrahedron** for 4 breaths.

TOTAL 36 BREATHS– Return to normal breathing for 60 seconds.
We finish here in the **Sun tetrahedron**. Your whole system should now be energised and pulsing. If this is stage one of your first training run, then end here. Otherwise, change your hand position to *Relaxation Mudra*. Left hand placed over right hand (or vice versa – whatever is comfortable), thumbs lightly touching. CONTINUE:

Relaxation Mudra either postion is fine

20. Focus consciousness to the **Heart Chakra** for 4 breaths.
21. Focus consciousness to the **Solar plexus Chakra** then pull the energy up into the Heart Chakra. Let the energies merge. 4 breaths.
22. Focus consciousness to the **Throat Chakra** then pull the energy down into the Heart Chakra. Let the energies merge. 4 breaths.
23. Focus consciousness to the **Sacral Chakra** then pull the energy up into the Heart Chakra. Let the energies merge. 4 breaths.
24. Focus consciousness to the **Third Eye Chakra** then pull the energy down into the Heart Chakra. Let the energies merge. 4 breaths.
25. Focus consciousness to the **Base Chakra** then pull the energy up into the Heart Chakra. Let the energies merge. 4 breaths.
26. Focus consciousness to the **Crown Chakra** then pull the energy down into the Heart Chakra. Let the energies merge. 4 breaths.
27. Focus consciousness to the **Earth tetrahedron** then pull the energy up into the Heart Chakra. Let the energies merge. 4 breaths.
28. Focus consciousness to the **Sun tetrahedron** then pull the energy down into the Heart Chakra. Let the energies merge. 4 breaths.

TOTAL 36 BREATHS – Return to normal breathing for 60 seconds,with all your Chakras now centred into your heart. If this is stage two of your first training run, then end here. Otherwise, for the rest of the breaths, use the same mudra for both inhale and exhale. The thumb, the first, and second fingers touching together, palms up:

Final Mudra

CONTINUE:

29. Visualise a spiral of energy like a rope coming up from the **Earth tetrahedron**, spiralling in a counter-clockwise direction. 4 breaths.
30. Visualise a spiral of energy like a rope coming down from the **Sun tetrahedron**, spiralling in a clockwise direction. 4 breaths.

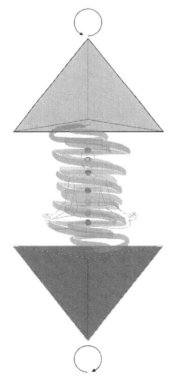

Steps 29 & 30

31. Visualise both spirals at the same time surrounding your body, moving up and down. 4 breaths.

32. Visualise both spirals vibrating faster and faster for 4 breaths.

33. Visualise both spirals vibrating so fast that they become a solid energy field of golden light, surrounding your body from head to toe. 4 breaths.

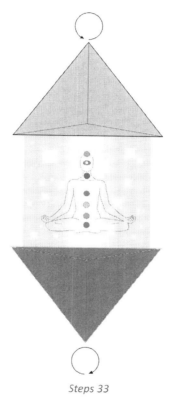

Steps 33

34. Visualise this column of golden light quickly act like a lightning bolt. This starts a chain reaction from your **Star Chakra** down to your **Heart**, and from the **Earth Chakra** up to the **Heart**.

35. Visualise your **Heart Centre** expanding outward with each breath in an implosion and explosion of gold light. 4 breaths.

36. Visualise your **Heart Centre** expanding out in a perfect sphere around you. It expands out to enclose the tetrahedrons. 8 breaths.

Steps 35 & 36

37. Breathe normally. You are now lighter than air. You can no longer feel your body. Everything is vibrating at a very high frequency. Hold this for 4 breaths.

38. Draw the **Earth Tetrahedron**, spinning clockwise up so that the base is about level with your Throat Chakra.

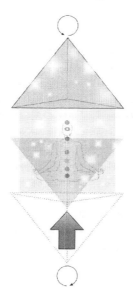

Step 38

39. Draw the **Star Tetrahedron**, spinning counter-clockwise, down so that the base is about level with your knees. It locks in with the spinning Earth Chakra, and spins in the opposite direction.

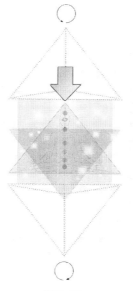

Step 39

40. Your MERKABA is now activated. As your Heart Chakra expands out further, your 12 strand DNA is activated. Visualise your DNA changing from two strands to 12 strands, populating your body at light speed. By your Will alone, you can now go into the 5th Dimension and anchor there, never to return to the 3rd Dimension. If you are ready – Go!

Step 40

TOTAL 144 BREATHS– Return to normal breathing if you remain on the 3rd Dimension. Carry out Grounding Meditation.

ANNEX 19.5.1

LINKS TO MY DOWNLOADS

Files:

Go to my website> www.dannysearle.com

Go to > Downloads >

- Life Lessons Survey.pdf

Audio Files:

- Merkaba Activation Meditation (Advanced).mp3
- Ascension Activation Meditation Final.mp3

Videos

Go to my YouTube Channel:

https://www.youtube.com/user/PathToAscention

Go to Playlists >ASCENSION - A STEP BY STEP GUIDE - BOOK FILES:
(Use this link to access files: http://tinyurl.com/ycqv9xsl)

1. Basic Chakra Cleansing
2. Aura Cleansing Meditation
3. Ascension Meditation 1 (Physical): Whole Body Alignment
4. Ascension Meditation 2 (Emotional): Forgiveness Meditation
5. Ascension Meditation 3 (Mental): Release Fear
6. Ascension Meditation 4 (Spiritual): Cosmic Consciousness
7. Ascension Meditation 5 (Physical/Spiritual): Life Lessons Healing
8. Merkaba Practice Meditation 1 (Basic)
9. Merkaba Practice Meditation 2 (Intermediate)

References and Further Reading

Brennan, B. (1993). *Hands of light*. 1st ed. Toronto: Bantam Books.

Dyer, Dr. Wayne W. (2010). *How To Forgive Someone Who Has Hurt You: In 15 Steps* [online] Available at: http://www.drwaynedyer.com/blog/how-to-forgive-someone-in-15-steps/ [Accessed 3 Apr. 2017].

Judith, A. (2004). *Eastern Body, Western Mind*. 1st ed. Berkeley: Celestial Arts.

Leadbeater, C. & Leland, K. (2013). *The Chakras*. 1st ed. Wheaton, Illinois: Quest Books/Theosophical Publishing House.

Maor, R. (2013). *Ray's 8 Days With No Food Or Water Television Exposure | Ray Maor*. [online] Raymaor.com. Available at: http://raymaor.com/watch/the-8-day-television-experiment/ [Accessed 3 Apr. 2017].

Mccasker, T. (2014). *Breatharian Leader Wiley Brooks Lives On Light, Air, And Quarter Pounders*. [online] Vice. Available at: https://www.vice.com/en_us/article/breatharian-leader-wiley-brooks-lives-on-light-air-and-quarter-pounders [Accessed 3 Apr. 2017].

Peirce, P. (2011). *Frequency*. 1st ed. New York: Atria Books.

Ray, A. (2015). *Walking the Path of Compassion*. 1st ed. Inner Light Publishers.

Rother, S. (2006). *Spiritual Psychology*. 1st ed. Las Vegas, NV: Lightworker Publications.

Searle, D. (2014). *The Truth Chronicles: Book 1 Secrets of the Soul*. 1st ed., http://amzn.to/2obQdKr

Sharamon, S. & Baginski, B. (2000). *The Chakra Handbook*. 1st ed. Delhi: Motilal Banarsidass.

OTHER BOOKS BY THIS AUTHOR

THE TRUTH CHRONICLES BOOK I: Secrets of the Soul

Your birth was not an accident. You chose your parents, your family, your friends, and your enemies. You also chose your gender, your race, and your appearance.

How is this possible?

In **The Truth Chronicles Book 1: Secrets of the Soul**, spiritual guidance counselor and YouTube sensation Danny Searle explains exactly what happens when we die, what our life in the spirit world is like, and what preparations our souls make before they return to the living world. Our souls grow through challenging experiences, and only life offers opportunity for such development.

Basing his explanations on a series of personal encounters with his spirit guide, Searle reveals how knowledge about the different soul ages can help us understand how people behave and why the world works as it does.

As Searle reveals the secrets of the spirit realm, he uncovers the hidden truth about humanity's origins—a secret locked within our DNA and recorded in ancient Sumerian texts.

Light-hearted, accessible, and entertaining, Searle's insights don't require previous experience in spiritual matters. But though this book is designed to be easily understandable, its consequences are profound.

Secrets of the Soul will change how you live and how you perceive death.

ISBN-13: 978-0992598105
ISBN-10: 0992598109
Availlbale on Amazon and Amazon Kindle.

THE TRUTH CHRONICLES BOOK II: Secrets of the Illuminati

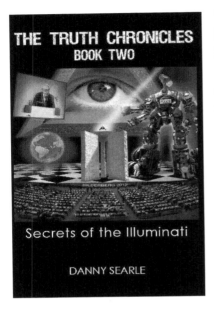

You have felt it all your life. Something is not right in the world. That question has led you here.

In **The Truth Chronicles Book II: Secrets of the Illuminati**, YouTube sensation Danny Searle explains exactly who the true "owners" of the planet are.

We build their cities, we fight their wars, and we slaved ourselves to keep them wealthy. But most of us do not even know "their" names.

What drives them to murder millions, hoard wealth, and place themselves above the rest of humanity?

After years of research, Searle can now answer these questions and much more. He details their crimes, sex scandals, and systems of control. He names, names.

As Searle states, "*Our so-called leaders do not care about you or me. They do not want to save us from bad things, find a cure for cancer, or feed the starving billions. No, they only exist for one reason – to maintain their status-quo.*"

So get ready for some shocks, oohs, and ahhs, and the odd giggle.

The Truth Chronicles Book II: Secrets of the Illuminati, is easy to read and follow, full of amazing truths, and it is a book that will impress and inspire even the most hardened Truth seekers out there.

ISBN: 0992598125
ISBN-13: 978-0-9925981-2-9
Availlbale on Amazon and Amazon Kindle.

Made in the USA
San Bernardino, CA
08 January 2019